The Housing Authority as Enabler

Other titles in this series

Social Housing and The Social Services by Paul Spicker

Housing Finance by David Garnett, Barbara Reid and Helen Riley

Housing Practice and Information Technology by David Hunter

The Housing Service of the Future edited by David Donnison and Duncan Maclennan

Maintaining Home Ownership: The Agency Approach by Philip Leather and Sheila Mackintosh

Effective Sheltered Housing: A Handbook by Imogen Parry and Lyn Thompson

Longman/Institute of Housing

The Housing Practice Series

THE HOUSING AUTHORITY AS ENABLER

INSTITUTE OF HOUSING

Robina Goodlad

Published by The Institute of Housing (Services) Ltd, Octavia House, Westwood Business Park, Westwood Way, Coventry CV4 8JP and Longman Group UK Ltd, 6th Floor, Westgate House, The High, Harlow, Essex CM20 1YR

Telephone (0279) 442601; Fax (0279) 444501

Published in the IOH/Longman Housing Practice Series under the General Editorship of Peter Williams

© IOH (Services) Ltd and Longman Group UK Ltd 1993

All rights reserved. No part of this publication may be reproduced, stored in a retrieval system or transmitted in any form or by any means, electronic, mechanical, photocopying, recording or otherwise, without either the prior written permission of the Publisher or a licence permitting restricted copying issued by the Copyright Licensing Agency Ltd, 90 Tottenham Court Road, London W1P 9HE

A catalogue record for this book is available from the British Library

ISBN 0–582–08188–2

Typeset by The Midlands Book Typesetting Company, Loughborough
Printed in Great Britain by BPCC Wheatons Ltd, Exeter

Contents

Preface	vi
Acknowledgements	vii
1 Origins of the enabling role	1
2 The meaning of enabling	22
3 The strategic housing authority	41
4 Enabling house building	60
5 Enabling house improvement	80
6 Influencing property management	103
7 Reducing disadvantage	127
8 Providing information and advice	145
9 Managing the enabling role	165
10 Performance and prospects	179
References	194
Index	207

Preface

This book has its origins in the teaching of housing policy to students on the Diploma in Housing Studies course at the University of Glasgow. The topicality of the enabling role of housing authorities led to its inclusion as a subject for a short optional course. A closer look at the meaning of the term led to the conclusion that while there is much that is new about 'enabling', including the widespread use of the word itself, there are also significant historical antecedents for its practice. However, there is little written specifically for those who are concerned to understand the meaning of the term and to explore its application in today's housing policy climate.

Other objectives contributed to the conception of this book. A belief that some of the available ways of improving housing conditions have been neglected by some housing authorities is one. Secondly, the book aims to examine whether this aspect of government policy provides local authorities with more than a nominal role in the network of public, private and voluntary agencies which increasingly determine the nature of local housing conditions.

The book is intended to help its readers to consider the nature, purpose and possibilities of the enabling role. This is done in five ways. First, it considers the nature of the current interest in the enabling role, by reference to the historical development of the role of local government in influencing housing conditions and by reference to the current policy debates. Secondly, the variety of meanings the term can convey are explored to provide some alternative models of the enabling role. This exploration is inevitably concerned with the role of the state (or more accurately local government) in influencing local housing conditions. Thirdly, the book examines the place of strategic planning in the enabling housing authority. This involves an exploration of the administrative systems for housing planning which apply in Britain, and of the extent to which the planning models implicit in them can be a help or a hindrance to the enabling housing authority. Fourthly, the largest part of the book is intended to provide an elaboration of the enabling role in practice, by devoting a number of chapters to different aspects of enabling, starting with new building and finishing with the pursuit of social policy objectives. Finally, the book attempts to assess the potential and achievements of the enabling role of housing authorities.

While not being a manual, the book should nevertheless provide some ideas about the conduct of enabling housing authorities. While not being a legal textbook, it provides a variety of models of the enabling role and the nature of the type of action an enabling authority might take. While not being a comprehensive guide to good practice, it provides some examples of the enabling role in action, and tends to leave the reader to decide if they *are* good practice.

The book is a study in housing policy. It draws on writings on local government and politics, on legal powers and their use, on housing policy and practice, and on planning and policy making. It is intended to assist housing practitioners, students, policy makers and anyone interested in current housing policy issues to make up their own mind about the potential of today's housing authorities to improve local housing conditions. It is intended to encourage a questioning approach to the claims made about the potential of the enabling role, without imposing a conventional wisdom based on the lowest common denominator of non-controversial action.

Discussions of the enabling role can arouse deep emotions. The greatest controversy surrounds the issue of whether or not an enabling authority should provide housing directly. This author takes the pragmatic view — seen as contentious by some — that providing council housing is, in principle, one of the most effective ways of enabling the improvement of housing conditions, and should not therefore be excluded from the panoply of action open to a housing authority concerned to influence housing conditions in its area. For three reasons, though, little discussion of direct provision and management of council housing is to be found in this book. First, the subject is covered in many other works. Secondly, in the current policy climate and possibly in future there is little prospect of retaining, let alone increasing, the present supply of council housing in Britain. And thirdly, although direct provision of council housing remains a popular idea with councils of all shades of party opinion and with tenants and potential tenants, it is by no means the only means open to housing authorities to influence housing conditions in their area.

Acknowledgements

I am indebted to many people whose contributions in various ways have made this book possible. All my colleagues at the Centre for Housing Research are a source of stimulation and assistance, but I would particularly wish to thank Duncan Maclennan, Suzie Scott, Keith Kintrea, Eleanor Lang, Yvonne Shannon, and finally Kirsty Neilson, whose assistance in tracing references was invaluable. Peter Williams and John Perry have been models of constructive support and practical assistance and advice. John Harper of Longman has combined forbearance and diligence in the most effective manner imaginable. Peter Taylor has supported and assisted me in many ways, not least in his comments on draft chapters, and Sarah and Alice have suffered the consequences of my efforts. At the University, the students on the Diploma in Housing Studies course have contributed to this book in ways they may not realise, but I hope will accept were invaluable. The responsibility for what follows rests, of course, with me.

Robina Goodlad

Chapter 1
Origins of the enabling role

Introduction

In a sense, there is nothing new about the idea of housing authorities as enablers. Local authorities have had powers to assist the improvement of housing conditions since at least the middle of the nineteenth century. Powers and duties to provide came later.

The notion that local authorities should have an indirect role in improving housing conditions was a feature of early government action to improve living conditions before 1919. The period from 1919 to 1979 or perhaps 1987 may best be viewed with a longer historical perspective as the more idiosyncratic in its emphasis on the role of housing authorities as providers of housing.

Yet today's housing authorities are very different from those of one hundred years ago. The role seen for them is more ambitious — no less than to assist the improvement of housing conditions in all tenures, by encouraging market and non-market processes. The range of powers and resources available to housing authorities is also much greater than in the last decade of the nineteenth century. But the capacity of housing authorities to act is also restricted in ways many housing authorities deplore, and the development of the enabling idea owes much to the attempt by governments since 1979 to change the nature of intervention in the housing market, abandoning direct state provision. This apparent conflict between a wide ranging role and a narrower vision of the role of the state is at the heart of many confusions and uncertainties about the contemporary meaning of the role of housing authorities.

One hundred years ago there was no such confusion — most of the time central government and most local authorities sought to restrict state involvement to the least and narrowest range possible. Today's enabling role for housing authorities is new and different, but it can only be understood with reference to the nature of the changing role of housing authorities over the last century. This chapter traces that history in relation to building new housing, clearance and improvement, financial and other assistance to consumers and providers, regulation, and strategic planning. But first the role of local government, and the changing nature of central–local government relations is examined as an essential backdrop to the more specific consideration of housing policy.

2 The Housing Authority as Enabler

Local government

Local authorities had a minimal but growing role in influencing living conditions in the nineteenth century. The dominant *laissez faire* ideology restricted state intervention to the minimum necessary to protect the population from the worst of diseases such as cholera or to placate the occasional uprising of working class dissent or middle class dismay about the nature of urban living conditions for the mass of the people.

Local authorities in any case were, in the main, inadequately placed to respond to any new legislation or any local pressure to act in relation to housing conditions. A plethora of local bodies, with overlapping boundaries, some elected on a limited franchise and some non-elected, provided a range of services or regulated a range of activities carried out by others in most parts of the country. Only a few were willing to go further than the duties imposed upon them, to take advantage of the powers available to them including the right to promote private legislation.

From the 1830s a network of local authorities began to be established in urban areas, especially following the 1835 Municipal Corporations Act. In the middle years of the century concern about living conditions and their effect on the middle and upper classes grew. The public health movement of this period was motivated by the desire to protect rate and tax-payers and profit margins from the consequences of disease and ill health, rather than as a result of working class or democratic movements or altruism on the part of those in authority. Early working class organisations were relatively powerless until the last quarter of the century, and even then any gains were sporadic and minimal although significant in influencing events at times (Englander 1983).

By the end of the century a network of local authorities existed which are recognisable to twentieth century eyes. In Scotland the origins lie in the Royal burghs of medieval times, and in 1889 county councils were established (Kellas 1984). Following the Acts of 1888, 1894 and 1899 England and Wales also had a system of councils which conformed to the four criteria which have been taken throughout much of the twentieth century to define the British system of local government. The criteria are contiguous but not overlapping boundaries at any one tier of government; tax raising powers; some autonomy from the central state; elected rather than appointed members; and multi-purpose functions (Hampton 1991, p 3).

In the years up to the outbreak of the Great War in 1914 local government was increasingly looked upon as an important part of the state. 'As new responsibilities were taken on by the state, so many of these were placed in the hands of local authorities' (Stoker 1991, p 2). The growing labour movement placed emphasis on the role of the municipality in improving living conditions, and argued, *inter alia*, for the building of council houses for the working class. To the old concern with public health and law and order were added education and public utilities such as gas and water services.

Some local authorities saw it as their role to improve conditions in their area rather than simply to save ratepayers money. Where Parliament had not given the power to local authorities to act, some took steps to promote private legislation to gain the powers necessary. Others waited until powers or duties were provided by Parliament. Some were reluctant to act unless mandatory duties were set down.

Some commentators see the 1930s as the high point in the achievement of the British local government tradition. Writing in 1954, Professor W. A. Robson argued:

> The most conspicuous tendency in recent years has been the removal of functions from local government control. (p 15)

and:

> The centralising tendency which is undermining local government assumes several forms. One form is the straightforward transfer of functions from local authorities to Government Departments or similar organs. This has occurred in regard to civil airfields, trunk roads, hospitals, public assistance, and the valuation of property for rating. A second form consists of the transfer of services and undertakings to *ad hoc* bodies subject to varying degrees of central control. This has happened in the case of the licensing of passenger road services, gas and electricity supply, and other public utility services. Yet another form consists of increased central control over local authorities.
> (Robson 1954, p 36)

This general diagnosis of the ills of local government is familiar to late twentieth century ears, although today's commentators would substitute alternative examples of lost functions and powers. To defenders of local government it always seems to be the case that 'the most conspicuous tendency of recent years' has been increasing centralisation and central interference. The relationship between local and central government has been a matter for disagreement throughout the history of local government, and has crucial importance in defining the role of local government

4 The Housing Authority as Enabler

generally, and local housing authorities in particular. So has the period since 1979 been any different from previous periods?

For most of the twentieth century local government's share of national resources has expanded. This is partly because of the simultaneous growth and decline in local government as new functions, such as consumer protection and social work services were added or extended while old services and functions, such as gas and electricity, were taken away. More significantly, alternative views about the nature and purpose of local government have shaped these developments over the years.

In the years after 1945, local government played an important part in building the welfare state, and there was little doubt in the minds of Labour ministers that the municipalities should be major actors in this. From the mid-fifties onwards local authorities continued to expand their activities despite sporadic attempts by governments of both major parties to minimise their role in general or in particular areas of activity. Current expenditure by local government in Great Britain rose (at constant 1975 prices) from £4,676 million in 1955 to £13,598 million in 1975. Capital expenditure also more than doubled in this period, with a dip in expenditure between 1955 and 1965. By 1976 local government represented 15.4 per cent of the Gross Domestic Product (compared with 9.1 per cent in 1955), a peak which a Labour and then several Conservative governments would not tolerate (Stoker 1991, pp 7–8).

The Thatcher governments from 1979 mark the start of a new episode. Tighter control on spending was not new as it had been a characteristic feature of the later years of the Labour Government 1974–79, after the economic slump of 1973–75, and the successful but conditional request for a loan from the International Monetary Fund in 1976. Under the Thatcher governments the scale of fiscal control intensified, and was accompanied by a new concern to reduce the role of local government in the locality as well as in the national economy. Measures of privatisation such as those contained in the 1980 Local Government Planning and Land Act required competitive tendering for much of the work of direct labour organisations (DLOs). 'Within three years the Act had led to widespread reductions in direct labour workforces, improved efficiency among many DLOs, and the total closure of others' (Ascher 1987, p 36). The biggest act of privatisation of all was the sale of council houses under the Right to Buy (RTB) provisions of the 1980 legislation (Forrest and Murie 1988).

Capital and revenue spending restraint was imposed on local government in the early 1980s, if necessary with the introduction of new legislation. Asset sales funded increasing proportions of capital spending, and, until 1991 and the switch from poll tax to value added tax announced in the March budget, more revenue was raised from local taxes than previously as central support was cut. However, although capital expenditure declined, revenue spending grew in all but one year between 1976–77 and 1986–87 (Stoker 1991, p 12). Local priorities for spending were also potentially distorted by greater targeting of revenue grants and capital allocations for specific purposes.

Local government changed in ways other than through measures of privatisation, expenditure control and redistribution of the source of revenue. Stoker identifies an additional three ways in which central government intervened in the 1980s: legislation which provided greater powers than previous governments had to intervene in local affairs; by-passing local government by setting up appointed public bodies such as Urban Development Corporations or Housing Action Trusts; and the reorganisation and reform of local authorities, including the abolition of the Greater London Council and the six metropolitan counties in England (Stoker 1988, pp 142–46). The political attack on local government has extended as far as reducing the payments councillors receive as well as abolishing types of local authority completely, so creating an impression of a central government which does not value local government as an alternative source of political power in a pluralist state.

The government's objectives for local government have not always been achieved and in some ways not achieved at all, yet the measures taken have helped to shape the nature of local government and individual authorities' reactions to the centre. These measures are unprecedented in the post–1945 period. But comparisons with earlier periods are akin to comparing apples with oranges. The growth of local government in the years after 1945 had been unprecedented, too, and was achieved partly as a result of broad consensus between local and central government about the need for such expansion. That consensus has been destroyed by the changes made to local government since 1945.

Academic theorists and writers on local government provide some further assistance to us in attempting to understand the nature of these developments. Loughlin (1986, p 5) has described the type of service provided by local government as falling into one of three types. Some of the action taken by local bodies and by local authorities in the nineteenth century were far more effectively provided collectively than individually. The economists' term *public goods* describes such services, since they cannot be satisfactorily handled by the private market. 'The classic example is that of street lighting. Once the street lamp has been provided fifty people might as well benefit as five' (Charles and Webb 1986,

6 The Housing Authority as Enabler

p 68). Public parks and public health measures also illustrate this characteristic of public goods.

In addition local authorities began to develop *trading services*, which could have been provided by the market, but which tended to be monopoly services, justifying municipal provision rather than allowing private monopoly profits. Examples include markets, swimming baths, gasworks, and some transport services.

Finally, local authorities provided *redistributive* services, such as poor law relief. Education followed in the nineteenth century, and then housing after 1919. These services were intended to benefit particular groups, but not necessarily the poorest. Loughlin argues that an important aspect of change since 1919 within local government and in the expectations held of local government by central government has been the increasing emphasis on redistributive services and the removal of trading services from the ambit of local government, 'In 1975, for example, 65 per cent of local expenditure was devoted to redistributive services' (Loughlin 1986, p 6).

From this perspective the objective of central government in the late 1980s has been to reduce the range of redistributive services provided by local government, by seeking alternative suppliers as in voluntary parent governors opting schools out of the education authority, or housing associations, trusts and co-operatives taking over council housing. The recent emphasis on the enabling role of housing authorities can thus be seen as an attempt to establish the ascendancy of public goods as the role of local government, although some important elements remain of redistributive services, such as repair and improvement grants.

The legitimacy of local government as an agency for change in localities is open to challenge on a number of grounds. Public choice theorists point to the alleged tendency of elected local authorities to over-provide and expand service provision beyond the point that can be justified to the minority who contribute through taxes (Stoker 1991, p 238). This view has informed the writings of those such as Nicholas Ridley, who provided one of the best known recent expositions by a Right Wing politician of the idea of enabling local authorities (Ridley, 1989). Public choice theorists favour the idea of local authorities as regulators and facilitators, rather than as direct providers of services.

Local government can also be criticised for its unreliability in delivering the quality or quantity of services that critics consider appropriate from a national perspective. This criticism can come from the political Left or Right. From the Left, the concern is to ensure at least a minimum level of service, and rural or Conservative-controlled authorities are sometimes singled out for criticism about the inadequacies of their housing, social work or educational services, for example. From the right the tendency is to pick out high spending Labour authorities and compare them to the allegedly more efficiently run Westminsters and Wandsworths.

In contrast, even among the severest critics of local government, there are few who wish to replace local authorities entirely with non-elected public bodies or voluntary organisations, or the private sector. The view that local authorities have a legitimate interest in the welfare of the communities they represent is a widely-shared value within the British political tradition. Three grounds or justifications for a system of local government are invoked. Local government provides for welfare, pluralism and participation in the political system, it is claimed.

The claim of welfare (sometimes referred to as efficiency) is that local authorities are better-placed than central government, to gear their services to the needs of the locality and particular groups within the community. The claim for pluralism arises from fear of the concentration of political power in a centralised government system: local government provides a bulwark against the power of the central state. The claim of participation is that local government provides councillors and their electorate with the opportunity to practise citizenship, which is seen as an educational process in its own right, as a training ground for participation in national political affairs, and as a valuable means to the end of defending the interests of citizens and localities. In the last 20 years, the value of consumer and citizen participation has been a dominant theme within local government, encouraging speculation about the adequacy of early twentieth century theories of democracy (Pateman 1970; Richardson 1983).

Local authorities are not in fact empowered by law to do whatever they consider in the interests of their areas. The legal doctrine of *ultra vires* requires that they must find a statutory provision justifying their actions. However, a degree of discretion exists in the way duties can be interpreted, and where powers are discretionary, local authorities can act or not as they wish. In addition, local authorities have often found ways of innovating by using powers intended for one purpose in slightly unexpected ways, or by using the limited general competence powers of the Local Government Acts in ways only they could have devised. But powers alone do not lead to action unless the political will, the resources, and the necessary expertise exist within local government.

The degree to which local authorities are free to pursue their own view of the public interest, accountable locally to the electorate or to local interest groups, is an issue of importance in considering the role of local government. If local authorities are not free to define their role or to pursue it as they please, then there are important consequences. First, more conformity with central government objectives can be expected than when local government is more autonomous, and, secondly, when local authorities have objectives which differ from central government, conflict will result. This has been the situation for many local authorities since 1979.

The developing role of housing authorities

The precise role of the state in relation to housing is a topic which has divided British politicians within and between parties for over a century. Government policy has consistently aimed to provide a decent home for everyone at a price within their means, but this commonplace statement raises more questions than it answers about issues such as the use of the tax system, the level of public spending on housing, the nature of the providers to be encouraged, and the meanings of 'a price within their means' and 'decent'.

The scope for mixing policy measures is wide, and council housing has often symbolised the broad approach in favour of high levels of state action. Others have seen it as undesirable. Both views are held for different reasons on the political Left and on the Right, but the Labour Party has been traditionally associated with the more positive view of council housing, and Labour councils have traditionally built the largest stocks.

For relatively short periods in the years since 1919, particularly in the immediate aftermath of both World Wars, council house provision has been seen as the only way in which government housing objectives to provide decent and affordable mass working class housing could be effectively pursued. In the years of the 1930s and from 1953 to 1979, council housing was tolerated by successive governments of both the major parties.

The political Right's concern with the role of council housing in the 1980s concentrated on the alleged inefficiency of the sector. An initial concern to reduce public spending was combined with an attempt to reduce the role of housing authorities as providers of housing. Housing policy was rarely far removed from the conflict between local and central government which characterised the 1980s. All the major housing legislation of the 1980s was opposed at the time by Labour housing authorities and the Parliamentary Opposition. Council house sales under the tenants' 'Right to Buy' provisions of the 1980 legislation were followed by the 'Tenants' Choice' legislation of 1988, and perhaps most significantly of all, the reforms of council house finance in England and Wales following the 1989 Local Government and Housing Act.

These measures, and the central government policy objectives which underlay them, provide the backdrop against which current meanings of the enabling role of housing authorities have to be understood.

Whatever view is held of council housing, politicians have supported, with varying degrees of enthusiasm which appear to show little correlation with party allegiance, the regulatory, planning and grant making powers of local authorities. This wide role continued alongside or including that of provider, but it varied in emphasis over time, assuming greater importance after 1977, and after the 1979 election of the Conservative government, especially after 1987.

Thomas describes the development of state housing policy from the point of view of central government:

> Successive British governments since the mid nineteenth century have been concerned with the condition of privately owned houses. The problem has been tackled by removing the worst substandard property and encouraging the construction of new housing conforming to certain minimum standards. Over time, the emphasis on public-sector involvement has varied. Generally, however, it has been recognised that, if left to itself, the private housing market will fail to provide acceptable conditions for low income groups; will attempt to maximise profits at the expense of space standards, densities and building quality; and, once housing has been built, will fail to provide adequate investment in maintaining the stock. Consequently, legislation has provided for the regulation of quality, for subsidy towards the cost of rehabilitation, and for building by local authorities and housing associations to meet directly the housing needs of poor and disadvantaged groups. (1986, p 1)

The visitor from outer space could be forgiven for thinking that the role of local authorities in all this is only to build council houses, and that central government takes responsibility for the other measures mentioned by Thomas. These measures are the historical antecedents of the enabling role. The British reader knows implicitly that the main agents for regulating new housing and assisting the rehabilitation of old housing are local authorities. However it would be too simple to view the relationship as one in which central governments invariably forced action by reluctant or compliant local authorities. The relationship has been more iterative, involving some local authorities in innovation and in pressing for additional powers and resources.

The nature of state intervention in housing has been a political issue throughout the twentieth century. The rest of this chapter

10 The Housing Authority as Enabler

provides the historical and contextual background necessary for an understanding of the factors which shape today's enabling housing authority. Broadly, involvement by housing authorities has taken one or more of six forms — clearance, improvement, building, grants and other assistance to consumers and providers, regulation of the development and management of housing by others, and assessment of need and strategic planning. These, with the exception of building council houses which has been discussed above, are outlined up to the 1970s, providing an essential historical introduction to the discussion of the contemporary role of housing authorities which follows in the next chapter.

Clearance and improvement

From the middle of the nineteenth century, legislation provided local authorities with powers to improve housing. Discretionary powers allowed (but did not require) local authorities to erect or improve lodging houses, then dwellings for the labouring classes. Powers of inspection were backed up with enforcement powers, including closure and demolition, initially of individual houses, then of areas of housing. These relatively cumbersome provisions were little used. The alleged sanctity of private property rights proved a severe deterrent against all but the most enterprising local authorities (Gauldie 1973).

In the years immediately after World War I the emphasis was on building council housing, but by 1933 the role of local authorities was seen as clearing slum areas and providing poor quality housing for those displaced. The 1930 Greenwood Act required local authorities to draw up plans for slum clearance. 'In all, 273,000 houses were dealt with' by 1939 when war disrupted the programme (Cullingworth 1966, p 24).

As in 1919, so in 1945, the impact of the war meant the first priority was to build new housing, then clear old housing beyond repair, and only then repair existing housing. However, there was some effort devoted to repair as early as 1949 when the Housing Act of that year extended to urban areas improvement grants for basic amenities and conversion. These measures were not uncontroversial, because many local authorities were reluctant to be seen encouraging or assisting private landlordism. Few were sympathetic to the position of landlords who may have been struggling to maintain, let alone improve, their property after 30 years of various sorts of rent control. 'Between 1949 and 1953 only 7,000 grants were given in the whole of Britain' (Cullingworth 1979, p 75).

The worst properties were to be demolished in a new programme of slum clearance. A new improvement grant system introduced in the 1954 Housing Repairs and Rents Act was intended to provide the carrot to property owners to improve housing in disrepair: around 35,000 grants were made per year in the second half of the decade, most for the installation of baths and hot water systems. These grants were discretionery and inevitably some local authorities were more inclined to promote them than others. These were extended and became mandatory (that is, local authorities had no choice about awarding them) in relation to the five basic amenities (a fixed bath or shower, a wash-hand basin, a water-closet, a ventilated food store, and a hot and cold water supply) in 1959. These mandatory grants were known as standard grants, and their use declined after the early 1960s, partly because the pool of houses remaining without the standard amenities had declined. The number of grants exceeded 100,000 per year in the five years from 1959 to 1964. Take up was concentrated in the owner-occupied sector, rather than the private rented sector, and this had consequences for whom the beneficiaries were and where geographically the grants were concentrated.

If grants were the carrot, the stick was intended to be a renewed commitment by local authorities to use their compulsory powers to ensure the improvement of housing which, although considered unfit for human habitation, was nevertheless capable of improvement.

In 1964, local authorities in England and Wales were given duties to inspect their areas and identify areas suitable for comprehensive improvement. Landlords, but not owner-occupiers in such areas, could be compelled by order to improve their property, with the tenants' consent. The procedures involved were cumbersome and little used. By 1968 only 379 areas had been designated by 136 housing authorities (Cullingworth 1979, p 80).

The Labour government had been elected in 1964 on a promise to build and clear more houses, but increasing criticism of slum clearance and relocation programmes led to growing interest in the idea of larger scale improvement and repair programmes. The post-war emphasis on clearance and redevelopment was criticised on a number of grounds — social, economic and practical. A number of studies and official reports pointed to the social dislocation created by large scale demolition and rehousing. Economic analysis compared the costs of rehabilitation and redevelopment. And there was a growing perception that the problem of poor housing could not be handled adequately using existing policies. There was a perception that the worst housing had already gone, and that the remainder could be tackled partly through demolition and partly through rehabilitation. However 'the constraint on public sector expenditure (following the

12 The Housing Authority as Enabler

1967 Balance of Payments Crisis) was the most important single reason why policy shifted towards improvement' (Thomas 1986, p 65), just as the clearance programme reached its peak with around 85,000 demolitions a year in Britain in the early 1970s.

The 1969 Housing Act introduced General Improvement Areas (GIAs) (Housing Treatment Areas in Scotland), intended to encourage area renewal by voluntary take-up of grants for housing and environmental improvement. The take-up of grants certainly increased from around 230,000 in 1971 to 300,000 in 1974 (Great Britain), but Thomas shows that this was more a result of the higher levels of grant made available in development areas (part of regional policy) than to any intrinsic success with GIAs. Local authorities had a role as initiators and co-ordinators, and sometimes had to act in default of owners. Private landlords had little incentive to co-operate. In England and Wales 904 GIAs containing 273,000 houses were declared (Hansard 1975). In Scotland few HTAs were attempted, partly because they were seen as unsuitable for rural/suburban areas, partly because Glasgow was still preoccupied with its slum clearance and redevelopment programme.

Amidst a background of growing criticism about the rate of progress in GIAs the 1974 Housing Acts introduced Housing Action Areas (HAAs). The Acts confirmed the switch in emphasis from redevelopment to rehabilitation, after a period of ambiguity from 1969. HAAs were intended to tackle the worst areas but in the interests of the residents, on the important assumption that most of the worst housing in post-war England had already been demolished, and that areas with particular concentrations of certain types of household would require special help. Separate provision for demolition remained. In Scotland, however, the legislation allowed for a continuing programme of area demolition, where appropriate, with its three-fold classification of HAAs for Demolition, for Improvement, and for Demolition and Improvement.

An important new feature of the acts was the higher level of grant in renewal areas, 75 per cent of approved costs, up to a limit, with the possibility of 90 per cent grants in cases of hardship. Grants in HAAs were for standard amenities, housing improvement, environmental improvement, and repairs, a new feature of housing legislation which challenged old assumptions about where the responsibility for ongoing maintenance lay. HAAs were expected to last about five years. The 1974 legislation also boosted the role of housing associations by providing housing association grants through the Housing Corporation. In some parts of the country the growth of housing associations has proceeded directly from the desire of local housing authorities to favour them as the means to housing improvement, especially in Housing Action

Areas. The GIA legislation remained broadly in place (except in Scotland). And measures were taken to restrict exploitation of improvement grants by speculators.

Grants and assistance

Grants by housing authorities provide arguably one of the most direct means of improving housing conditions. Grants aimed at improving the housing stock have already been mentioned. Other grants — in the form of housing allowances — are aimed at assisting those on low incomes to meet their housing costs, and have developed since 1930 when the Greenwood Act gave local authorities powers to draw up and operate rent rebate schemes for their own tenants. Few authorities used these powers, disliking the parallels with the hated means test of the Public Assistance Board. A Conservative controlled Birmingham introduced a rebate scheme which 'caused the largest and most successful council tenants' rent strike in the inter-war years (Malpass and Murie 1990, p 59). In the mid-1950s and again in the late 1960s local authorities were encouraged to increase council house rent levels and introduce or extend rent rebates. In 1972 the controversial Housing Finance Act imposed a rent rebate scheme on all authorities. By this time around two-thirds of authorities had a scheme. The Act also introduced a new rent allowance scheme for private sector tenants, following Birmingham's example in gaining Local Act powers in 1968. Very little discretion was given to local authorities to vary the national scheme by making small additional payments (Cullingworth 1979, p 133).

Housing authorities have had powers to lend money for house purchase since 1899. Loans have normally been given to lower income applicants, on lower price and older properties than building societies and banks lend on. These powers have supported the tenants 'Right to Buy' since 1979. Grants and loans to housing associations have also been a possibility since the nineteenth century, and local authorities have had powers to carry out many of their housing functions through housing associations since the 1930s. Grants to other types of voluntary organisations, such as local councils for the single homeless, or advice agencies, are also a long established feature of local government.

Regulation

From the middle years of the nineteenth century, the role of local government in regulating the development and use of urban areas was becoming well-established. The public health reforms of the later decades of the century had by 1900 achieved a significant improvement to living conditions in most towns and cities. These measures were most effective in influencing the construction of new urban areas, in the rapidly expanding towns and cities of Victorian Britain. Local authorities used the powers given them by the Public Health Acts of the nineteenth century to make and operate building by-laws and regulations. These covered a wide range of aspects of the siting, construction and materials involved in house building. The detail of these regulations was justified on the grounds of health and safety, ensuring for example, fire resistance, damp-proofing, and the installation of sanitary conveniences. By the 1960s the arguments for conformity in building regulations across the country were accepted by Parliament and the 1961 Public Health Act gave the relevant minister power to make regulations for England and Wales. Similar provisions had already been made for Scotland in 1959 (Cullingworth 1966, p 134).

Also in the Public Health Acts of the nineteenth century, in relation to overcrowding, local authorities acquired powers to deal with houses likely to be dangerous or harmful to the health of their inhabitants. Overcrowding was defined precisely much later in the 1935 Housing Act. The provisions were written to control exploitation by private landlords, with the possibility of prosecution for offending landlords. Increasingly, though, overcrowding was dealt with by rehousing by the local authority — an option which is increasingly problematic, as is the assumption in legislation that overcrowding is a phenomenon solely associated with the private rented sector. Concern about the case of housing in multiple occupation (HMOs) led to legislation in 1961 and 1964 which defined multiple occupation and granted powers to local authorities to register HMOs, with ministerial consent, to make management orders, and to require physical improvements.

A wider role in influencing the creation of a better living environment was envisaged by early supporters of the 'Garden Cities' and town and country planning movements. The earliest Acts with Town Planning in the title were dated 1909 and 1919, but these provided weak, complex and discretionary powers which were little used. Their broad intention was to give local authorities a role in the layout of new urban areas, and even if they had been taken up more enthusiastically, their influence on existing urban areas would have been minimal. A more effective system for regulating the location and nature of urban development in new and older areas had to await the reforms of the post-1945 era.

The framework of the British system of town planning was established in the 1947 Town and Country Planning Act (there

Origins of the enabling role 15

was a separate, essentially similar, Act for Scotland). The system was regulatory, in controlling development through a requirement to seek planning permission, and positive, in seeking to guide development in line with the authority's view of what was in the public interest through a system of development plans. Plans were based on the results of a survey of the social, economic and physical characteristics of the area, and required ministerial approval. The size, layout, design and density of developments such as new housing could be controlled by the necessity to gain planning permission, sometimes by requiring developers to observe certain conditions in the course of the development, through granting a conditional planning consent. Development plans could include provision for comprehensive development areas, which were used along with separate housing legislation in the 1950s and 1960s in some of the most unpopular programmes of the post-war welfare state, with enforced redevelopment and dislocation of inner city residents.

Almost 20 years later some parts of the country were still not covered by development plans. The development plan system was substantially revised in 1968 (1969 in Scotland) to include two types of plan — structure and local plans. Structure plans, covering larger areas such as a whole city or county (or even the whole of Strathclyde Region, which contains half of Scotland's population), were intended to provide a broad brush indication of desirable land uses, based on a diagram rather than a precise base map. Emphasis was placed on the written statement of policies accompanying the 'key diagram', rather than the precise geographical implications of the development proposals. Local plans, in contrast were expected to cover smaller areas such as neighbourhoods, small towns and their surrounding countryside, or segments of a city. They were expected to conform to the broad policies of the structure plan, and were to be approved by the planning authority after a public inquiry. Three types of local plan were possible, and there was nothing to prevent a particular geographical area being covered by more than one local plan.

The 1968 legislation required that the public were given opportunities to comment on both types of plan, at the draft stage. Structure plans have no longer to be approved by the relevant minister (except in Scotland), and planning authorities are responsible for convening an examination in public, intended to be an informal and unconfrontational public debate on the issues raised by the plan.

Broadly, responsibility for the new plans was split between the two tiers of local government created in the reforms of 1972 and 1973, with development control and local plans being the responsibility of the lower tier of local government. In Scotland,

16 The Housing Authority as Enabler

the three more rural regional councils have responsibility for both types of plan, and for development control.

Assessment of need and strategic planning

The 1919 Addison Act gave housing authorities new duties in relation to surveying housing conditions in their areas, as well as providing for needs found. In 1935 local authorities were given duties to survey their areas for overcrowding. For decades the focus of attention was on provision of housing rather than on the investigation of housing needs. This began to change in the 1960s. The Cullingworth Report (CHAC 1969) on council housing allocation policies and procedures was critical of the weaknesses perceived in the approach taken to the management of council housing. The needs of groups such as single people were neglected, it was alleged. Housing authorities were seen as neglecting their general duty to examine the housing needs of their area — issues such as the condition of stock across all tenures and the needs of all social groups. The conventional nuclear family with a desire to rent a council house was the client group councils were dealing with best. But this represented only one part of the population. The Cullingworth Committee, a sub-committee of the Central Housing Advisory Committee, concluded: 'If local housing authorities are to ensure that the needs of their area are being met, they must know what these needs are and how they are changing' (CHAC 1969). The committee urged local authorities to pay more attention to the housing needs of those such as single people, the homeless, students, and 'coloured people' who had, it was argued, been relatively neglected in the drive to provide council housing after the war.

This led to a view of the housing authority's role which emphasised a concern with investigating the housing needs of all social groups in the area, and seeking to take action in relation to all types and tenures of housing. A guide to action — a housing plan or strategy — was increasingly seen as the essential prerequisite of a housing authority's work, which extended beyond the provision and management of council housing to a wide range of activites intended to assist other housing providers, including owner-occupiers, builders, and housing associations. This idea of the comprehensive housing authority was the 1970s precursor of the enabling authority (see Chapter 2).

During the 1970s the focus of attention at central and local government level moved increasingly to the role of planning in local housing policy. This coincided with debates about the future structure of local government, and the distribution of functions within local government. The number of local authorities in England was reduced from about 2,000 to around 400, creating generally larger housing and planning authorities. In Scotland 56 housing authorities were created from 234. In Wales 37 district councils took over housing responsibilities (Hampton 1991, pp 20–49). Part of the argument for reorganising local government was the wish to create larger authorities that could be better relied on to take a more strategic view of their areas, and attempt to provide for the variety of needs that existed. There was a potential conflict here with another intention — that of creating local authorities autonomous enough to determine their own priorities, even if they were not as wide or strategic as the Redcliffe-Maud Commission hoped they would be.

The new local authorities which took over responsibility for housing policy at the local level in 1974 and 1975 were influenced by 'the corporate planning theories advocated through the Institute of Local Government Studies and elsewhere' (Hampton 1991, p 81) and by the contents of the Bains Report on the internal organisation of the new authorities. For housing authorities this meant that the administration of the housing stock within an authority should be seen as only part of a more general responsibility for housing conditions. Each council's housing policy objectives should be reflected in its committee system, rather than have a committee system based on traditional departmental boundaries which had in the past so often meant a committee for each department. In practice, these recommmendations seem to have been observed more in the letter than the spirit their advocates intended by most authorities (Power 1987a, pp 84–87).

The view of the housing authority's role as strategic planner was endorsed in the housing policy 1977 Green Papers (Cmnd 6851, 6852), which also introduced a new planning tool through which the strategies of the comprehensive housing authority could be set down. The Green Papers set out the Labour government's view that, 'Only the local authorities can take a comprehensive view of what should be done locally "across the board" in both the public and private sectors. Consequently it is for local authorities to assess the local housing situation as a whole, and keep it under regular review, through ... local housing strategies' (Cmnd 6851, p 75) and:

> Responsibility for making assessments and devising strategies must lie with local housing authorities. They are well established as providers and managers of rented housing but their role goes further. By statute their responsibility extends to securing adequate

housing in their localities. They are therefore concerned with the broad formulation and execution of housing policies for their areas, and it is this strategic aspect of their role which the government believe should be developed further.

(Cmnd 6852, p 43)

These new housing plans, called Housing Strategies and Investment Programmes (soon abbreviated to HIPS) in England, Housing Plans in Scotland and Housing Strategies and Operational Plans (HSOPs) in Wales, are discussed further in Chapter 3.

Conclusion

Consensus about the purpose and tasks of local government has broken down since 1979, as central government has altered the post-war central–local government relationship by reducing the role of authorities in direct provision of services, by fiscal controls, and in other ways. The loss of a role in providing new council housing has meant more emphasis on other ways in which housing authorities might play a part in improving local housing conditions. This review has shown that the role of housing authorities has been wider than that of provider of council housing for many years. A variety of powers and duties fall into five broad overlapping categories:

— clearance
— improvement
— grants and other assistance
— regulation of housing management and development
— assessment of need and strategic planning.

These have developed and changed over the decades to suit the perceived needs of the time. Some powers, such as the power to give mortgages, have remained on the statute book and served slightly different purposes at different times — in this case, most recently in support of the public sector tenant's Right to Buy. Housing authorities can act only within the powers available to them in statute. But it is too simple to see them only as the agents of Parliament or the government in power. Legislation has followed local discontent, as in 1919. Housing authorities have pioneered new ways of working, as in the development of some innovative improvement programmes, which were then followed by legislation making it easier for others to replicate the experience. Legislation is, in any case, only part of what is needed for local government action. Also required are resources, expertise, and a will to seek improvements in a particular way. The range of powers open to housing authorities are wide and varied. The 'enabling role' as developed in the 1980s and 1990s has not involved the acquisition of significant new powers by housing authorities — more a reiteration by central government of the importance of some existing powers, but in a new context, which the next chapter will examine in greater depth.

About this book

The role of local government and the part played by local authorities in housing policy has been examined in this chapter. This historical introduction is an essential means to understanding the nature of recent debates about the role of housing authorities, and a necessary preliminary to exploring, in Chapter 2, the variety of emphases the role of housing authorities has received. This chapter suggests that the confusion which surrounds the meaning of the term 'enabling housing authority' is a consequence of the variety of meanings which different commentators have suggested for housing authorities. Chapter 2 concludes by presenting a model of approaches to defining and conceptualising the enabling role.

One important emphasis in recent accounts of the enabling role has been the need for strategies. What should a housing authority enable? What housing needs and demands exist and who should have what role in dealing with them? What targets or standards should it seek to achieve for the housing conditions of its area? What policies should be adopted? These questions are addressed in Chapter 3 which starts with an examination of the concepts of standards, need, and demand. The administrative framework for housing authority strategies is examined, and its link to the capital bidding system is discussed. The conflict between central and local government which characterised the Thatcher governments and its consequences for local housing strategies are explored.

The production of housing to ensure a decent house at a price that can be afforded for every household has been a policy objective of successive governments since the First World War. The role local authorities have had formerly in providing directly for this need has given way to a concern that housing authorities should assist other providers in ensuring that alternatives are available to those who cannot afford to buy in the market-place. Chapter 4 is concerned with the variety of means available to housing authorities to assist non-municipal investment in housing. The emphasis is on 'social housing', defined to include non-profit rented housing,

20 The Housing Authority as Enabler

usually provided by housing associations and co-operatives, and subsidised housing for shared ownership or for owner-occupation. The use of town and country planning powers, and related means of influencing housing production are the main focus of this chapter. Partnership with housing associations is also considered. The capacity of housing authorities to use these methods to enable the production of sufficient housing is examined.

One of the earliest functions carried out by local authorities in the growing towns and cities of an industrialising Britain was the improvement of the physical condition of the housing stock. The variety of approaches taken to this aspect of their role is used to explore the scope and autonomy housing authorities have to develop their role as enabler in Chapter 5. The examples of area renewal, improvement and repair grants, and various means of improving former municipal stock illustrate the main points.

The book goes on to look at the management of the housing stock, outside the traditional concerns of council housing management, and in particular, at ways in which housing authorities can work with and influence the management of housing owned by housing associations, private landlords and others. Chapter 6 considers the scope and nature of the variety of approaches taken by housing authorities in relation to private sector leasing, the allocation of housing association dwellings, and the development of tenant participation.

Chapter 7 is about the inter-relationships between social policy and housing policy. Housing authorities have a role in improving the housing conditions of particular groups of people, as well as a concern with the physical fabric of housing more generally. Community care and equal opportunities policies are given special attention, and the role of housing authorities in reducing disadvantage is considered. Can social objectives be pursued effectively? Can the housing system serve needs which housing authorities articulate with, or on behalf of, disadvantaged groups such as black people, women and other people with specific disadvantages in the housing system?

The provision of advice and assistance to consumers or potential housing consumers has for a long time been accepted as a role for housing authorities. The assumptions on which this conventional wisdom is based are scrutinised in Chapter 8. The nature of housing advice and assistance is considered, and the experience of local authority housing advice work is examined. The growth of independent specialist services such as Care and Repair is discussed.

The capacity of housing authorities to undertake an enabling role depends largely on the willingness of others to co-operate, or on the bargains which can be struck between housing authorities and others. This creates new challenges for those housing authorities which have for a long time relied on their capacity for direct and unilateral action to solve housing problems. Chapter 9 discusses the management of the enabling role in relation to the relationships and skills it involves, and considers whether the traditional skills of housing and local government professionals are adequate for the tasks of the enabling housing authority.

The final chapter considers how well housing authorities are carrying out their enabling role, and evaluates the adequacy of enabling as an aspect of national housing policy. The future role of housing authorities is considered in the context of developments in central–local government relations, and the role of the state.

Chapter 2
The meaning of enabling

The current role of housing authorities can only be understood with reference to the debates that have taken place about local government generally, especially in the period since 1979. The role of the state has been the subject of bitter disagreement during this period. The role of local authorities, and of housing authorities in particular, has at times been the most visible focus of these disputes. In particular, the issue of whether local authorities should be landlords has divided politicians, and caused divisions within and between local authorities, housing associations, and tenants' organisations.

The Conservative governments of the 1980s had no doubt that the enabling role meant ideally the end of direct provision. Many local authorities and tenants' organisations disagreed. In the midst of the heat, little light was thrown on what 'enabling' should or could mean in practice. There are few detailed elaborations of the 'enabling' role to be found in party political, academic, or official literature. There is instead a good deal of confusion and uncertainty about what this role is supposed to mean and how to conceptualise it. And yet in the mid-1970s there appeared to be a good deal of political and professional consensus about the direction of housing policy, and the role of local government within it. This chapter traces the development of ideas on the role of local housing authorities since the 1970s, showing how and why an apparent consensus broke down in the 1980s, leading to such confusion in the 1990s. After describing a number of ways in which the enabling role has been visualised, a discussion follows of how to make sense of the competing views about the nature and meaning of the role of housing authorities. Three separate aspects or dimensions in many accounts of the enabling role are detected, and a schema is presented as an aid to conceptualising the housing authority as enabler.

The accounts discussed here come from a variety of sources, such as carefully couched government literature, academic writing, and housing practitioners' reports. Every account of the 'enabling' role should be carefully examined to understand the political, professional or other context within which it has been developed.

The comprehensive enabling authority

Housing policy in the immediate post-war years was dominated by a common perception that the priority had to be the construction of new houses within the public sector for the many families who were inadequately housed. To this was added a role in slum clearance and redevelopment.

A growing challenge to large scale council house building emerged in the 1960s, for a number of reasons (see Chapter 1). As the priority attached to slum clearance declined, and the idea of rehabilitation as an alternative took hold from the late 1960s, so the need to build council housing was seen by central government to be reduced. And increasingly in the 1970s, council housing management was the focus for criticism for its insensitivity and ineffectiveness. But arguably one of the most influential critiques of local government's role in improving housing conditions came from a committee set up to examine the role of social services departments in local government.

The Seebohm Report provides a classic statement of the social policy objectives of housing policy at the local government level as seen by many people in central and local government in the 1960s. Housing provision, design, management, policy towards the homeless and others in great need such as elderly and disabled people — all are seen as properly organised and carried out in order to meet social need. The implications of the report for the role of housing authorities is clear in these extracts from the summary of conclusions and recommendations:

> (3) All housing authorities should take a comprehensive and extended view of their responsibilities; in particular, they should be concerned with assisting a family to obtain and keep adequate accommodation, whether it be in the council house sector or not.
>
> (4) Local authorities should know more about the total housing situations in their areas. . . .
>
> (7) A local authority should provide a centre for housing advice and guidance to which the public, as well as workers in statutory and voluntary social service agencies, can turn'.
> (Committee on Local Authority and Allied Social Services 1968, p 133–34)

The following year the Cullingworth Report (CHAC 1969) warmly endorsed this comprehensive view of the housing authorities' role. Both reports provide an illuminating insight into the thinking of academics, professionals, civil servants and some politicians at the time. They do not speak, however, for the local housing authorities who were expected to take steps to understand better the housing needs of their areas, and assist more diverse provision. No evidence was provided that such an approach would be more effective or economical in improving housing conditions. Neither is it clear that the funding and institutional mechanisms and the skills required were in place or could easily be put in place. However, equally it should not be assumed that the approach of Seebohm and Cullingworth was opposed by all housing authorities. Some experience existed of all the approaches recommended in these reports. And since council housing as a solution to housing problems was increasingly unpopular with central governments, it became increasingly important for authorities to pursue other means of improving housing conditions.

The concept of a 'comprehensive housing service' was a direct descendent of Seebohm and Cullingworth's ideas, translated into administrative terms. Practitioners advocated new larger housing departments which would bring together the full range of housing functions carried out by a housing authority (Institute of Housing Managers 1972). Two reports from the Housing Services Advisory Group (HSAG) of the Department of the Environment, in 1977 and 1978, dealt with planning and organisational arrangements respectively. The second report, *Organising a Comprehensive Housing Service*, set out 'the responsibilities which derive from a comprehensive housing service' as:

i. to take an overall view of the demand for housing in an area, to assess housing conditions and develop a strategy designed to meet the requirements revealed in both the public and private sectors;

ii. to encourage an appropriate provision of housing for sale or rent in different ways by all agencies, including private builders, landlords and housing associations and to promote freedom of tenure choice through the development of alternative forms of tenure;

iii. to provide local authority housing . . .;

iv. to allocate the local authority's own housing to the greatest benefit of those in need . . .;

v. to manage the local authority's housing stock in . . . the best possible (way) . . . including, where appropriate, the development of management and other co-operatives;

vi. to provide the necessary stimulus for action in the private sector, including proposals for area improvement, in order to improve standards and make the best use of the private sector stock;

vii. to provide advice and assistance to members of the public on their housing and related problems;

viii. to integrate these activities both inter-departmentally within the authority and in consultation with other bodies. . . .;

ix. to enable the housing service effectively to play its part in contributing to the achievement of broader social and economic policy objectives.

(HSAG, 1978, p 2).

The emphasis on council house provision and management places this account historically before the election of 1979. The relative lack of attention to the private sector and to promoting private forms of provision is also significant.

The 1977 Housing Green Papers (Cmnd 6851 and Cmnd 6852) provided government support for the view of the role of local housing authorities which had by now become something of a conventional wisdom in academic and professional circles, and was adopted by some of the larger housing authorities after local government reorganisation in the mid-1970s. The government's view downgraded the importance of council house building programmes, but did not foresee any elimination of the role of provider, arguing instead for more plurality of provision, and in particular for the growth of owner-occupation.

> To be fair, the review did recommend that local authorities should take a strategic view of housing needs and resources in their areas and adjust policies not only in relation to the demand and supply of housing but also in relation to transport, employment, health and social service policies. But without central guidelines on how this is to be achieved and with the continuing bifurcation of the market, it is difficult to envisage already hard-pressed housing departments so radically altering their policies to ease shortage and eliminate injustices, simply on this recommendation.
>
> (McKay and Cox 1979, pp 147–48).

The non-providing housing authority

The most recent major government statement of policy in relation to the role of local housing authorities is contained within the White Papers for England and Wales, and Scotland published in 1987 (Cm 214, 242). The key sentence from the paper for England and Wales is:

> The future role of local authorities will essentially be a strategic one identifying housing needs and demands, encouraging innovative

26 The Housing Authority as Enabler

> methods of provision by other bodies to meet such needs, maximising the use of private finance, and encouraging the new interest in the revival of the independent rented sector.
>
> (Cm 214, p 14)

In Scotland, though:

> Housing authorities' dominant concern is bound to continue to be the condition and management of their existing stock. Alongside this, local authorities also have an essential strategic role, in identifying the overall housing needs of their areas, particularly the needs of the homeless, and considering the means by which they can be met most effectively.
>
> (Cm 242, p 21)

This different approach recognises the different tenure structure of Scotland, where public sector renting still exceeded 40 per cent in 1991. The White Papers provided a brief account of the role seen for housing authorities, confirming the direction of policy since 1979, when the Conservatives came to power partly on the promise to grant public sector tenants the right to buy their homes. As Malpass and Murie point out, policy after 1979 was directed at boosting owner-occupation through the Right to Buy and in other ways, at encouraging repair and improvement of existing housing in all tenures, and at targeting public spending on those most in need (1990, pp 88–89). By the late 1980s the emphasis lay more on the expansion of the private rented sector, partly through the privatisation of remaining council stocks. Housing associations were seen by central government as the favoured owners of social rented housing.

While there are some striking similarities between the roles seen for housing authorities in the Labour government's 1977 Green Papers and the 1987 White Papers, there is also a big difference. Taken along with other developments in local-central relations and in housing policy and finance, the role proposed in 1987 can be seen as essentially supportive of the private sector. Local housing authorities are to be relatively weak actors on the stage, with diminished powers and capital resources to apply to the task of furthering their local housing objectives. Their primary task is to assist others to pursue ends which do not always match those of the housing authority. The White Paper does not address the issue of the nature of the bargaining and leverage processes that might be involved where the needs identified by the housing authority are not the same as the demands identified by the private investor.

The Housing Acts, and the Local Government and Housing Act

The meaning of enabling 27

1989 (for England and Wales) which followed the 1987 White Papers provided part of the legislative framework within which the role of housing authorities could develop. Powers to fund private rented and shared ownership schemes were clarified and extended. The deregulation of private renting included housing associations, against the wishes of the housing association movement. The legislation allowed for alternative landlords to take over council stock, with voting arrangements which made it easier for transfers to take place in England and Wales than Scotland. However, most transfers took place under previous legislation which allowed housing authorities, under certain conditions, to transfer stock to landlords approved by a majority vote of tenants.

Further legislation and regulations followed in 1989 and 1990. These provide a financial framework for housing authorities in England and Wales which encourages 'enabling' schemes such as private building under licence, improvement for sale, and nomination arrangements with developers. No further legislative clarification of extension of the enabling framework has been forthcoming, but by 1991 the government had begun to promote more actively the 'enabling' role of housing and planning authorities, by the publication of a circular (DoE 1991a) (see Chapter 4), and in the form of unpublished letters of guidance to housing authorities about capital allocations and the role of housing authorities, for example.

A note by the Department of the Environment in June 1990, produced as guidance for authorities preparing their HIP submissions, and entitled *Local Authorities' Housing Role*, provides probably the fullest elaboration of the government's view. The key passage is:

> The housing role of local authorities is changing; in particular there is growing emphasis on their role as enablers of private sector provision. Ministers wish to encourage this trend. . . . Local authorities are ceasing to be the main providers of subsidised housing for rent; but they retain their statutory duties under housing legislation and will remain responsible for ensuring, so far as resources permit, that needs for housing in their area are met, by the private sector alone where possible, with public sector subsidy where necessary. This will require some of them to take a broader view of their responsibilities than they have in the past, and to develop their information sources and monitoring arrangements accordingly. Much of the HIP submission itself will be about public expenditure needed to provide for people who cannot afford housing at market prices or cannot maintain their homes without assistance. The case for extra public expenditure should be justified, however, by reference to the extent to which

> the private sector is able and willing to make provision for low cost housing, and the steps that the authority is taking both to maximise the private sector contribution and to make best use of its own stock.
>
> (DoE 1990a, paras 2–3)

This paints the clearest picture yet of a housing system provided by the private sector, apparently with minimum public support. Nothing is said about the tax position of owner-occupation. The note goes on to examine the role of housing authorities under three headings — owner-occupation, new rented provision, public sector renovation. In relation to owner-occupation, authorities are asked to consider their planning and land release policies (see Chapter 4), to discuss affordability with housebuilders and financial institutions, to consider partnership schemes with the private and housing association sectors (see Chapter 4), and to consider their new powers for renovation and clearance under the 1989 legislation (see Chapter 5).

In relation to new rented provision, authorities are asked to consider whether they can use the existing stock better, and how they can focus provision on 'people who really need it' (para 11). 'Authorities in areas of excess demand should also review their allocation policies to ensure that lettings — including any nominations to housing association tenancies — go so far as is practical only to people who could not provide for themselves in the private sector' (para 11). They are also asked to examine low cost ownership schemes including cash incentives, and shared ownership, for those who can afford it, and private rented provision, with public subsidy if necessary. 'Where new subsidised housing for rent is the only way of meeting need, Ministers intend that housing asociations should be the main providers, relying to the maximum practical degree on private finance' (para 17). The Department 'Would not normally expect to see plans for building new council houses in significant numbers except where other approaches have been exhaustively considered and it is clear that unmet demand from people who cannot afford to house themselves, and who need to live in the area, is unlikely to be met in any other practicable way' (para 18).

This is one of the clearest statements of a residual and ever-diminishing role for council housing available. Ironically, it comes at a time when the public subsidy for council housing in England and Wales is virtually restricted to supporting the Housing Benefit system. There is a hint that the DoE suspects housing authorities are not establishing a clear enough separation between those who cannot meet their need in the private market, and those who

The meaning of enabling 29

can, who should be left to do so. This begs the question of whether people's housing needs are capable of such clear and permanent categorisation, and neglects the tax advantages of owner-occupation.

In relation to public sector renovation, authorities are asked to target resources on selected estates, including those at risk of becoming unlettable; and to consider sales to private developers or others. As far as possible, housing authorities are to reduce their role in these estates by introduction of the private sector, or through tenant participation. There is an implicit recognition that there is a limit to the Right to Buy, where people are too poor to exercise it, and where the housing stock is so run-down and unattractive that those who could are more likely to move out than buy.

A year later the note was supplemented by another of the same title (DoE 1991b), which indicated the Department's intention to make performance of housing authorities the primary criterion in the distribution of discretionary HIPs allocations. The performance criteria would include, 'The extent to which the authority is likely to use its allocation to develop its enabling role in co-operation with housing associations or other parts of the private sector' (para 9).

A third note (DoE 1992a) expands upon the factors to be taken into account in assessing authorities' efficiency and effectiveness under two broad headings — commitment, and activity. The Department will be looking for evidence of housing authority commitment and activity in relation to housing providers and housing consumers. Providers are listed as:

— Housing Corporation and housing associations
— Financial institutions
— Private landlords
— Voluntary and charitable agencies
— Developers
— Housebuilders.

Consumers are:

— Tenants groups and individual tenants
— Private owners and renters
— Families seeking homes.

(Annex A)

The use of the word 'families' is presumably deliberate, and intended to exclude single people. This is a puzzling omission, given the emphasis on assessing all forms of need in previous statements.

30 The Housing Authority as Enabler

The Department provides a number of examples of the types of activity authorities are expected to engage in. In relation to housing providers these are:

— use of planning powers to achieve affordable housing;
— funding capital investment through LA HAG and improvement grants;
— disposal of land;
— use of compulsory purchase;
— partnerships with the private sector, including housing associations;
— 'special initiatives' to make best use of private space, such as flats over shops;
— support and guidance to housing providers and agencies.

In relation to housing consumers authorities are recommended to provide:

— housing advice and promotion of housing options, rights and duties;
— alternative options for council tenants, such as cash incentive schemes to encourage moves into owner-occupation;
— funding through home improvement grants etc.

(Annex A, DoE 1992a)

These notes, and the 1987 White Paper, provide the fullest account of the government's view of the housing authority's role available. Some additional guidance relates to specific aspects of this role, in particular the use of the planning system to create affordable housing (see Chapter 4), and the improvement and renewal provisions of the 1989 Act (see Chapter 5). But little has been done by the DoE to address the issue of the general adequacy of the powers and resources available to authorities, or to consider the nature of the bargaining processes that are involved, or to consider the cost effectiveness of the approaches recommended.

Alternative conceptions of the enabling housing authority

Other writers have provided their own elaborations of the role of housing authorities, differing in important respects from the government's. One of the best known accounts is given in *The Inquiry into British Housing* (1985, p 43):

> We believe that local authorities should increasingly be co-ordinators and enablers of housing activity at local level. It

is essential, we believe, that there is a strong local democratic base for housing policy, and that there should be bodies with the powers to ensure its implementation. Our proposals ... call for a greater variety of agencies to be involved in the provision and management of housing in the future. Some may need help if they are to make a contribution; all will require co-ordination if housing resources are to be fully used in order to meet needs. These functions can be fulfilled by local authorities

The report goes on to elaborate the dimensions of the enabling role. The first is concerned with strategy — assessing needs and devising a plan to meet them. The second is concerned with 'social responsibility' — meeting the needs of the most vulnerable, not necessarily through council housing, but certainly through effective control over some lettings of good quality housing. Thirdly, the report sees local authorities having a role in enforcing minimum standards, using enforcement action where necessary, as in relation to unfitness, overcrowding, and other environmental health concerns. Next the report recommends a breaking up of the larger council estates, with more varied ownership and management arrangements, including tenant involvement.

Finally authorities are said to require new powers, 'The most important' of which would give them the right to nominate tenants to other landlords in certain circumstances: 'If they (housing associations) were able to refuse whenever they considered the nominee to be "undesirable" the way would be open to further social segregation between council tenants and others ...' (p 45). The other new power specified is in relation to enforcing standards of housing management or maintenance by other landlords. The report recommends that central and local government should examine how a greater separation could take place between the authority's landlord and 'strategic/co-ordinating/enforcement' roles. But as more of the day-to-day management on council estates is taken on by housing co-operatives and other management bodies, so the two roles will become similar, it is suggested, with an emphasis on monitoring and enforcing standards.

This vision of the 'strategic/co-ordinating/enforcement' role had some similarities with the White Papers' view two years later, but it is different in that it shows greater commitment to housing authorities being able to achieve their housing policy objectives, and meet needs they identify, irrespective of the views of others if necessary.

In recent years the view of the role of the State encapsulated in the phrase 'enabling local authority' has been most often associated with the political Right, but by no means exclusively so. Clapham, for example, argues in a publication sponsored by the Fabian Society that:

> It is clear that the strategic housing authority even without any housing stock could play a major role in the housing system
>
> (p 64)

and

> putting down the burdens of dealing with day-to-day management could leave councillors and housing officers free to focus their attention on issues which are more important in achieving the social objectives of housing.
>
> (1989, p 65)

Clapham sees two key aspects of the enabling, strategic role: first, the need to ensure that sufficient housing of at least minimal standard is available. This requires both regulatory (for example, building standards), and facilitatory powers (for example, grants). And secondly, there is a need to ensure that all have access to housing of a decent standard. This could involve a variety of approaches, such as attaching conditions to developments aided by the authority, or through nomination rights and monitoring procedures in relation to lettings by co-operatives, housing associations, and others. Clapham devotes a separate section to the role of housing authorities in registering, monitoring and supervising all types of landlord in their area.

> For example it could offer an advice and conciliation service for disputes between residents and landlords. It could also offer aid and advice both to individuals and to co-operatives and other housing organisations
>
> (p 63)

Clapham is clearer than most about the objectives he seeks to pursue. They are equality, democracy, freedom and community. Clapham argues that these can never be met by the provision of council housing, or even through a diversity of provision of rented housing. What is needed is a fundamental transformation in the legal relationships involved, which 'removes the unequal power relationship between producers and consumers'(p 38). His prescription is for co-operatives to become the dominant form of rented housing, replacing council housing.

Local housing authorities would therefore lose

> what has generally been regarded as their major housing functions. However, they should still have a major role in achieving the

objectives of equality, democracy, freedom and community in the housing system. ... local authorities are the appropriate agencies to perform a strategic role because of their local scale and their accountability to the local electorate .... key issues such as the amount, location and distribution of housing should be the subject of local political debate and decision makers in these areas should be accountable

(p 53)

Clapham argues that local housing authorities should have stronger powers to regulate housing in their areas, and in particular to ensure that other landlords, especially the co-operatives he so much favours, make their contribution to achieving freedom, democracy, equality, and community.

His views have more in common with the Duke of Edinburgh's Inquiry Report than with the government. Superficially he shares the government's anathema for council housing, but he has very clear proposals for replacing it with publicly-funded rented housing, whereas the government wishes to substitute private provision or private funding as far as possible. He shares the Inquiry Report's willingness to control and regulate the market to ensure the achievement of social objectives. He takes it for granted that public expenditure will be required to fund housing for rent. He does not see the same strict division between market provision for those who can provide for their own needs, and public involvement in providing for the rest. He does not accept the view implicit in the government's policy statements that only those who can operate in the market-place are entitled to any choice. His book, and the Inquiry Report, have very different implications for the role of housing authorities than the 1987 White Papers.

Defining and conceptualising 'enabling'

There are a number of accounts of the role of housing authorities or local authorities in general, some of which have been reviewed above. Most are expressed in prosyletizing tones, and significant differences exist between them. The authors range from the Right to the Left in politics, and from professionals to academics. 'The exact meaning of the enabling role ... has been the subject of some debate' (Gyford 1991, p 1). Some accounts from the political Left (such as Clapham 1989) have something in common with Right wing elaborations, and yet enormous differences exist in the meaning and purposes of their visions of local government.

The Housing Authority as Enabler

The Left accuses the Right of attacking local government, while the Right claims it is instead liberating it from the burdens of direct service provision, a goal shared by some on the Left. It is clear that there is no single account or definition of the role of housing authorities on which everyone can agree.

There are a number of dimensions on which disagreements occur, explaining the confusing differences and similarities between accounts of the role of housing authorities. Here three dimensions are considered — concerned with models of policy making, with the way in which resources are distributed by the market or the state, and with the extent to which authorities act alone or with others.

The first dimension is concerned with the way in which policies are developed. Authorities can be placed at points along this dimension or continuum, the ends of which could be seen as ideal types against which the real world might be compared. At one end is the 'bottom up' approach to determining what gets done or provided. 'Bottom up' planning involves citizens and consumers determining the type, amount and quality of housing services to be provided. This ideal type is applicable equally to private and public sector provision. Within the public sector citizens or consumers would determine the nature of housing services, as in a co-operative, for example. Within the private sector, services, including new housing, would be supplied in response to consumer demand. On this continuum it is irrelevant whether the consumer or citizen is operating in the public or private sector.

Several examples of accounts favouring this end of the continuum can be mentioned, such as the government's exhortations to housing authorities to assist the private sector to respond to demand in the market, and to involve tenants in management. The Citizen's Charter as it applies to housing can also be seen to be about supporting this view of the role of housing authorities. Clapham's view of the rented sector dominated by consumer co-operatives is another example. And Gyford's 'bottom up' model of the enabling role is intended to address 'some of the particular preoccupations of the political left' (1991 p 2). This model emphasises the community development and empowering opportunities of local government, in which they operate as a 'training agency, resource centre and support service for local community groups' (Gyford 1991, p 4).

At the other end of the continuum is the planned approach. This end of the continuum suggests a model of policy making in which local authorities — through the legitimacy of elected councillors, and the expertise of professional officers — are the decision makers who determine policies on the nature and distribution of housing services at the local level. Residents may object, but housing authorities know best. In the 1970s this was to be achieved as a result of comprehensive, rational planning systems such as PPBS (Planning, Programming, Budgeting Systems) (Hogwood and Gunn 1984). Housing plans, HIPs, and HSOPs were conceived at this time as the epitome of rational, 'top down' planning by housing authorities (see Chapter 1). The Seebohm (1968) and Cullingworth (CHAC 1969) Reports provide prescriptions for housing authorities to take on this planning role.

In theory, most contemporary accounts emphasise 'bottom up' as well as 'top down' elements, placing importance on citizen or consumer involvement. Of the accounts considered in this chapter, the Duke of Edinburgh's Inquiry Report (1985) comes closest to the 'top down' end of the continuum in its emphasis on assessing needs and developing a strategy, but then goes on to encourage housing authorities to promote tenant management in its own housing and that of other landlords. In practice, however, many housing authorities appear to be placed on this continuum near to the 'top down' end of the spectrum. Evidence from surveys of housing authorities suggests very little involvement by tenants over most housing issues in the late 1980s (Cairncross, Clapham and Goodlad 1989, p 47).

The second dimension is concerned with the extent of state or market provision. The opposite ends of the spectrum are defined by whether state action or market forces are the determining feature in the distribution of resources. At one end is the enabling role seen by those such as Ridley (1988) and Henney (1985) which minimises intervention in the market to the least provision of services and 'public goods' which cannot be easily provided in the market-place. Exponents of this view see the market as the best — most efficient and socially just — mechanism for the distribution of resources, and criticise public bureaucracies and representative democracy for being wasteful, inefficient and profligate (Stoker 1991, 238–242). The DoE's account of the enabling role of housing authorities falls clearly towards this end of the continuum, with its commitment to private provision and financing, and its reluctance to condone public provision, unless all other avenues have been exhausted.

Ridley claims:

> The role of the local authority will no longer be that of the universal provider ... it is for local authorities to organise, secure and monitor the provision of services, without necessarily providing them themselves ... authorities will need to operate in a more pluralist way than in the past, alongside a wide variety of public, private and voluntary agencies
>
> (Ridley 1988, pp 17,22,25)

Henney's Centre for Policy Studies pamphlet *Trust the Tenant* (1985) couches its attack on municipal ownership in the language of choice and consumer control.

At the other end of the continuum is the interventionist view that local government should provide or act in whatever way the local authority considers reasonable and effective at securing the desired outcome. The adoption of such an approach might involve a decision to provide directly or not, depending on the authority's view of what is likely to meet social need best. This need not involve rejection of market mechanisms, providing the distribution of resources resulting is in line with the authority's desired outcome. It implies, though, that authorities have freedom to act in a wide variety of ways, and have the powers and resources to ensure their plans are implemented, directly or indirectly.

The Duke of Edinburgh's Inquiry Report is near this end of the continuum, with its emphasis on the assessment of local needs, and of housing authorities having the powers and resources to act in meeting need. Clapham's account places a restriction on the type of action open to local authorities, and is thus placed on the continuum slightly nearer to the market distribution end — he wishes the housing authority's actions always to be mediated by consumers' views, in the case of rented housing through the quasi-market of a housing co-operative. In other ways, though, he is a long way away from the market end of the continuum.

John Stewart's account of the role of local government provides another example. He argues that every local authority in Britain should have a power of 'general competence' like many of our European neighbours, 'That is, the right to take any action on behalf of its local community, that is not specifically barred to it' (1989 p 238). He sees the 'primary role' of this type of local government as being 'concern for the problems and issues faced by local communities' (p 240). He goes on to criticise the Thatcher governments for their limited view of local government, which he says was a view of local authorities as (preferably indirect) providers of a limited range of local services. Stewart is undogmatic about whether local authorities should provide services directly or not (p 242). The enabling authority might:

— provide services directly;
— regulate provision by others;
— provide grants;
— use its influence as a major employer or purchaser;
— assist through the provison of knowledge, skills or information;
— contract with others for the provision of goods and services;

- bring people and organisations together;
- assist new organisations;
- involve service users in running services;
- speak on behalf of the area and its people.

Within a Labour authority this is likely to mean, in practice, a commitment to higher levels of direct provision. But there are many people in local government who believe that housing authorities should have more freedom and resources to do as they like in the interests of their community, without necessarily taking the same approach as Labour controlled authorities. Authorities such as Wandsworth and Westminster are unusual amongst Conservative authorities in their commitment to this minimalist view of the role of local government.

The third continuum is concerned with the extent to which housing authorities might act alone or with others in achieving their objectives. Housing authorities which see the provision of council housing as the only solution to housing needs are at one end of the continuum, sharing their position on this dimension with those who see housing associations as the only means to improved housing conditions. Those who seek to develop a working relationship with a wide variety of other agencies and actors are at the other. The government's view favours working with the private sector to achieve better housing conditions. This is a somewhat restrictive view compared with Clapham and Brooke (1989) who suggest a wider range of involvement with voluntary and statutory as well as private sector agents.

Brooke, a former Chief Executive in local government, sees the erosion of local government powers in the 1980s as providing an opportunity to develop collaborative working with other agencies (for example, housing, health and social work services in relation to community care; police, health and social work in relation to child abuse). He emphasises the different types of relationships that can be formed between local authorities and their electorate, the private and voluntary sectors, and so on. Relationships may be of a number of types:

- control
- partial control
- partnership
- part ownership
- purchaser/vendor
- support
- regulation
- influence.

(1989)

38 The Housing Authority as Enabler

There are some similarities between the accounts of Brooke and Stewart, but the major difference is that Stewart sees the local authority as one actor amongst others in an intrinsically political process. What local authorities do will be determined at least in part by their relationship to the electorate, community groups, local industry, central government and so on. Brooke sees the local authority as the principal participant on the local policy scene, able to determine the nature of relationships through its own choice. This point will be examined further in Chapter 9.

In practice it is hard to suggest examples of the 'act alone' type of authority, despite the myth of the single-minded Labour authority committed to council housing and no other form of action. However, Militant's ascendancy in Liverpool in the 1980s is a recent example. There are many examples of the 'act with others', or networking local authority, including most of Britain's large towns and cities such as Birmingham, Leicester, Cardiff, Glasgow, and Newcastle, and London boroughs such as Islington and Kensington and Chelsea. A characteristic of such authorities is the effort devoted to developing relationships with housing associations, private funders, residents' groups, specialist voluntary organisations, social services and health service agencies, government departments and other funders.

At some unknown point along the continuum are the 20 authorities which have sold their housing stocks to housing associations, and which aim to achieve their objectives through other agencies. It is hard to place them precisely without knowing more about the number of agencies with which they seek to collaborate. It may be that they attempt to work only with the housing association which took over their stock. If so, they would be placed further towards the 'acting alone' end of the continuum than many authorities with substantial stocks of their own. Divesting itself of its housing stock does not guarantee that an authority's role is managed in the pluralist way consistent with most accounts of this dimension of the enabling authority.

The schema which results from this discussion of three dimensions of the role of housing authorities (Figure 2.1) provides a useful device for examining different accounts of the 'enabling' role. The government is placed at or near the bottom on all three dimensions. Over the last 20 years the government view of the role of housing authorities has moved from a position near the top of the first dimension and mid-way along the other two, to the position occupied by the Conservative governments of the 1980s and early 1990s.

Clapham's views are at the bottom on the first dimension, in the top half on the second, and in the middle on the third. The Duke

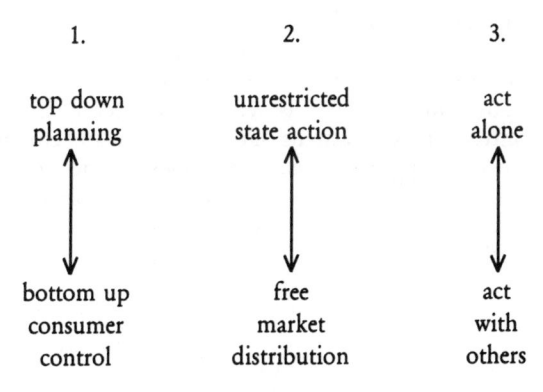

1.	2.	3.
top down planning	unrestricted state action	act alone
↕	↕	↕
bottom up consumer control	free market distribution	act with others

Figure 2.1: Dimensions of the enabling role

of Edinburgh's Inquiry Report is somewhere in the middle of the first two dimensions, and near the bottom of the third. Ridley, in contrast, argues for the bottom end of all three dimensions.

Finally, it is perhaps surprising that the Thatcher governments which were so committed to a particular view of the role of housing authorities were so reticent about setting out in detail what they meant by it. The explanation may lie in the position that view occupies on the schema — near the bottom in all three dimensions — where the role of the local authority as a planning agency is minimised in favour of consumer control, where the scope of enabling is minimised in favour of market mechanisms, and where the involvement of other agencies required bargains to be struck and compromises to be agreed. Perhaps the enabling role was not elaborated because it was so minimal.

Conclusion

This chapter has examined recent debates about the role of housing authorities in some detail, and contrasted the 'comprehensive' housing authority with different elaborations of the 'enabling' housing authority. The government's view of the housing authority's role places emphasis on assisting private provision, including housing associations, and involving consumers in the management of housing where it remains in the public sector.

The 'enabling' concept is then unpicked, so that different elements or dimensions can be examined more closely. Three aspects are considered, concerned with the extent to which housing authorities or consumers should determine local housing policies, with the extent to which state or market mechanisms of distribution should apply to housing services and provision, and the extent to which housing authorities should operate alone, or in collaboration with others. The government's view is seen to fall clearly in favour of consumer control, market systems of distribution, and collaboration with others, especially private sector agencies, in the local housing system. This minimalist view has not been spelled out very clearly, helping to cause confusion about the meaning of the 'enabling' role of housing authorities.

Chapter 3
The strategic housing authority

The process of considering the future in order to influence it — which priorities to set, how to achieve objectives, and so on — is referred to as planning. The product or outcome of such a process is a plan or strategy. This chapter examines the place of planning in the enabling role. It starts with a discussion of the purposes of analysis and planning, and goes on to describe the administrative systems within which housing strategies have been developed, and their relevance to the work of housing authorities. The central concepts of standards, need, and demand are then considered. The chapter concludes with a discussion and evaluation of a variety of approaches commonly used in developing housing strategies.

It is not self-evident what should be enabled by housing authorities in their enabling role. Enabling one housing initiative involves *not* enabling others, or at least spreading the jam more thinly. Supporting one tenure has an impact on others. Facilitating renewal or rehabilitation in one place has implications for renewal or new construction or other programmes elsewhere. Helping one special needs group may involve not helping others. Even where a minimal view is held of the role of the housing authority, decisions have to be taken about how to exercise that role. At least some differences of emphasis will exist between or amongst officers or councillors within an authority and from one authority to another. At an extreme, fundamental differences of policy separate one council from another, or central government from local government. Choices have to be made as clearly as in the allocation of council houses to one applicant rather than another. Enabling is a political process.

Why plan?

The case for planning the use of housing resources can be stated strongly whether applied to the individual, to central government, to housing providers in the private or voluntary sector, or to the work of housing authorities:

- Housing is an expensive and long-lasting good and merits careful consideration before expenditure decisions are made. It has a life span which usually exceeds the life span of its occupants. Spending money or expending resources of other kinds unwisely on housing is more serious in its consequences for individuals and society than an unwise decision to purchase a pair of shoes or even a pair of battleships, for example.
- Housing planning and analysis provide valuable information about the nature of housing problems or issues. Housing policy making shares with other types of planning the potential benefits of looking systematically at the nature of the problems or issues to be addressed. Housing problems may be hidden from superficial view, and a systematic examination of housing circumstances and people's needs may reveal previously unheard of problems and issues, as in the case of domestic violence for many years. Knowledge of the condition of the housing stock, for example, is a key aspect of deciding whether to spend resources on repair grants for individual houses or on area renewal programmes. Knowledge of the demographic structure of households and how it is changing is a key aspect of providing for the housing needs of elderly people, for example.
- Housing planning aids the democratic process. It allows the clear adoption of priorities for using whatever the resources of money, staff and so on that are available. Explicit statements of priorities and objectives are an aid to political debate. Policies and priorities can be disagreed with, and those responsible for them held to account.
- Housing planning involves assessing policy options against each other so that the option most likely to achieve the desired objective at least cost — in financial, social and other terms — is seen to be best and can be adopted as policy.
- The planning process can be used to evaluate the outcome of past policies, so that future policies are more effective.
- Planning provides a guide to action. An unambiguous strategy ensures that resources are devoted to programmmes and activities that are in line with the housing authority's priorities. It also provides a means to consider opportunities which arise — if they enable the plan's priorities to be furthered, then they should be grasped.

Given these advantages it is surprising to encounter resistance or failure to engage in comprehensive, rational planning of the type implied above. It is important to look at why this is the case. A number of reasons can be identified:

- Even when a strategy exists, it is commonplace to make decisions about particular issues as and when problems or opportunities arise, taking account of whatever views or information is judged appropriate at the time. The future is uncertain and unpredictable, and it is tempting to wait until the future becomes the present before taking decisions.
- There are practical, political and resource constraints on the collection of information on which strategic decisions can be taken. There is a fear that housing authorities could consume disproportionate amounts of time and money on research and analysis with no guarantee that this would be a cost effective use of resources, or result in additional capital allocations, for example. Also there will be at least some who claim that they do not need more research and analysis of housing problems they know to exist.
- There are difficulties with some of the techniques of planning. It is difficult to predict demand or need in the future, for example. The unpredictable often happens. It is sometimes not clear that there are sound enough techniques available for comparing one policy option against another, and in any case, politicians may make an intuitive choice between options on the basis of their values rather than on the results of a cost benefit analysis or other evaluation of options.
- Many plans are so bland that they provide no guide to action. They are the outcome of a process intended to reconcile competing views, and the only way conflict has been removed is by the parties adopting an indisputable statement such as 'a decent home for every household at an affordable price'. This sort of 'strategy' has the benefit of being a policy around which everyone can unite, but it hardly provides a guide for choosing between alternatives in particular circumstances.
- Some politicians and professionals may prefer to leave objectives and policies unstated, since to be explicit is equivalent to inviting criticism if objectives and targets are not achieved, or if consistency is not observed.
- Some politicians would prefer to leave the future to the working of the free market. Any role for planning is restricted to the minimum necessary to assist markets to operate.

There is, however, widespread support for the view that despite the difficulties and weaknesses of strategic planning, there should be an attempt to develop local housing strategies (see, for example, Inquiry 1985; Merrett 1986; Maclennan 1991). A belief in the value of planning is a characteristic of a democratic society which values rational scientific inquiry. The arguments for planning are therefore considered to be overwhelming, especially when the process is undertaken with an appreciation of the limitations and of the political nature of what is involved (Hogwood and Gunn 1984).

Local housing plans

The main statements of housing strategy by housing authorities to be found in a written form in Britain are associated with or contained in Housing Strategies and Investment Programmes (HIPs) in England, Housing Strategies and Operational Plans (HSOPs) in Wales, and Housing Plans (in Scotland). These were introduced in the 1977 Housing Policy Green Papers (Cmnd 6851 and 6852). The Green Papers had concluded that Britain no longer had a single housing problem, but a series of local problems and difficulties for which local strategic housing plans could help provide remedies. The Green Papers mark a significant change in perception of the role of housing authorities in the post-war period.

> Central Government must lay down an overall national policy framework, and provide advice where necessary. But the key to the success of national housing policy now lies in the development of effective *local* housing strategies, planned and carried out by local authorities with the minimum of detailed intervention from the centre.
>
> (Cmnd 6851, p 42)

These local housing strategies were expected to incorporate assessments of the housing needs of the area, across all tenures. They should take account of policies in related fields such as town planning, social services and health, and should ensure that other housing providers could play their part, for example through the allocation of land or planning permission. The enabling authority was expected to clarify its role through the strategy set down in a local housing plan. The answer to the question of what should be enabled was to be contained there.

For England and Wales the Green Paper went on:

> The Government therefore propose to institute and develop a system of local authority housing investment programmes (HIPs).

These will be drawn up as part of the local housing strategy. They will set out the authority's proposals for investment in the whole range of its housing activities for the following four years, within the context of the expected activity of other public housing bodies in the area and private housebuilders.

(Cmnd 6851, p 44)

Elsewhere, in a series of circulars, the Department of the Environment referred to Housing **Strategies** and Investment Programmes (author's emphasis), making clear that the capital programme set down in the HIPs was part of a larger strategic statement.

In Scotland, Housing Plans were expected to incorporate:

— an analysis of housing provision in the area and an assessment of local housing needs;
— a statement of the objectives and policies which the authority proposes to pursue. This will include an assessment of the contribution which other housing agencies ... may be expected to make to meet the assessed needs;
— and a costed capital programme presenting the authority's own contributions to meeting needs over the next five years.

(Cmnd 6852, p 44)

It is important to emphasise that HIPs, HSOPs and Housing Plans are part of a national system of public spending control. They contain bids for capital allocations and there is no requirement on central government to make the allocations requested. The system is intended to provide the information necessary to assist central government to weigh the needs of one area against another, and to influence the balance of spending particularly between public and private sectors, and between new housing construction and modernisation or rehabilitation. Hambleton summarises the four objectives of the system at its inception as:

1. To improve central direction over the broad priorities for housing expenditure.
2. To bring housing expenditure fully within the arrangements for public expenditure control.
3. To increase local discretion by giving local authorities greater responsibility for deciding the right mix of investment.
4. To encourage a more thoughtful approach to the formulation and implementation of housing policy at local level . . . .

(Hambleton 1986, pp 120–21)

This 'more thoughtful approach' was intended to be comprehensive, rational, and systematic. Housing authorities were expected to examine the housing situation of their areas across all tenures, and to consider the needs for renovation as well as new building. They were expected to follow a rational planning model involving a stage by stage process of planning. The first stage should involve an examination of need including an estimate of future housing needs derived from projections of households set against estimates of the future housing stock across all tenures; then objectives should be adopted; and policy options examined to see which would best meet the objectives (HSAG 1977; SDD 1977).

Some changes have taken place since the system was introduced. English and Welsh local authorities still make annual submissions, and receive a capital allocation in one block, instead of the three used in England when the system was first introduced. Capital allocations to particular English authorities are influenced by a number of factors of which the HIP submission is arguably least important. Other factors include the previous pattern of spending; use of the Generalised Needs Index (GNI) which 'is intended to summarise the many dimensions of housing need by giving appropriate weights to indicators of different types of need' (Gibb and Munro 1991); and the role of the Department of the Environment's Regional Controllers, who by 1991 exercised discretion over 60 per cent of HIP funds. In 1992 the Department proposed the elimination of the GNI element altogether. Increasingly discretion has been exercised in favour of authorities which demonstrate the most effective performance and the best quality housing strategy:

> To give some examples, the Secretary of State will want to see whether the local authority has established a well-defined housing strategy for the area, with a realistic view of the resources likely to be available from all potential sources. He will want to know whether an authority has made the best use of available stock, for example by offering cash incentive schemes, and kept voids to a minimum ... he will be interested in the authority's involvement with housing associations, ... Evidence of cooperation with private sector developers ... will be looked for. Similarly he will want to hear how active the authority has been in consulting and involving its tenants and other local people, and in using its planning powers to meet its objectives.
> (DoE 1992a, para 29)

In other words the primary criterion is the extent to which the authority has taken on the enabling role seen for housing authorities by the government, rather than the extent of need. Authorities have quickly adapted to this situation, putting on as impressive a display of their activities as possible when Ministers visit their authority, and writing their HIPs statements to echo the government's approach. Many have been disappointed with the results. The process has been described as a lottery by the Association of Metropolitan Authority's Under Secretary for Housing, Matthew Warburton (1992), but is defended by Ministers for its flexibility and encouragement of efficiency (Blake 1992).

As the role of housing authorities as providers has diminished, and the role of housing associations as the principal providers of new social rented housing has grown, there has been growing disquiet about the existence of two separate systems for channelling resources into social housing in local areas, operated by the DoE and the Housing Corporation. The Department has, therefore, stated its intention of bringing the two systems together 'in support of the objective of a coherent strategy for each area' (Local Authority Housing Division 1992, para 9).

In Wales, part of the capital allocation is entirely determined by a formula in which the Welsh House Condition Survey plays an important part. The remainder is determined through a competitive system aimed at ensuring the Welsh Office's priorities are implemented through special initiatives (Audit Commission 1992, pp 33–34).

In Scotland Housing Plans are prepared every four years (with the exception of Glasgow which submits biennually), and are intended to provide a strategy for a five year period, with a costed capital programme for three years which is then rolled forward on an annual basis. A 'housing checklist', based on a questionnaire providing statistical information, and a capital programme, is submitted each year. Capital allocations are made in two blocks, for use in relation to public and private sector expenditure. There is no GNI in Scotland, and capital allocations appear to be based on past spending patterns, conformity with national policy objectives, and some assessment of relative need by the Scottish Office influenced by the content of Housing Plans and other contact between local authorities and government.

Finally, one objective of HIPs, HSOPs and Housing Plans — to assist in meeting demand in the private sector — has been promoted by central government as the primary purpose of the system. Strategies are intended to provide guidance to developers and individuals about the policy framework within which decisions about grants, planning permission and so on will be taken.

This is not the place to set out a detailed history of the HIPs, HSOPs and Housing Plan systems. That has been done effectively elsewhere (Bramley, Leather and Murie 1980; Leather 1983; Hole and Brindley 1983; Midwinter, Keating and Taylor 1984; Hambleton 1986; Carter and Brown 1991; Maclennan 1991; Audit Commission 1992). It is sufficient here to set down the main reasons why the system has 'been transformed from a mechanism which emphasised the importance of developing local strategies into an instrument of central financial and policy control' (Hambleton 1986, p 121). There are several reasons concerned with the politics of housing planning and the technical aspects of it.

The rational planning model which authorities were intended to use was greeted with less than enthusiasm by many housing authorities despite the apparent consensus between central and local government surrounding its introduction. Authorities did not always have the staff and other resources to engage in the sort of exercise envisaged, and there was a lack of political will to devote the necessary resources. Many authorities in any case did not have the management information or statistics which would enable them to plan comprehensively. Systematic data on house condition, for example, was absent from many of the first and subsequent strategies.

The planning techniques recommended for the drawing up of plans (HSAG 1977; SDD 1977) were deficient in some respects, and were in any case more suited to assessing need in the public sector than forecasting demand in the private sector which increasingly dominated housing provision. Housing authorities did not have well established links with the private sector agencies concerned with housing in their areas. Strategies, therefore, had very little to say about the contribution such bodies would make to solving housing problems.

There developed very quickly a clash between the political objectives of central government and some local authorities. The possibility of such tensions were built in at the beginning in the multiple objectives of the strategic planning system. The conflicts have arisen from the determination of the government to restrict public spending, and to attempt to influence the substance of housing policy at the local level.

The government would have met less opposition if it had offered extra inducements to local authorities to implement central government programmes, such as low cost home ownership, as well as local authorities' own schemes. But through a variety of legislative and administrative devices the government made it difficult for some authorities to do what they wanted to do, especially if that involved building council housing, and easy to do what the government wished. By 1991 it was also clear that housing authorities who wished to use part of their capital allocation to build new council housing would be treated less favourably than those who proposed to assist housing associations to build. The capacity of housing authorities to determine their own priorities has, therefore, been reduced by this sort of discrimination or by top-slicing the total capital allocation for projects considered a priority by central government (Gibb and Munro 1991). The Estate Action Programme has been the most significant example of that process, with as much as 37 per cent of HRA capital funding devoted to Estate Action work in one region in 1992–93 (Audit Commission 1992, p 35).

A few authorities have pioneered a more proactive and systematic approach to strategic planning, as in the analysis of needs, options and strategies carried out for the Wrekin District Council (Leather and Murie 1989), and Glasgow District Council's Inquiry (1986). These take account of changing aspirations and demands in the housing market, as well as more traditional concerns with need and housing conditions. Before looking in greater detail at the ways in which plans have been drawn up, it is necessary therefore to make a closer examination of the concepts of need and demand.

Need, housing standards and demand

Need is a fundamental concept in social policy and it can only be defined with reference to some criterion or standard. Someone is 'in need' if they fall below that standard.

Housing standards set down in legislation and circular are particularly complex and wide-ranging. People's housing needs can be defined in terms of particular physical or design aspects of housing, or with reference to aspects of management, location, or access. Statements about need are therefore implicit or explicit in standards set within building regulations for new housing; in fitness regulations for existing housing; in design guidance for special housing intended for particular groups such as older people and people with physical disabilities; in housing benefit income thresholds, below which people are not expected to contribute to their housing costs; and in homelessness legislation. Making sense of this requires a closer look at different types of need. Forder (1974) discusses three different approaches to identifying need.

- 'Normative' approaches involve the definition being made by 'outside' groups or individuals not themselves in need, for example through political processes, or by application of expert opinion. Many examples of such needs can be cited from housing policy. Public health, building and fitness standards reflect the normative values of society at particular times. Surveyors apply a normative standard in reaching an expert opinion that a property should have certain remedial work carried out before it is mortgaged. Housing benefit provides assistance to those whose income is considered insufficient to cover their housing costs in specified circumstances. Expert medical opinion may be required to substantiate claims to need in a housing allocation system.

- 'Felt' need or subjective need is defined by people who consider themselves as in need. Households with young children living in a flat may consider that they need a house with a garden. The majority of British households consider that they need central heating and many aspire to double glazing. Individual needs may be unpredictable and idiosyncratic: academics need a study, cat lovers a cat door, and shift workers a quiet location. Or they may be consistent with broad normative policies: victims of domestic violence feel the need for refuge and social workers consider this a reasonable view; people with learning difficulties feel a need for social support and professional social workers and doctors judge it is needed; and the homeless feel the need for a home, and for some this is achieved through the official standard which is the homelessness legislation. Differences between normative definitions of need, and consumers' own needs, can make an estate difficult to let, or a house difficult to sell.

Subjective, or 'felt' definitions of need are least well developed in the field of social policy. But a recognition of their importance lies at the heart of developments in citizen participation and consumerism. Enabling housing authorities will ignore at their peril the aspirations for improvements to their housing conditions of the people of their area. If an authority sets itself only the task — difficult as that is — of bringing everyone's housing circumstances to at least the minimum normative standards that apply, it will find itself surprised that there are people who feel their housing circumstances are inadequate. The notion of subjective or felt need also lies at the heart of moves to extend consumer choice by means of the market, or by creating quasi-markets. At an extreme, purist exponents of public choice theory would abolish all state standards of need — with the exception of those essential to protect the lives and welfare of all — and leave everyone free to choose the level and nature of housing services they wish to consume. At this point, for some, the concepts of need and demand become inter-changeable.

- Forder's third category of need — 'comparative' need — is defined in relation to 'standards actually achieved by different groups within a society' (p 41). Comparative need is demonstrated in community care policies to design or adapt housing for particular groups, such as disabled people, so that they are enabled to live what is considered to be a normal way of life.

These approaches share in common the fact that need is defined in relation to a standard — the expert's standard of suitability for mortgage, the consumers' standard of what is acceptable, the government's standard of low income, and so on. The application of standards for housing is one of the longest established features of state involvement in housing. Some of the measures adopted were outlined in Chapter 1. They included the Parker Morris Standards of the 1960s and 1970s, overcrowding standards and fitness (England and Wales) or tolerable (Scotland) standards. They represent a target — the elimination of all unfit or sub-tolerable housing — which governments are willing to acknowledge. This is set at a level which minimises state involvement and expenditure. Ideal norms, such as the achievement of a decent house for every family at a price they can afford, for example, are left deliberately vague. Housing authorities have an important role in defining these standards, in regulating conformity with them, and in assisting people to meet them.

In contrast, 'demand' is a concept borrowed from economics and increasingly used in the public sector to help define the role of the state. The demand for housing is the amount of housing purchased at a given price in a particular market area. 'Latent demand' is the amount that would be purchased were it to be available. The housing authority's role, therefore, involves assisting the private sector to provide for the demand and latent demand in the area, and perhaps to assist those households with aspirations which cannot be met in the market to achieve their housing objectives.

With two thirds of the housing stock of Britain in the owner-occupied sector it is increasingly seen as important to consider the strategic role of the housing authority in relation to this housing, which is traded and repaired and renovated in the private market. The demand for housing, however, cannot be predicted from the type of demographic data which has so influenced the estimation of need in the public sector. Much economic analysis has taken place in relation to the demand for new owner-occupied housing. Yet many local housing strategies have not taken into account the economic factors which influence demand (Blincoe 1987; Maclennan 1991).

Demographic factors certainly have an influence on demand for housing (Ermisch 1991), but they create the potential for household formation and demand for housing in the private sector rather than housing demand itself. Whether demand appears is a product of economic factors such as income, price (influenced, amongst other things, by interest rates), and preference (Charles and Webb 1986).

If anyone needed convincing of this the slump in the housing market in most parts of Britain starting in 1988 should have provided demonstration. The challenge for the professional housing planner is to estimate housing demand, and assist the policy maker to decide whether to assist in accommodating or resisting it. To do so requires an understanding also of the importance of supply. Excess demand will create a tendency for house prices to rise, if all else remains the same. This has led some economists to use changes in house prices as an indicator of unmet demand, and in particular as a sign that more development land needs to be made available with planning permission for housing (Keogh and Evans 1992, p 694).

The difficulty for the strategic housing planner is that there is little in the way of readily understood, and tried and tested techniques for estimating the demand for housing, although this is a fast-developing area of housing research (Maclennan 1986; Ermisch 1990; Hancock and Maclennan 1990). This is at least partly due to the intrinsic difficulty of developing techniques of planning for such a complex commodity as housing, which is traded in an environment affected by the national tax system, the local planning context, and the unique social geography of particular areas. But the lack of such planning has also been ascribed to the paucity of research and advice to housing and planning authorities from central government. 'Government advice to authorities on how to monitor the private housing sector is appalling' (Maclennan 1991, p 200). Arguing for better use to be made of existing or new systems of price monitoring Maclennan goes on:

> This database may serve the local authority in a number of ways. Is there a long tail of low price properties concealed in aggregate figures? Are there areas of sustained market depression or resilience? Are there gaps in the lending patterns of societies? Even wider insights may be gained by examining the temporal evolution of the system. . . .
>
> (Maclennan 1991, p 201)

Unfortunately, housing authorities are, in the main, still a good distance away from having such monitoring systems in place, and recent advice from the Audit Commission is as deficient in this respect as previous advice from central departments. In their report, *Developing Local Authority Housing Strategies* (1992), they concentrate largely on the physical condition of housing in the private sector, clearly a crucial area of concern, but a much narrower one than is implied by government advice about meeting needs and demands. A brief discussion of rehousing needs calls for 'more complex models', and suggests that 'waiting lists, homeless acceptances and other internal information' can be as useful to councils for five year forecasts as demographic projections, which are inadequate in some respects. No advice is given about whether the 'more complex models' are within the grasp of housing authorities, or what sort of information they might need to collect in order to understand the dynamics of the market better (Audit Commission 1992, p 27).

Developments in house prices are carefully monitored by building societies and estate agents and some of that information is available to housing authorities. Also available is the house price information in the English Land Registry. The Scottish Register of Sasines has been a public record for many years (Williams and Twine 1992). Data on incomes is available from several sources, or from special surveys. The economic factors involved in housing demand cannot be denied, and an awareness of this is the first step to developing better systems for taking them into account. To do so does not necessarily imply any particular commitment to the government's view of the role of local authorities in improving housing conditions.

Analysing need

Broadly, housing authorities consider needs (and possibly demands) as a first stage in their strategic analysis and planning. Having identified needs (and demands) authorities have been advised, for example by the Audit Commission (1992), to consider alternative options for meeting them. Few have done so in any sort of systematic way, often moving straight on to assume that the best way of meeting need is self-evident. This leads to a programme being adopted, usually a capital programme, given the HIPs', HSOPs' and Housing Plans' relationship to the capital allocations process.

Revenue and administratively-intensive methods of meeting housing needs have been relatively neglected in the planning process, if not in the work of the authority overall. The proposal to incorporate housing management plans in Scottish Housing Plans may encourage a more comprehensive approach (SOED 1992).

In assessing need, housing authorities have looked traditionally at two different aspects of need — the needs of the housing stock, particularly the oldest housing, and at the needs of the people of the area, particularly those who have applied for housing to the local authority.

Housing authorities have a statutory duty to consider housing conditions in their areas. Legislation does not lay down how exactly that consideration should take place, but guidance (SDD 1988; DoE 1990a) suggests at least some systematic house condition surveys from time to time. House condition surveys undertaken at the national level by government departments or agencies can provide only the most general indication of condition and trends within any local area, unless sufficiently large samples are drawn to make the results significant at a local authority level. Local surveys should provide valuable information about disrepair and deficiencies in individual types and tenures of house and by neighbourhood, and assist judgements to be made about appropriate remedial action, including costs. Household surveys carried out alongside condition surveys help 'explain and identify the causes of house condition which will assist in targeting resources and is therefore a most valuable supplement to the physical survey' (SDD 1988).

Few housing authorities carry out systematic and regular house condition surveys, although the numbers may have risen recently, (see Chapter 5). In the absence of such information, housing authorities rely on smaller scale local surveys, out-of-date or unsystematic data, assumptions that the oldest stock will be in worst condition, or the knowledge of the stock which officers or councillors may have acquired, perhaps from unsystematic sources such as grant applications.

In relation to the needs of the people of the area, several different approaches can be used singly, or in combination, as some Scottish and English housing authorities do. The methods focus particularly on people who cannot meet their needs in the market, and should be seen as complementary to the consideration of demand discussed above. They are:

- waiting list analysis
- demographic analysis
- social groups needs analysis.

Waiting list analysis

Using waiting lists as a measure of need has been the subject of much criticism (SDD 1977; National Housing Forum 1989). Waiting lists contain a proportion of 'dead wood' estimated at 25 per cent or more in one study (Prescott-Clarke, Allen and Morrissey 1988, pp 50–53) and are updated less than every two years by a substantial proportion of English local authorities (CHR 1989). Ability to get onto waiting lists varies according to differences of practice and policy from one authority to another (Bramley 1989 pp 23–4). The level of applications is affected by economic factors such as migration and income. And applications to housing authorities vary according to the perceptions of applicants and potential applicants about the likelihood of housing being available. The net effect of these factors is unclear and studies disagree about whether waiting lists understate 'real' need significantly, as the National Housing Forum (1989) argue, or whether they overstate it, as a DoE-sponsored study found (Prescott-Clarke, Allen and Morrisey 1988).

Despite the criticisms, waiting lists have been used probably more than any other indicator to estimate the extent of need for new housing to rent, and exhortations to use this method appear regularly (for example, Maclennan 1991; Audit Commission 1992). Some at least of such estimates are based on inaccurate information, spurious assumptions, and inadequate understanding of the dynamics of the local housing situation. However, there are circumstances in which waiting lists can yield valuable insights into the nature of the local housing situation.

Assuming they are reasonably up-to-date, which is increasingly possible with the aid of information technology (Hunter 1991), waiting lists can be used to monitor changes in patterns of demand or popularity of particular estates or areas; changes in demand from particular household types or sizes; and changes in the pattern of refusals of offers. This analysis can extend to applications for transfers, and to applicants who are homeless. However relatively few authorities can benefit fully from such analysis. Two thirds of authorities do not collect information about applicants' incomes or assets (Audit Commission 1992, p 24). Many authorities do not have computer or other systems for analysing whatever information is collected in the applications and allocations process. If allocation systems were extended to encompass surveys of the type now established within housing associations in England, Wales and Scotland then even more valuable analysis could take place of the impact of income and other factors on patterns of preference and demand (Maclennan 1991).

Demographic analysis

Perhaps the most commonly advocated system of assessing need is the type of demographic analysis recommended by the Department of the Environment and the Scottish Development Department for the early HIPs and Housing Plans (SDD 1977; HSAG 1977). This is essentially a 'top down' approach, applying official standards of housing fitness to projections of houses and households for a period of years ahead. It has become the standard approach to assessing need contained within development plans prepared under the Planning Acts, and in many housing strategies. The analysis is easily described as a step by step process.

1. State existing population of plan area.
2. Estimate future population five years from now, taking account of migration, mortality and birth rates (or more usually start here by using the estimates published by the Registrar General).
3. Convert population to household figures, preferably separating out different types and sizes of households five years from now. Or alternatively, use the estimates produced by the Department of the Environment, the Scottish Office and the Welsh Office, or by local planning department colleagues.
4. This gives a preliminary estimate of the number of houses required — one for each household — but to this figure must be added an allowance for vacancies which are required to allow mobility within the system.
5. Now state the number of houses available today, preferably broken down into the same size categories as the household projections.
6. Add any potential new houses which are known to be 'in the pipeline' and deduct any existing houses which it is anticipated will be lost due to poor condition or demolition in the next five years: this provides an estimate of housing supply, assuming no further action by housing developers.
7. Subtract the figure (or figures for each house size) produced at 6 from the figure or figures produced at 4 to give an estimate of crude shortages or surpluses for each household and house size.
8. Analysts then usually proceed to estimate the likely level of completions required over the next five years. This will be done either by estimating the likely level of public sector completions and treating the private sector as the residual supplier, or by the opposite method, treating the public sector as the residual supplier. In other words private sector completions are estimated 'either by linear extrapolation of past performance or by assuming that developers will close the gap between total households and needs' (Maclennan 1991, p 193).

This approach has been subjected to growing criticism for its inadequacy on a number of grounds. There are reasons why the projections of households produced by government departments and sometimes by planning authorities should be used with great caution. They are based on trends in household formation which were perceived in a period several years previously. Factors such as growing relationship breakdown and increasing numbers of older people in the population could render them useless as predictions of future household numbers. The analysis also ignores the effect of economic factors on the formation of households, on the demand for owner-occupation, and on the breakdown of demand for different tenures. And even if the projections of households set against houses are sound, a crude balance between the two cannot be credibly accepted as an indication that there are no housing issues or problems to be addressed in an area. For these reasons the technique needs to be supplemented with the sort of economic analysis of demand advocated in the previous section.

Social needs groups analysis

The needs of particular social groups — often termed 'special needs groups' — has received increasing attention from housing authorities as the growth of interest in community care policies has developed. Housing strategies might be expected to identify priority groups, and programmmes of action to enable the improvement of the housing conditions of such groups. This is most commonly done with reference to the incidence of particular types of need within the general population, and the ratio of provision which should, by some standard, be made. Groups which are most often identified in local housing strategies include older people, people with learning difficulties, people with mental illnesses, ex-offenders, and people with physical disabilities.

For every 1,000 elderly people in the population, housing authorities in Scotland are encouraged to enable provision of 20 'very sheltered' houses, 46 'sheltered' and 80 'medium dependency' houses (Scottish Office 1991, p 11). This sort of approach has encouraged the provision of housing and support services associated with community care policies. But this 'top down' method of planning is not without its difficulties. While possibly of value at the regional level, it may or may not be appropriate to provide 20 'very sheltered' houses, 46 'sheltered' houses and 80 'medium dependency' houses within a particular town with 1,000 older people. And it is even less certain what is required in a neighbourhood with 100 older people. Only the perception of large-scale overall deficiency in special needs provision has prevented such issues emerging as problems of resource distribution. The planning for special needs which community care policies now require calls for a 'bottom up' as well as a 'top down' element in planning.

Conclusion

This chapter has discussed the place of strategic planning in the work of housing authorities. After establishing that planning has positive advantages in attempting to clarify what might be done to improve housing conditions, the administrative systems for housing planning by housing authorities were described and reviewed. It was seen that the conflicting objectives of the HIPs, HSOPs and Housing Plan systems have distorted their role from that of providing potentially valuable opportunites to develop and state local strategies towards weakly researched bids for capital resources. The key concepts of housing needs, standards and demands were then discussed in order to demonstrate their complexity and centrality to strategic analysis and planning. The lack of attention to estimating and planning for demand was noted. This has important implications for the capacity of housing authorities to take on the role seen for them by the government in assisting the private sector to provide for housing demand. Yet little guidance has been given housing authorities in this admittedly complex area of analysis. Three ways of measuring need — through waiting lists, demographic analysis, and special needs groups — were then reviewed for their strengths and weaknesses.

The general conclusion of this chapter is that strategic planning by housing authorities is at a limited stage of development. Authorities clearly vary across a wide range in the quality and quantity of information they have available to them about local housing conditions, but for most there is a great deal more that could be done to collect up-to-date and systematic information. Few authorities ever engage in an analysis of alternative options for dealing with housing needs. And few are well placed to review and monitor the action they nevertheless take. There are a number of reasons for this state of affairs, not all to do with the lack of expertise or political will at the local level:

- Little advice and encouragement has been offered to local authorities by central government since 1980.
- Disincentives to engage in systematic and comprehensive analysis of need have been created by the government's use of the capital allocations system to achieve its own ends. What is rewarded is a partial analysis combined with a statement of policy measures in line with Ministers' predilections.
- Difficulties exist in operationalising some of the techniques of planning.

- Local authorities are sometimes too busy doing things to devote much time to planning what they should do, and they are not convinced that the resources required for planning would be effectively spent.

Housing Plans, HSOPs and HIPs remain the single most significant opportunity for housing authorities to state the strategies which drive their capital spending and other programmes. But the documents themselves became more concerned with making a bid for increased resources for the public sector, often within a short planning horizon. The analysis of needs and demands which was supposed to underpin the strategic plan was rarely developed into the sort of sophisticated examination of the local housing system which the process called for.

Despite this, housing authorities and central government continue to hold the view that analysis and planning are important. They may do so for different reasons, and may put the emphasis on the role of housing strategies in meeting demand, or in meeting need, depending on their view of the role of local government. For housing authorities which have developed their information and analysis furthest, however, the prime motivating factor seems to be the value to the authority itself in knowing about unmet needs and demands, and being clear about which will receive priority in a situation of scarce resources.

Chapter 4
Enabling house building

This chapter considers a variety of ways in which housing authorities can encourage the provision of housing for rent or low cost owner-occupation, without direct provision of council housing. Two types of measures are discussed — working in partnership with housing associations and private developers, and using the planning system. These are not mutually exclusive, but are discussed separately for the sake of clarity. Most attention is devoted to the use of the planning system, which, it is argued by the English Housing Minister, Sir George Young, can be used 'to get more affordable housing. We've hardly scratched the surface of Circular 7/91, which enables councils to get affordable housing with no public expenditure cost. They can turn down applications from developers who don't include affordable housing' (*Roof* March/April, 1992). Working with housing associations has also received considerable attention (Fraser 1991; Dunmore 1992a and b).

The chapter starts with a description of the way in which town and country planning influences the nature, tenure, size, design and location of new housing developments. It continues with a discussion of the scope for using the planning system to achieve the production of more affordable housing, and includes a review of the evidence available about the extent to which the planning system is being used creatively in this way, and the prospects for the future. It concludes with a discussion of the opportunities for collaboration between housing associations and local authorities in the production of housing. Full details of the methods and powers used are provided elsewhere (Fraser 1991; Northern Consortium of Housing Authorities 1991; Dunmore 1992b).

Housing authorities which have traditionally seen their role as being to provide council housing for families on their waiting list have fared increasingly badly in the 1980s and 1990s. The council stock has declined for three reasons — the impact of the right to buy; the difficulty of expanding the council stock in the face of capital spending restrictions which make it hard to maintain the condition of the existing stock let alone expand it through new provision; and the development of a financial regime which has pushed existing and projected rent levels so high and investment levels so low that the option of large scale transfer to housing

Enabling house building 61

associations has become increasingly popular with some housing authorities and some tenants.

In the face of these developments, the provision of 'affordable housing' — new subsidised housing for rent or for low cost owner-occupation — has become one of the most pressing issues housing authorities face. The phrase 'affordable housing' has been defined as:

> New housing provided with a subsidy to enable the asking price/rent of the property to be lower than the prevailing market prices/rents in the locality, and which is subject to arrangements that will ensure its availability in perpetuity.
> (London and South East Regional Planning Conference 1992, p 1)

The most common forms such housing takes are housing association housing for rent and 'low cost' home ownership projects such as shared ownership. The nature of the subsidy can vary, but at least sometimes is a hidden one commonly called a cross subsidy, resulting from developers foregoing the opportunity to build housing at market prices on part of a site. The adequacy of the subsidies as a method of keeping prices or rents low enough for the low paid, for example, is one of the controversies surrounding the issues raised by this approach to the provision of new housing.

Another issue — and arguably the most important — is the quantity of housing which can be created in the ways described in this Chapter. The government has been reticent about the numbers of new social housing units required in Britain. There is little agreement about the methods to be used in assessing need, and any analysis requires many assumptions to be made about household formation rates, the role of the private sector, and so on. The crudest estimates compare the number of dwellings with the number of households, showing more dwellings than households, but this method takes no account of house condition, the need for vacancies, or other factors. Other estimates of the need in England over the next decade vary from 18,000 to 250,000 units per annum, but the most systematic review and analysis so far published narrows the range to a point of around 100,000 units per annum. However, 'even this level of social provision implies a far more active improvement policy than that currently being implemented or even discussed' (Whitehead and Kleinman 1992, p 16). It is also at least twice the size of the current programme of social housing provision, largely funded by the Housing Corporation. Assuming, optimistically, that a level of new provision of 40,000 to 50,000 houses will be achieved by housing associations in England, an additional number of at least

50,000 houses will require to be built, to prevent housing conditions from deteriorating further. This is the scale of the task housing authorities face, and for many it is the ultimate test of the 'enabling' role.

Town planning

Chapter 1 outlined the system of town and country planning developed in Britain after 1945. A dual system of development planning and development control was intended to encourage the right building projects in the right places, and regulate the developments that took place through a system requiring planning permission, which could be granted subject to conditions. In most parts of Britain structure plans are prepared by the top tier of local government, and local plans are prepared by district councils, which also operate development control. However, in these urban parts of England where a single tier system of local government exists, a new system of unitary development plans has been introduced, following the 1990 Town and Country Planning Act. These plans are prepared in two parts: Part I will ... 'be very similar to the structure plan for a metropolitan county ... consisting of a written statement formulating the authority's general policies in respect of the development and other use of land in their area. ... It seems that Part II will consist of a number of separate parts each similar in effect to a local plan ... additional "parts" can be added from time to time' (Telling 1990, p 69).

The government was dissatisfied with the rate of local plan preparation so the 1991 Planning and Compensation Act required that local plans cover the whole administrative area of a district council. District councils no longer have discretion about preparing them, so references to district plans (and unitary plans) will be increasingly common.

The 1991 Planning and Compensation Act confirmed a new commitment to the planning system by the government when it introduced a new legal status for plans. There is now a legal presumption in favour of the provisions of the development plan, rather than in favour of development. These developments may lead to 'a large number of developers chasing a limited number of (land) allocations', and so enhances the local authority's prospects of achieving the type of development it favours (Dunmore 1992b, p 69). However, designation of land in a development plan, helpful as it may be to a willing developer, does not bring forth applications for planning permission in a depressed housing market, and nor does

Enabling house building

it ensure that any applications for planning permission will contain proposals for 'affordable' housing.

To explain why the planning system is now seen as providing scope for enabling such construction it is important to look at aspects of the planning system not yet considered, as well as the scope for using the system of development plans and development control already outlined. The London Research Centre suggests that there are as many as nine 'policy options for securing affordable housing in England' (LRC 1991a, p 18). As will be seen this is an optimistic account of the number of options, but all nine are listed and discussed, four of them taken together since they involve attempts to use the development plan and development control system as it has been described above. However, although most of the viable options are discussed separately, they are often combined in practice.

Possible uses of the planning system to create affordable housing

1. Residential land release policies.
2. Local/community needs policies.
3. Tenure policies.
4. Cross-subsidy and quotas.
5. Conversion and rehabilitation policies.
6. Dwelling densities and standards for private amenity space.
7. New settlements.
8. The 'exceptions' policy for rural areas.
9. Planning agreements.

Conversion and rehabilitation policies

Existing housing may be affected by planning as well as housing policy. In London 'since the early 1980s the conversion of houses into flats for sale has become the most important way in which new owner-occupied housing units are produced'(Barlow 1989, p 18). Conversions are seen by the DoE as providing for London 'a valuable source of lower cost housing' (DoE 1989a, para 54), but some evidence suggests that higher than average incomes are still required to be able to afford them (London Research Centre 1991a, p 20). No assumptions should be made about who gains from conversion and rehabilitation policy. It is unlikely, even when it benefits those on low incomes, that it offers a sufficient solution to the creation of affordable housing.

Dwelling densities and standards for private amenity space

Planning authorities have some control over the internal and external design features of new developments, through attaching conditions to the grant of planning permission. Internal and external space standards may be used to provide higher or lower density developments, potentially affecting land costs and ultimately housing costs. But there are pressures from government, and local residents, to enhance amenities through low densities and high levels of private amenity space. So some kind of trade-off will be required, with the knowledge that comes with hindsight, about the consequences of attempting to build to high densities to save land, as in the non-traditional mass housing programmes of the 1960s. On its own, a high density policy could create as many problems as it solves, and, at best, is unlikely to make more than a marginal contribution to the problem of providing affordable housing.

New settlements

Many new settlements have been proposed in recent years, and few have been built, partly because of the opposition any such proposals engender in rural areas. Any new villages provide scope for housing of all types, including low cost housing, and this has been recognised in the DoE's Planning Policy Guidance Note 3 (1992b). But to secure 'affordable' housing would probably require the use of some of the measures discussed elsewhere in this chapter.

Land release, local needs, tenure, cross subsidy and quotas

The planning system of development plans and development control is intended, according to successive governments, to ensure adequate land for housing and other needs. In the 1980s authorities have been encouraged to respond to demand in the market-place as well as their estimates of need. But development plans were not intended to show the tenure of future housing developments — the planner's concern was about the suitability of land for residential development, not the tenure of the housing.

The existence of controversy about the need and demand for housing, and the effect on land prices of development plans, makes this part of the town planner's role less easy than it at first sight may appear. Planners have attempted to designate land in their development plans which is sufficient to ensure an adequate supply for housing needs. But this could not guarantee that the housing built as a result would be within the means of those in need. In addition, price and demand pressures in some parts of England led to land and house prices rising and making the construction of affordable housing even more difficult.

Local and community needs policies, tenure policies, and quota and cross subsidy policies are an attempt to overcome the restrictions of traditional town planning with its interest in land use rather than with who is the user of the land. Increasingly, a number of local authorities had sought to insert into policy statements or grants, planning permission conditions which attempted to ensure that some of the houses built in new residential developments were in the form of housing to let. The London Borough of Brent was unsuccessful in imposing conditions of this type, after the applicants appealed to the Secretary of State. Another way of attempting something similar was to adopt a quota policy, in an attempt to ensure a quota of 'affordable' housing as part of a bigger development. 'Affordable' was usually defined to include shared ownership and rented housing. Cross subsidy involves proceeds from housing built for disposal in the private sector to be used for creating affordable housing, on the same or some other site. It may be asked why landowners would agree to forgo the profits which could have been realised on their land. The most frequent answer has been that the land was owned by the local authority itself, working in co-operation with a housing association and a private developer.

After resisting some of these attempts for years, the Department of the Environment took steps to assist in using the planning system to create 'affordable' housing in 1991 and 1992. A DoE Planning Policy Guidance Note, PPG 3, stated, 'A community's need for affordable housing is a material planning consideration which may properly be taken into account in formulating development plan policies' (DoE 1992b, para 38). A similar policy applies to Wales, and Scotland. This approach opens the way for planning authorities to seek to ensure that planning consents for housing developments are not granted without some provision of 'affordable' housing. In effect, the developer is asked to forgo the profit that could have resulted from developing the land entirely for disposal at market prices.

Planning authorities are, therefore, entitled to take a view about the affordability, and by implication the tenure mix of housing they would wish to see developed. They are allowed to suggest a target

66 The Housing Authority as Enabler

for the provision of affordable housing, and even to set targets for individual sites. But it would be erroneous to consider that a consistent tenure or quota policy would be enforceable. Planning Policy Guidance Note 3 is clear that, 'Policies should not, however, be expressed in favour of any particular form of tenure', (para 38). And, 'Policies should not seek to impose a uniform quota on all developments, regardless of market or site conditions' (para 39).

An additional difficulty for local authorities is that it is not clear that affordable housing can be achieved only by means of the normal operation of the planning system, even with the developer's willingness to include an element of affordable housing as a 'material consideration which the planning authority should take into account' in considering an application for planning permission (DoE 1992b, para 39). How can this ensure the ultimate and successive users of the house will be those the policy is intended to assist? Some other method may be necessary.

These issues are examined by SERPLAN (London and South East Regional Planning Conference) in a study which looked at the building of affordable housing in the South East Region in the years 1989-90 and 1990-91, and estimated results for 1991-92. Structure and local plans in preparation are increasingly incorporating quota policies, in the case of local plans all at around 20 per cent, and 20 to 30 per cent in structure plans. Within London the majority of boroughs are seeking to pursue such policies, usually in association with planning agreements (see below). In relation to cross-subsidy between social housing and housing for sale or let on the open market, a 'small number' of schemes have been forthcoming and 'only modest amounts of affordable housing' are being built (SERPLAN 1992, p 10). The SERPLAN report does not distinguish the numbers of houses created by different uses of the planning system. To do so would be difficult because of the way a variety of mechanisms are used in combination in most schemes. However, overall, the total provision of affordable housing identified in the South East in 1989-90 was 8,728, in 1990-91 it was 8,589, and in 1991-2 it was expected to be 9,854.

Ultimately, land release through the development planning and development control system is a necessary but not sufficient condition for affordable housing to be built. Its release does not guarantee any housing will be built, 'affordable' or otherwise. Even in promising circumstances — a housing developer seeking permission for a site designated as suitable for housing, and a housing authority with a desire to achieve affordable housing and a tenure policy to back it up — the normal planning framework cannot be used to force the developer to include affordable housing in the development, or to ensure it remains affordable once built.

What of the other possible options? Can they be used in combination with tenure and quota policies to achieve new affordable housing?

The 'exceptions' policy

The 'exceptions policy' is called after the willingness of the government to condone the use of land for social housing in exceptional circumstances. The use of the 'exceptions policy' in rural areas was sanctioned in DoE Circular 7/1991, after a number of authorities had experimented with it in the 1980s (London Research Centre 1991a, p 73). Circular 7/1991 was superseded by Planning Policy Guidance Note 3 in 1992 and preceded by a ministerial statement on 3 February 1989:

> 'The question of who is to occupy premises for which permission is to be granted will normally be irrelevant. I recognise, however, that in some rural areas there are genuine difficulties in securing an adequate supply of low cost housing for local needs. In such areas the need for low cost housing and the existence of arrangements made by the developer, or between the developer and the landowner or the local authority, to ensure that new low cost housing is made available for local needs could be material considerations which the local authority would take into account in deciding whether to grant planning permission. Such considerations might be particularly relevant to the release of small sites within or adjoining existing villages which would not otherwise be allocated for housing.
> (*Hansard*, H.C. Deb., Vol. 146, cols. 433–4)

The 1989 statement goes on to suggest that, since planning conditions cannot normally be used to impose restrictions on tenure or occupancy or to ensure continuing benefit, additional steps need to be taken to ensure 'affordability'. These could include:

— involvement of a village trust or housing association with a suitable lettings policy;
— covenants giving priority to local first-time buyers;
— a planning agreement between developer and planning authority (see below).

The first stage in the use of the exceptions policy is in the preparation of a development plan, which should, according to PPG3, make clear that so-called 'off-plan' sites, that is sites not shown as for residential development, would be released for affordable housing, in addition to the plan's general provision for new housing development.

The reason for such obfuscation — in not showing the sites on the plan — is to do with the rise in land values associated with designation as land suitable for housing in a development plan. Land so designated will be attractive to developers and landowners for the development of relatively high price housing, rather than 'affordable' housing, whether for rent or shared ownership. (In Scotland, designation in a development plan is recommended (SOED 1992)).

The approach of allowing planning consent in exceptional circumstances for low cost housing on land which would not otherwise be allocated for housing development is arguably a rather peculiar use of the planning system, which is normally expected to provide for acceptable and desirable land uses in a development plan. It might be argued that if a piece of land is suitable for development it should be so designated; if not, it should not. Further, what credence can be attached to a process of public participation in the preparation of development plans when planners may later admit to having ideas about exceptions they would be prepared to allow? This more surreptitious approach is justified in the interests of making land available which has not increased in value as a result of being designated as suitable for housing. Some landowners may not mind being part of such an altruistic endeavour, and the research evidence shows that parish councils are often its most enthusiastic advocates (Williams, Bell and Russell 1991; Williams and Bell 1992), but one fear is that the approach could bring the planning system into disrepute, with some land owners enjoying the benefits of increased land values as a result of the development plan system, and others being asked to sacrifice such gains in the interests of a few. An additional difficulty is highlighted by the Royal Town Planning Institute. 'It (the exceptions policy) threatens the integrity of the planning system where conflicts may arise at a local level between housing and planning objectives' (RTPI 1992, p 10).

A number of other possible problems raise more pressing issues about the capacity of the approach to provide sufficient additional housing. First, it is not clear that the advantage of lower price land will be sustainable in the longer term, especially if planning authorities identify suitable small parcels of land and this becomes known, even without being included in planning policy statements. Secondly, it is not clear that the level of subsidy represented by a lower land price will be sufficient to secure 'affordable' developments. This emphasises that other resources apart from land will be necessary to ensure 'affordable' housing is built. Third, it is not clear that the housing created through this approach would continue indefinitely to be available to the people for whom it is intended. And fourthly, it is not clear that the control over access to such affordable housing, through a village trust, for example, will conform to the equal opportunities and other good practice guidelines which apply to the activities of local authorities and housing associations. Will this mean the reintroduction of the sort of 'local connection' policies which housing professionals have sought to outlaw over the last 20 years?

Only one safeguard — 'staircasing' restrictions on shared ownership schemes in settlements of less than 3,000 population — was outlined in Planning Policy Guidance Note 3. This confirmed that state subsidy (normally through the Housing Corporation) would be given on shared ownership schemes which restrict the shared owner from staircasing to full ownership. This allows shared owners to purchase a high proportion 'not less than 80 per cent', but the housing association or other developer is able to retain some equity and therefore control over succeeding shared owners.

The contribution the exceptions policy has made in its early stages of implementation is examined in two studies. Research sponsored by the Department of the Environment (Williams, Bell and Russell 1991; Williams and Bell 1992) looks at the first year of operation of the policy. A survey of relevant housing authorities carried out early in 1991 showed that three quarters had drawn up an exceptions policy, but fewer than half had so far approved a housing development within the policy (Williams and Bell 1992, p 143). Most authorities had involved a variety of interests in the policy process, including landowners, parish councils, county councils, housing associations and developers. The survey identified 264 proposals for development, of which 153 had received planning permission, involving 1,710 units of housing. A further 111 proposals were under discussion.

There was a concentration of policies and development proposals in the South of England where development pressures were greatest. The largest scheme was for 46 houses, and the average was 11 (p 144). Overall just over one quarter (27 per cent) of the schemes were intended for rent, over one third (36 per cent) had both rent and shared ownership components, and under one third (31 per cent) were wholly shared ownership schemes (p 144). Planning agreements were used to secure the original use and purpose of the housing for the future. Delays in bringing schemes to fruition were caused by the multiplicity of agencies involved, and co-ordination and funding difficulties. More worrying, the cost of completed schemes was found to exceed comparable rented or shared ownership housing, showing that lower land prices may not be a sufficient subsidy for 'affordable' social housing. 'The study has concluded that significant increases in public sector subsidy ... would be necessary if this is to become a significant component of a wider strategy for the provision of affordable housing' (Williams and Bell 1992, p 144).

Overall, the study suggests that the impact of the exceptions policy is 'limited', and 'the schemes which are coming forward may not fully reflect local needs. Those least able to compete in the private market are not being catered for at all in those parishes where no rental housing is being provided and there appears to be little provision for the needs of particular groups such as the elderly or disabled' (p 86). However, as a housing measure the policy has had 'some success' (p 86), with around 60 schemes on site or completed, and others under discussion. But, as a planning policy, there have been a number of problems, including 'tension between district council departments', and 'a tendency to compromise planning principles' (Williams, Bell and Russell 1991, p 87).

The second study, carried out by SERPLAN (The London and South East Regional Planning Conference), examines the use of the exceptions policy in the South East, outside London, one of the areas of greatest housing pressure in the country, in the years 1989–90 and 1990–91. The results echo those of the other study. Most of the shire districts are found to be seeking to use the exceptions policy in their local plans, and even one structure plan, for East Sussex, hardly a rural area, includes a general exceptions policy. But the results obtained are small. Proposals typically refer to small developments of less than 12 houses, on sites of no more than one acre. Sites 'are difficult to identify, and even if this is possible, finance is not always forthcoming'. As a result, SERPLAN's fears that the exceptions policy would compromise the environmental objectives of planning have not been realised.

It seems that, so far, like the other planning approaches considered here, the exceptions policy is a possible contributor to housing production, rather than a sufficient solution.

Planning by agreement, or planning obligations

The 1991 Planning and Compensation Act introduced the term 'planning obligations' to describe the planning agreements which Section 106 of the 1990 Town and Country Planning Act enabled a planning authority to enter into 'with any person interested in land in their area for the purpose of restricting or regulating the development or use of the land'. (Section 50 of the Town and Country Planning (Scotland) Act makes a similar provision.) Planning law has included this provision since the 1930s, and the process involved is referred to as 'planning by agreement'. Such planning involves an element of bargaining between landowners and planning authorities in which the planning authority is likely to use the provision of planning permission for some proposed development as its bargaining tool.

Planning by agreement allows the planning authority to impose 'conditions' on the developer's proposed development which are not possible under the normal system of planning control. The developer might concede such a bargain in the interests of achieving planning permission for a lucrative or much sought after development.

> There entered into the business of granting planning permission an element of bargaining, and in the development boom of the late sixties and early seventies many developers were ready to make concessions rather than court a refusal of permission and incur the delay involved in exercising the right of appeal to the Secretary of State.
>
> (Telling 1990, p 209)

Examples of agreements reached include allocation of a portion of land for public use, provision of buildings for community use, agreement by the developer to pay for statutory services to be provided for a site, and provision of land for 'affordable' housing (Telling 1990; Rowan–Robinson and Young 1989). The use of planning agreements has been seen as controversial. They can be portrayed as a positive feature of the planning system which can be used to secure for community benefit some part of the increase in land value created as a result of planning permission. Others see dangers in the process of bargaining between planners and developers which might encourage collusion, abuse of discretionery power, lack of accountability, and secrecy (Jowell 1977; Loughlin 1981; Heap and Ward 1983).

Despite their long history, planning agreements were relatively little used until the 1980s, at least partly because they required ministerial consent on an individual basis until 1968 (1969 in Scotland). The number did not exceed 157 in any one year in the 1960s (Telling 1990, p 209). In Scotland only six agreements were entered into in the period up to 1969, but from 1975 to 1982 no less than 165 had been agreed, and 'in the five years from 1982 a further 496 agreements had been completed (Rowan-Robinson and Young 1989, pp 72–3). Estimates suggest that by 1990 agreements were being entered into at the rate of 6,000 per year, with a growth of 20 per cent per annum in the three years from 1987. Six in ten (61 per cent) of the agreements were concerned with housing developments, a higher percentage than housing represents as the subject of planning applications generally (Grimley J. R. Eve et al. 1992, p 20).

The use of planning agreements for housing purposes has received little serious attention until recently. Two studies carried out in the early 1990s (London Research Centre 1991a; Barlow and Chambers 1992a, 1992b), provided in the words of one subtitle 'an examination of the potential for the plannning system to secure affordable housing with special reference to planning agreements' (LRC 1991a), and a third study for the Department of the Environment provided a general overview of the use of planning agreements in the planning system (Grimley J. R. Eve et al. 1992).

The DoE study found that most of the housing related agreements were for small sites averaging 2.8 acres. One of the most common features of agreements (in 55 per cent of cases) was limitations on the use of the development. In three quarters of these (76 per cent) the occupancy was affected with specifications such as age (sheltered housing), occupation (agricultural workers' housing), and housing priority (social housing). Other, less common, features of agreements related to financial payments, highway and other infrastructure improvements, environmental measures such as landscaping and street furniture, and community facilities such as recreational space near housing (Grimley J. R. Eve et al. 1992, pp 22–4). In some cases agreements merely replicated the conditions attached to the planning consent, but it seems unlikely that those concerned with creating social housing would be of this kind since tenure, price and future ownership and occupation cannot be made effective conditions of planning permission it was felt by planning officers, but can feature in planning agreements. Delay was caused by the negotiations required for an agreement. This was likely to take from six to twelve months from the date of the resolution to grant planning permission (Grimley J. R. Eve et al. 1992, pp 40–44).

Barlow and Chambers found that almost one in five (18 per cent) of the authorities surveyed had been involved in planning agreements involving provision of a quota of 'affordable' housing. These authorities were concentrated in the South and Midlands of England, and in West Central Scotland. Many more, about three-quarters of authorities, had had discussions about the use of such agreements (Barlow and Chambers 1992a, p 19). Some authorities had gained experience because of the enthusiasm of officers, others because of the desire of elected members. Motivations arose largely from previous experience in the land market, and from a desire to provide more 'affordable' housing in difficult circumstances. Barlow and Chambers identified about 130 schemes involving about 35,000 open market and 10,000 'affordable' housing units at January 1992 (1992a, p 36). Most schemes provide for few 'affordable' houses — the largest ten account for more than 5,000 (1992a, p 37). The average 'quota' was about one quarter (23 per cent) of the total number of units, but this accounts for less than that proportion of the land area of the site (p 38). The exact nature of the agreement varied, from transfer of land at no cost or at less than market value, (generally 20 per cent to 30 per cent discount), to transfer of completed houses to a local authority or housing association (p 38).

The nature of the agreement is important in evaluating the use of planning agreements. If the agreement provides low cost or free land, or in other words allows for a cross subsidy scheme, but housing association finance is still required to provide 'affordable' housing then it is open to question whether any additional units are being provided. Developers and land owners preferred shared ownership housing as the 'affordable' element in their agreements, and local authorities preferred rented housing. In the 61 schemes for which data was available, around 2,650 houses for rent and 2,130 for shared ownership were to be provided (p 39). The most successful schemes involved housing authorities with clear policy objectives based on good information about needs, and good lines of communication between housing and planning departments, and with housing associations (p 56).

Given that many planning permissions, without planning agreements, remain extant for the next few years, the authors conclude:

> Even if all the schemes we have identified come to fruition during the period 1992-95, the total number of affordable housing units produced annually during the mid to late 1990s is unlikely to exceed 1,500 to 2,000. We should, however, make one proviso. By the mid-1990s LAs will be allocating new land and the possibility for entering affordable housing agreements will therefore rise towards the end of the decade. Assuming that private sector housebuilding levels recover to (say) 150,000 units per annum by the late 1990s, and that 50 per cent of these completions are in areas where house and land prices are high enough to justify affordable housing "gain", use of a 20 per cent quota would yield 15,000 affordable housing units per annum.
>
> (p 37)

However:

> We believe that while affordable housing agreements have some limited potential, they are a messy and imprecise tool for achieving affordable housing objectives.
> (Barlow and Chambers, 1992a, p 57)

The London Research Centre express similar caution about the use of planning agreeements, based on their research into the experience of the 33 London Boroughs since 1985. Only just over a third of boroughs (12), under Labour, Conservative and Liberal Democrat control, claimed to have used such agreements in the period from 1985 to 1991, but over two thirds said they intended to if they had not done so in the past (pp 50–51). The years 1987 and 1988 were the most successful (p 53). Two boroughs had reached more agreements than the rest put together, but the size of the gains in numbers of houses was relatively small, varying up to 80 units. The LRC's overall evaluation is that 'Planning gain is not a policy alternative but is a useful supplement' (p 67).

Partnerships

Housing authorities in some parts of Britain have for many years seen housing association housing as a complement to council housing. Housing associations with experience of developing special needs housing or of rehabilitation of older stock, for example, were seen as bringing additional resources for the provision of rented housing. In the 1980s and 1990s housing associations have been seen increasingly as a substitute for new council housing, especially since the 1988 housing legislation and the impact of the Right to Buy on council housing. Few, if any, housing authorities would discourage housing associations from providing housing in their area, but the question of interest to many housing authorities has been whether they can do anything to encourage housing associations to make more provision than would otherwise be the case. As has been seen already there are a number of ways in which housing authorities, housing associations and private developers can co-operate in the use of the 'exceptions' policy in rural areas, and in the use of quotas and planning agreements. This section, however, looks at the possibilities for partnership between housing authorities and housing associations, and sometimes private developers as well, with or without any extraordinary use of the planning system.

Dunmore (1992a, 1992b), Fraser (1991) and the Northern Consortium of Housing Authorities (1991) provide many examples of partnership schemes for the provision of new housing involving housing associations, private developers and housing authorities. These often involve the sale of local authority land and the provision of financial assistance to housing associations. These may be used alone, or in combination with each other, or with the planning powers outlined in this chapter.

Local authorities have been substantial landowners in the postwar period, with significant powers to acquire land, including powers of compulsory purchase in specific circumstances. Sometimes land acquired for council housing or for some other purpose which the authority is no longer able to fulfil may be suitable for housing development. Land should normally be sold to the highest bidder by local authorities but that would not necessarily achieve any of the housing authority's objectives. The authority would only have succeeded in enabling whatever the developer wanted, subject to anything that could be gained through a grant of planning permission. To improve on what can be gained through the planning system, housing authorities can strike deals which enhance the prospects of achieving housing for homeless people or for people on the waiting list, for example. But a number of constraints limit what can be achieved, for example, the prohibition on using the cheap land to lower the rent levels in a HAG-funded scheme, and the requirement to allow 'staircasing' to full ownership in shared equity schemes on all but the most rural land. The most common mechanism is to bargain for enhanced nomination rights with a housing association, and then seek consent from the Secretary of State for disposal of the land at less than market value (Dunmore 1992b). This might be expected to bring a double benefit — some capital to use for housing purposes, as well as the housing association development. But in England the use of the capital receipt is regulated by the provisions of the 1989 Local Government and Housing Act and in Wales restrictions apply to the use of capital receipts from the sale of non-housing land (Fraser 1991; Dunmore 1992b).

Financial assistance by local authorities to housing associations in England can take a number of forms, of which 'local authority HAG', which is reimbursed by the Housing Corporation, and Section 24 funding under the 1988 Local Government Act are the main provisions. Local authority HAG is generally considered to be relevant only to larger authorities (Dunmore 1992b). Other financial assistance may be available for special needs projects from health or social services authorities. Despite an apparent array of powers to assist housing development financially, there 'is conflict between the DoE's objective to encourage local authorities in their enabling role whilst at the same time seeking to minimise capital expenditure and maximise receipts. The result is a system which is complex, subject to change without notice as schemes which meet the enabling role fall foul of controls on local authority capital spending and relies heavily on the discretion of the DoE' (Dunmore 1992b).

Fraser (1991) reports a partnership between Cardiff City Council and Hafod Housing Association which involves both the use of below market price land, and grant assistance to a housing association. The construction of 369 houses for rent was financed with financial assistance from the local authority, private sector cross subsidy, and private borrowing by Hafod. These and other schemes in towns and cities such as Leicester, Leeds, Darlington and Harlow (Fraser 1991; Northern Consortium 1991; Dunmore 1992b), attract a lot of attention, but it is less clear whether they create additional housing to that which would be built anyway, and if so, at what cost.

Part of the cost is in time spent in negotiating and co-ordinating the partnership between association and authority. The Institute of Housing has suggested that the relationship between associations and authorities should be the subject of a contract which sets out:

- The criteria to be used by the authority in deciding which associations to work with. These might include having a local office or committee, and having a satisfactory record in tenant participation or equal opportunities.
- The commitments the authority would make to approved associations. These might include the sale of land or housing and payments of renovation grants.
- The commitments the associations would make to nomination procedures, for example.
- Arrangements for monitoring the provisions of the contract.
- Procedures for associations to contribute to the authority's strategic planning process.

> The Institute believes that this type of formal arrangement will ensure that local authorities and housing associations work together in an effective, fair and equal manner. After all, their housing objectives are almost synonymous.
>
> (Fraser 1991, p 122)

In the past, while housing associations and housing authorities were seen as making complementary provision, it did not matter that their housing objectives were not 'synonymous'. In the 1990s, housing authorities may lose some of their capacity to provide for those they consider needy, if their objectives prove to be insufficiently 'synonymous' with housing associations'.

Too little is known about the extent to which associations and authorities are making successful partnerships. It is not clear, for example, to what extent the dozen or so examples cited by Fraser, the Northern Consortium and Dunmore are illustrative of a larger number of partnership schemes, or are isolated examples of innovative effort by a few housing authorities and associations. And whatever the scale of the achievement, any systematic evaluation would require to consider whether more housing could be achieved in alternative ways.

Conclusion

This chapter has reviewed the options available for the creation of new housing to rent or buy at 'affordable' prices. Four main methods have been identified — the rural 'exceptions' policy, quotas and cross subsidy, planning agreements, and partnerships between housing associations and local authorities. These are not mutually exclusive, and many projects involve elements of two, three or even four of these mechanisms.

There is a growing volume of research which evaluates the use of quotas, planning agreements and the 'exceptions' policy, but there is a lack of systematic research on the partnership approach to affordable housing. However, with some qualifications, it can be said that all four methods have been found to make a significant but small contribution to the production of new housing. A full evaluation of their capacity to create an adequate supply of 'affordable' housing must await a longer experience of implementation. But early evaluations have concluded that at the rate achieved in the early 1990s the planning-led approaches do not provide a substitute for a dedicated programme of subsidised house construction. They do not come anywhere near achieving the level of construction indicated as required at the beginning of this chapter. They did not constitute a social housing programme, and it is not yet clear that they can be a substitute for a programme of social housing:

> The planning system cannot address the scale of social housing need in isolation and it should not be regarded as a substitute means of redressing the inequities of the housing finance system.
> (RTPI 1992, p 10)

The weaknesses and difficulties vary from one type of measure to another, but can be summarised as concerned with the market, with finance, with management and with social consequences. Dependence on the market is unreliable, and any social housing programme which relied only on cross subsidy between private and social provision at the point of planning application is hardly worthy of the name of social housing programme, especially in a period of recession when the need for social housing may well grow and the development of private housing will probably decline. Planning gains and land deals do not necessarily provide the financial support necessary to hold rents or equity costs at a level comparable with conventional housing association or local authority housing. And it is not clear that any programme can be sustained in adverse market conditions, or in the event of a scarcity of local authority land combined with the reluctance of government to sanction active involvement in the land market by housing authorities. 'Bricks and mortar' subsidy may be required as well.

Management problems relate to the complexities of co-ordinating the multiplicity of actors involved in the schemes outlined in this chapter. The co-ordination and administration of any housing development is a complex process, but the schemes discussed here are even more difficult to bring to fruition than those funded and developed through conventional housing programmes, whether by local authorities or housing associations. It is possible, though, that authorities, associations and others will develop speed as well as expertise in the management of such projects, so that in time they will appear no more onerous than other forms of housing development. Authorities which have not experimented with such projects will be more inclined to do so. But they will continue to be more risky, because the links in the chain from conception to construction are more tenuous than in more conventional developments.

There are also uncertainties about who are the beneficiaries of the new housing. Does it address the needs of homeless people, and others least well served by the market? Does the emphasis on shared ownership mean that much of that housing will be lost to the social rented sector? Another cause of concern is the allocation and management policies which can apply to the rented housing built. Are the criteria of access defined in planning agreements, for example, too restrictive? Are discredited residential qualifications reappearing as a 'legitimate' device for defining 'local'? Housing authorities are not necessarily exemplary in their approach to handling these issues, but at least their allocation policies are public documents open to public debate, access to their waiting lists is relatively open, and they are accountable at the ballot box and in the council chamber. Future evaluations must examine the nature of the needs met and not met by the alternative new housing discussed in this chapter, as well as the number of units built.

Ultimately, the evaluation of the role of housing authorities in helping make provision for new 'affordable' housing will depend on the quantity, quality and management of the housing produced. The research so far available concentrates on the quantity, and even then draws only preliminary conclusions, complicated by the dangers of double counting and the lack of consensus about what an adequate social housing programme would be. However, it is clear that at the rate of construction applying in the early 1990s, housing authorities in aggregate would be performing unusually well if they managed to enable the construction of the necessary quantity of 'affordable' housing for rent or purchase. If housing authorities do not manage to enable the construction of sufficient social housing, the evidence suggests their 'failure' is a failure of the government's reliance on inadequate policy instruments rather than any failure of housing authorities to draw a pint from a half pint pot.

Chapter 5
Enabling house improvement

This chapter considers the role of housing authorities in improving housing conditions. The major part of the chapter deals with repair and improvement in the light of early experience of the 1989 regime, and earlier evidence from previous legislation. Where appropriate private and public sector housing are given separate treatment, and the special case of houses in multiple occupation are considered. Information on the physical condition of housing provides a context for the discussion of clearance, improvement and repair.

'Improving housing conditions' is a common objective of housing authorities, and has been for over a century. The nature of this concept is more wide-ranging than is sometimes understood, potentially extending across all tenures and income groups, and involving a wide range of types of assistance and improvement. 'Improving housing conditions' is used in this chapter frequently in preference to 'improving housing' since it emphasises more explicitly the relationship between the physical housing stock and people. An improvement in housing conditions could take place, for example, if a single person living in a three bedroomed house with garden were to exchange accommodation with a family of mother, father and two children living in overcrowded conditions in a one or two bedroom first floor flat in the same area. Few improvements are as easily achieved as this one might be, and even this one is not easily achieved if the two properties are not in the same tenure, or if the family cannot afford the cost of the larger house, or if either household has reasons for wishing to stay in their present house.

There are broadly four possible approaches to improving housing conditions, whatever its tenure, which can be used singly or in combination:

- providing new housing
- eliminating inadequate housing which for some reason cannot or should not be improved (this in itself is no more than a start, and would make conditions worse if the former occupants were not satisfactorily rehoused);
- ensuring repair or improvement to the existing stock;

Enabling house improvement 81

- changing the management arrangements (including allocations) of existing housing to meet needs, demands or aspirations.

The first of these was considered in Chapter 4 and the last is the subject of Chapter 6. This chapter concentrates on the role of housing authorities in eliminating or reducing disrepair and unfitness in the housing stock.

Condition

Housing authorities cannot expect to be effective in improving housing conditions without a clear idea of the state of housing conditions and and the sort of improvement they consider appropriate. Councillors and officers often operate with an intuitive knowledge of housing in their area which relies on observation and contact with the public, information about waiting lists, and information about grant applications, for example. For much of the post-war period this knowledge was used to frame clear policies — to eliminate unfit housing, and to build for rent. But this has been seen by central government and others as an inadequate foundation for local housing policy, valuable as the detailed knowledge of councillors, consumers and officers can be. With policy changes favouring rehabilitation rather than demolition, and housing associations and owner-occupation rather than council housing, the role of housing authorities is more problematic. Commentators have argued for a more comprehensive and systematic approach (see Chapter 2), involving more systematic evidence about housing conditions and the recognition of a role for housing authorities in relation to all tenures.

Information about the physical condition of the housing stock varies from one local authority to another. The first house condition survey carried out in England and Wales in 1967 showed that the number of unfit dwellings was more than twice local authority estimates (Cullingworth 1979). In many authorities the quality of the information has improved little since then, despite statutory requirements to undertake periodic surveys. In one authority studied by Houlihan, the extent of substandard housing in the late 1970s was found in a survey to be double the estimated level (1987 p 108).

The increasingly common remedy for poor information is to carry out a local house condition survey at regular intervals, and interest in such surveys appears to be growing, amidst encouragement from government (SDD 1988; DOE 1990a). In a three year period from 1989, no fewer than 27 housing authorities out of a total of 56 in Scotland carried out local house condition surveys (Scottish Homes 1990). Such surveys usually involve building surveyors inspecting a sample of properties from all tenures, if necessary with a boosted sample of types of tenure or property which would not otherwise be sufficiently well represented in the survey to ensure results that are statistically significant. At least some information about householders as well as house will be collected, usually by the surveyor, or in a separate more extensive household survey. Such information is required for a number of reasons. First, there are some obvious connections between the social characteristics of residents and their housing, which may affect the quality of the accommodation (for physically disabled people, for example) and prospects of achieving improvement (in the case of housing in disrepair occupied by owners on low incomes, for example). Secondly, the occupiers may be the best source of some sorts of information, for example, about sound insulation. Thirdly, the opportunity should be taken to survey the views of residents about their housing and neighbourhood (SDD 1988).

House condition surveys carried out at the national level are no substitute for local surveys, since it cannot be assumed that the same conditions will apply in local circumstances which can vary greatly by age, tenure and location. However, results from the Welsh and English House Condition Surveys do provide an indication of the policy objectives which should be pursued at national level, and a pointer to the sorts of issues that are likely to arise in some form at the local level, and in Wales they are taken into account explicitly in capital allocations.

The main findings are easy to summarise and are consistent with previous surveys. Condition varies by age, tenure and location — the oldest and most rural housing and the private rented sector have the highest incidence of poor condition (defined as unfit, lacking basic amenities, or in poor repair requiring at least £1,000 spent). Owner-occupation is second worst of the tenures, followed by local authority and housing association housing (DOE 1988; Welsh Office 1988). In greater detail, 2.5 per cent of houses in England lacked at least one of the standard amenities; less than 5 per cent were judged unfit, of which three-quarters were built before 1919; and 12.9 per cent were in poor repair (DOE 1988, pp 20–30). These houses contained particularly high concentrations of low income households (p 44). Repairs costing from a few pounds upwards were required in about three-quarters of the stock, and in 5 per cent of cases at least £2,900 required to be spent (p 22–23). The cost of repairing post-war council housing was estimated at almost twice the cost of equivalent owner-occupied property (p 23). Pre-war housing required an average of £2,090 to be spent on repairs and private rented housing required repairs costing £2,030, on average (p 23). Almost two-thirds of owner-occupiers claimed prompt attention to repairs, but most of the rest did only those jobs they felt to be essential, and 6 per cent postponed or neglected repair work. Although there was some association between attitudes and actual state of repair, the majority of housing in poor condition was occupied by those with a positive attitude (p 48). Those with a higher income were more positive in their approach to repair, but even at the highest income bands there were over 15 per cent who did essential maintenance only (p 112). Throughout England — with some substantial regional differences — there was a roughly one-in-five chance that those aged over 75, those who were unemployed and those on low income (less than £3,000 per annum) would be living in housing in poor condition (DOE 1988, p 45). The condition of the housing stock is worse in Wales than in England, with a higher incidence of disrepair and unfit housing (Welsh Office 1988). In Scotland a national house condition survey was carried out for the first time in 1991–92.

When compared with previous surveys the evidence about trends is mixed. There were small reductions in the proportions of houses defined as unfit, and in serious disrepair but the *number* of such dwellings remained relatively stable over 15 years, and in the case of absence of basic amenities the rate of decline has slowed down since the 1970s. There were some significant regional differences, showing 'some correspondence to local authority action in the private sector' in the North and South East of England. Some types of household, including single parent families and families with one or two children had suffered a deterioration in their housing conditions compared with the situation in 1981 (DOE 1988, pp 73–79).

The conclusions to be drawn from these surveys are open to dispute. It is likely, though, that housing conditions are not being improved quickly enough, and that there is a danger they are getting worse rather than better as a result of continued neglect, changes in the tenure balance, and inadequate public and private investment. Remedies proposed include selective demolition, comprehensive area action, much higher levels of public spending, and a more pro-active role for housing authorities (Institute of Housing 1992a). The role of housing authorities in this is crucial by common consent, and so too is the level of resources available to them.

Eliminating old houses

At its peak, the post-war slum clearance programme was responsible for demolishing over 90,000 houses per annum in both 1970 and

1971. In the 20 years from 1954 to 1973 around one and a half million houses were closed or demolished (Cullingworth 1979, p 83). In 1990 3,200 houses were demolished, a level so low as to lead one commentator to question whether 'it is any longer government policy to replace houses that are too dilapidated to be improved . . . . The average house standing now will have to last thousands of years at current replacement rates' (Perry 1991, p 28).

In practice there is an inevitable link between demolition and new building: no government could promote demolition without also promoting new building, unless it appeared that there were sufficient houses of decent quality for every household — a situation which has obviously not prevailed in the post-war period. Demolition has therefore not featured strongly in policy in the 1980s, when the emphasis was on private provision and improvement. The issue is now increasingly debated, but, unlike the 1950s and 1960s, in the context of unpopular council estates, and areas of predominantly owner-occupied housing.

Where problematic council housing is demolished, a variety of destinations for its residents is likely, involving existing council housing, and housing associations. Delays are bound to occur while residents are found suitable accommodation. Most such examples of demolition of council housing in the 1980s appear to have taken place in systems built estates which have become difficult if not impossible to let. Such estates have usually achieved a reputation of such notoriety that it is felt that no alternative to demolition would be acceptable to tenants, and no alternative involving the private sector would be feasible. Clearance is not usually a cheap option, especially in the case of systems built flats. And most post-war properties will still have a loan outstanding. But to do nothing also costs money for security, administration and some maintenance. In towns and cities where the level of demand for council accommodation has been affected by the growth of owner-occupation, or by migration and demographic trends, clearance has been a feasible option on a small scale. But in areas of acute demand for council housing, and in the absence of resources for replacement rented housing, a large scale programme of council house demolition is unlikely. However, in the light of growing evidence about the poor or unacceptable condition of some council housing it is likely that pressure for a larger programme will continue to develop.

Leaving aside the issue of what attitude should be adopted towards the owner-occupier on a high income who neglects maintenance, it is clear that substantial proportions of owner-occupiers are unable, through low income, to maintain their properties, and may only have been able to buy a house in the first place because of its poor condition, and hence low price. In 1986 in England and Wales the majority of houses in poor condition were owner-occupied (DOE 1988; Welsh Office 1988). In the worst cases there may be strong reasons to favour clearance and rebuilding rather than repair and rehabilitation. However, owner-occupiers are likely to resist the idea of demolition just as they did in the 1960s and 1970s. At least some demolition will be considered by housing authorities to be in the public interest, and two recent legislative changes acknowledge the sensitivity of the issues involved. The 1989 Local Government and Housing Act gave all owners of housing which is demolished the right to compensation at market values, and the 1991 Planning and Compensation Act provided higher home loss payments to home owners than to tenants. This measure may owe more to the imminent development of the Channel Tunnel rail link than to a concern with slum housing, but the measure applies to all such houses and demonstrates a new development in the recognition of home ownership as the dominant tenure.

Is there a role for housing authorities in assisting the owner-occupiers of property which should be demolished? In the past the housing authority's role was usually that of co-ordinating the clearance, compensating the owners of properties which inevitably had a low value, and finding council accommodation for the displaced. But what should the role be, if the owner wants to continue as an owner-occupier? The authority's role may well remain as co-ordinator, with a more difficult task of co-ordinating clearance and rehousing in line with tenure and affordability requirements.

The situation of owner-occupiers in clearance areas has been the subject of pioneering work in Birmingham, followed by a few other authorities. Research commissioned by Birmingham in 1985 confirmed the broad picture of home owners in clearance areas reluctant to leave their area and tenure, and unhappy with the delays and levels of compensation payable to them. In the light of these findings the Council developed the idea of a rebuilding grant (Morris 1992). This is being tested in Birmingham and Leicester through the Urban Programme, and Sheffield and Rochdale have shown interest in similar schemes to provide help for 'sensitive rebuilding in inner cities', but the statutory powers available to local authorities are inadequate in contrast with, for example, improvement grants, discounts under the Right to Buy, and other schemes to encourage owner-occupation for first-time buyers (Perry 1991, p 29). Formidable problems, therefore, remain to be tackled if a model for redevelopment in areas of owner-occupied housing is to be developed. 'Because of these detailed problems, it remains clear that owner-occupation represents a major constraint on future levels of demolition, with implications for the organisation and implementation of clearance programmes. The challenge is to make clearance socially and politically more acceptable, perhaps by increasing the element of consumer sovereignty' (Thomas 1986, p 193). It is hard to avoid the conclusion that this will require greater levels of public spending than governments have come to expect are necessary for the development of owner-occupied housing, and greater levels of local authority commitment than some authorities will consider appropriate.

Repair and improvement

At the local and national level there have been a number of recurrent controversies about the best approach to take to repair and improvement. These can be seen as part of the debate about the enabling role reviewed in Chapter 2, with policy options ranging from strong state intervention to free market solutions, and from high levels of planning to high degrees of consumer control and influence. But at the local government level the controversies tend to be posed more as a series of dilemmas, requiring political and professional judgements about the balance to be struck between different approaches and attitudes.

The most fundamental dilemma is the extent to which public sector or private sector remedies should be sought. It is not obvious that the housing authority has to be the agent of change in every instance, or that it even has to be involved at all in the case of privately owned housing. Private owners can be expected to pay for the repair and maintenance of their housing, just as they paid for it initially. On the other hand, housing in disrepair can have implications for the neighbourhood; people's circumstances can change after purchasing a house, making it difficult for them to maintain their housing; and in flats or houses in multiple occupation or with common parts, the implications for neighbours of poor repair and maintenance have for decades been seen to justify a role for the local authority.

A related theme is the relationship between state support and private profit. Local authorities have sometimes been concerned that their award of improvement grants, for example, would do more to assist the profit margins of private landlords than improve the housing conditions of their tenants. Similarly, owner-occupiers have not always been seen as deserving recipients of grants or attention, given — as a group — their relatively privileged position in the housing system. And partnerships, for example, involving the take-over of run-down council estates by private developers to create housing for owner-occupation have not always been welcomed because of the fear that the developers' interests will predominate over the remaining tenants. Attempts to improve housing in neighbourhoods of mixed or owner-occupied tenure have been influenced by fears about the possibility of improvement leading to gentrification, with a consequential loss of access to housing for poorer people. At its worst the use of local authorities' powers to enable improvement can provide 'opportunities for the unscrupulous to evict or harass tenants of potentially valuable improvable houses. . . . ' (Cullingworth 1979, p 90). In rural areas the concern is often one of improvement being used to increase the amount of housing used as second homes, or to raise price levels beyond the means of local people on smaller incomes.

A third dilemma relates to the extent to which improvement to private sector housing should be encouraged or required by the state, and the nature of the local government response when voluntary action is not forthcoming. This dilemma is commonly encountered in the case of individual areas of unfit housing where a local authority is trying to encourage the take up of improvement grants. How far should private landlords and owner-occupiers be free not to improve or maintain their properties? The exact answer for a housing authority might depend on the implications for others. Private tenants in HMOs, for example, are entitled to expect decent and safe housing for the rent they are paying, so may expect local authority intervention on their behalf. And residents of a dilapidated terrace or block of flats may expect action from the council against reluctant neighbours or absentee landlords. What should be the balance between use of the stick of compulsory powers and the carrot of grants?

Another common theme has been the debate about whether people, or properties should be the target of local government action. The balance at national level has swung clearly in favour of targeting the poorest people since 1989. This is consistent with other policies of the Conservative governments since 1979 — to concentrate subsidies and assistance on needy individuals rather than on 'bricks and mortar'. There are also questions about the balance to strike in state action between individual and area action, and the possibilities for area action when grants are targeted on individual people.

Finally, how far should housing authorities be free to pursue their own priorities, even if this means that some problems or issues are neglected? While many examples of greater administrative and financial controls by central government since 1979 can be cited, there are also areas of discretion which different local authorities use in different ways. Some argue that housing authorities have not made full use of the powers they have. Others suggest a lack of powers in legislation to do some of the things housing authorities wish to do. A final set of questions is concerned with whether housing authorities have got appropriate powers and resources in order to make the desired changes to housing conditions. There are renewed complaints from housing and other professionals about the unwieldy nature of the powers available for dealing with HMOs or renewal, for example, and persistent complaints about the inadequacy of capital and revenue resources.

Housing improvement

The development of the systems of grants and other provision for physical housing improvement in the private sector have been documented elsewhere (Cullingworth 1979; Thomas 1986; Mackintosh and Leather 1992). Here the main themes and events since the late 1970s are reviewed.

During the 1960s there was a growing perception that the worst housing had already been demolished, and that the remainder could be tackled partly through demolition and partly through rehabilitation. However 'the constraint on public sector expenditure (following the Balance of Payments Crisis of 1967) was the most important single reason why policy shifted towards improvement' (Thomas 1986, p 65).

The 1969 Housing Act introduced General Improvement Areas (GIAs) (Housing Treatment Areas in Scotland), intended to encourage area renewal by voluntary take-up of grants for housing and environmental improvement. Amidst a background of growing criticism about the rate of progress in GIAs the 1974 Housing Acts introduced Housing Action Areas (HAAs). HAAs were intended to tackle the worst areas but in the interests of the residents, on the assumption that areas with particular concentrations of certain types of household would require special help. Separate provision for demolition remained. In Scotland, however, the legislation allowed for a continuing programme of area demolition, where appropriate, with its three-fold classification of HAAs for Demolition, for Improvement, and for Demolition and Improvement. An important new feature of the Acts was the higher level of grant in renewal areas. Grants in HAAs were for standard amenities, housing improvement, environmental improvement, and repairs, a new feature of housing legislation which challenged old assumptions about where the responsibility for ongoing maintenance lay. The

1974 legislation also boosted the role of housing associations. In some parts of the country the growth of housing associations has proceeded directly from the desire of local housing authorities to favour them as the means to housing improvement, especially in Housing Action Areas. The GIA legislation remained broadly in place (except in Scotland). And measures were taken to restrict exploitation of improvement grants by speculators.

The 1974 legislation remained broadly in place until 1989, with some non-controversial amendments introduced in the 1980 Housing Act (1980 Tenants Rights etc (Scotland) Act). Changes to grant percentages made the system more complex and less effectively concentrated on area improvement. The most important change was the extension of repair grants beyond the boundaries of HAAs. The boom that followed an increase in the level of grant available in 1982 arguably provided a distraction from the priorities housing authorities had identified, while scarce staff resources were devoted to administering the repairs grant system. Little was heard from the government about whether the neediest people or properties were being targeted, or about whether the generosity of grants was tantamount to encouraging the neglect of routine maintenance which some owners could have afforded to undertake. Only the cynical commented on the proximity of the forthcoming general election.

By the mid-1980s the government was proposing a fundamental reform in which three main strands can be detected. One was the continuing levels of disrepair and unfit housing. Secondly, there were many criticisms of the existing system, especially from those in local government who tried to make it work. It was complex, lengthy, ill-suited for those on the lowest incomes who could not afford any contribution for housing improvements, and it was based on a standard of fitness considered by many to have long outlived its relevance to late twentieth century views of decent housing. Thirdly, the government's view of the state's role in housing policy — to target public spending only on those who could not afford to provide for themselves — was inconsistent with the system which placed the condition of the property as the dominant criterion for state aid. The government's view that the owner had primary responsibility for the upkeep of private housing was clearly stated in the 1985 White Paper, with its proposal for means tested grants (Cmnd 9513).

The legislation which eventually followed in the 1989 Local Government and Housing Act provides a framework on which regulations were based in the months that followed, making it difficult for housing authorities to prepare for the new system. The main provisions and changes are summarised here. First, under the terms of the Act, an enthusiastic Secretary of State could require and regulate periodic condition surveys. New provisions require an annual consideration of conditions by housing authorities. Second, the Act introduces a new unified renovation grant, following criticisms about the complexity of the provisions applying since 1980. The new grant is means tested, and, subject to certain conditions, mandatory for owner-occupied houses which are unfit. Landlords will not qualify unless notices have been served against them, which may deter some councils from taking action. Grant levels will be as high as 100 per cent of approved costs for those on the lowest incomes, but a limit of £50,000 was subsequently introduced following reports of the possibility of housing authorities having to pay grants of up to £200,000. There are fears amongst housing authority staff and councillors about some of those who do not qualify, but are not on high incomes. Other grants are available largely at the discretion of the authority. These are common parts grants, houses in multiple occupation grant, disabled facilities grant, and minor works assistance for thermal insulation, patch and mend, staying put, and elderly resident adaptation. Several of these have significant implications for community care policies.

Third, a new fitness standard lists nine criteria which have to be met if a property is to be judged fit, so bringing the standard broadly into line with the Scottish tolerable standard. The new standard provides a clearer basis for judging fitness, but does not essentially alter the state's definition of what is a decent house. The requirements are worth paraphrasing here, but the reader should also study carefully the advice offered on applying the standard in DOE Circular 6/1990:

(a) structural stability;
(b) free from serious disrepair;
(c) free from dampness prejudicial to health;
(d) adequate lighting, heating and ventilation;
(e) adequate piped supply of wholesome water;
(f) satisfactory facilities for preparing and cooking food, including a sink with hot and cold water;
(g) a suitably-located water-closet for the exclusive use of the occupants;
(h) a fixed bath or shower, suitably located, with hot and cold water, and for the exclusive use of the occupants;
(i) an effective system of drainage;

(DOE 1990b)

Fourth, new provisions are intended to simplify grants and procedures for group repair schemes. Fifthly, a new area approach — Renewal Areas (RAs) — is introduced 'to focus attention on the use of a broader based area strategy which may include environmental and socio-economic regeneration' (DOE 1990b, p 5). RAs are expected to be larger than GIAs and HAAs which they replace. An important feature of the procedure for their declaration is the carrying out of a Neighbourhood Renewal Assessment (NRA). This is intended to prevent authorities from going 'too far' with improvement as some are alleged to have done in the past 'where this seems not to have been cost effective in terms of securing the life of the stock and where there were no good social reasons why redevelopment should not have taken place' (p 6). NRAs are intended to provide an aid to decision making, but it is likely that some authorities will find it hard to undertake the 'series of logical steps' including a 'costing out of alternative strategies at net present values' which is involved (pp 8–10). The housing stock in RAs is expected normally to be in poor repair, with three-quarters unfit, or otherwise eligible for grant, and in addition, 30 per cent at least of the residents should be in receipt of welfare benefits such as Income Support, Unemployment Benefit and Housing Benefit. Information and advice services must be provided to residents, a new requirement following the success of Care and Repair and other advisory services (see Chapter 8). RAs are intended to target resources onto particular areas, but without the guarantee of any particular levels of grants, which can be varied by the Secretary of State. These provisions do not cover Scotland, which retains the 1974 framework (Robertson 1992).

Previous experience shows that it will take time for these new provisions to make any impact. The early experience is reviewed below, after an evaluation of earlier improvement activity by housing authorities.

Housing authorities as enablers of improvement

Early evaluations of the 1974 provisions for improvement were not too encouraging. Local authorities were reluctant to embark on a large programme using untried legislation; administrative processes were not always in place; grants were not always adequate to provide the incentive required and, for that and other reasons, co-operation was not always forthcoming from residents and landlords. 'In general terms, progress seemed to have been most dramatic where implementation included compulsory action and public sector acquisition', despite the generally unwieldy nature of the powers available to housing authorities (Thomas 1986, p 80).

Later studies show that more progress can be expected after several years of designation. In a study of six HAAs at least five years old Niner and Forrest (1982) showed that almost three-quarters of the houses had been reached by some kind of work. Some local authorities tackled their new responsibilities enthusiastically, adopting a clear strategy of identifying and dealing with the worst areas, sometimes through assisting housing associations and sometimes through local teams of officers working with residents to implement the improvement work. Leicester, Liverpool, Edinburgh, Glasgow, Newcastle and Birmingham — with its 'enveloping' schemes (DoE 1982) — are notable examples.

Enveloping developed from concern about the difficulties of using HAA powers to achieve effective improvement of blocks or streets, when the grant system was targeted at individuals. Birmingham tried to co-ordinate individual grant applications to achieve a comprehensive approach, but this was difficult and expensive in staff time. The council was able to take advantage of the government's inner city initiative, announced in the 1977 Budget, and owners had external repairs carried out at no expense, 'on the assumption that external renovation would encourage grant take up for external works'. The scheme was integrated into the HIP process in 1982, but 'the early response of local authorities was slow', despite 75 per cent exchequer contributions. Some authorities preferred to use repair grants, especially when set at 90 per cent, or found the approval procedures cumbersome and slow (Thomas 1986, pp 126–27).

Even in the most committed authorities, though, the rate of progress was felt by many to be inadequate. Birmingham City Council estimated (1981) that 93,000 houses needed repair or improvement, and throughout England in 1982, only 173,000 houses were included in HAAs (Thomas 1986), at a time when the DOE estimated that three-quarters of the property suitable for such treatment was not in the programme (DOE 1983, p 23).

The most recent systematic evaluation of local authority improvement activity is contained in the *English House Condition Survey 1986*. Although a good deal of activity by local authorities, affecting individual houses and areas of housing and involving 1.6 million properties between 1981 and 1986, is reported, the level of activity is much less than was possible given the scale of need. Although both area action and individual action affected a disproportionately high number of privately rented properties, the majority of home improvement grants (82 per cent) were paid to owner-occupiers. Area based activity was concentrated disproportionately in the north of England, and GIAs were the most common type of area action. Local authorities were apparently reluctant to use their compulsory powers to enforce improvement. Where they did in relation to individual properties, there was a greater than 50 per cent chance the dwelling would be privately rented. However only 5 per cent of the unsatisfactory housing identified in 1981 had been the subject of such action by 1986. In relation to area action, of the 1.78 million dwellings identified as suitable for inclusion in GIAs or HAAs in 1981, only 541,000 had been included in any sort of area renewal programme by 1986.

Some of the reasons for this bleak picture are revealed in Houlihan's study of area improvement in three councils, Stoke-on-Trent, Sefton and Liverpool in the 1970s and 1980s. Only Liverpool, under Liberal control, quickly adopted the new national enthusiasm for improvement rather than demolition, using housing associations as agents for rehabilitation. Liverpool was first to declare a GIA, and first to adopt an ambitious programme of HAAs. However the election of a Labour-controlled and Militant-dominated council in 1983 threatened this programme, because of the councillors commitment to a traditional policy of clearance and new build, which received a good deal of professional support in an authority where the Improvements Division was relatively isolated in the housing department. (However, the Council was not entirely successful because of housing associations, the Housing Corporation and the regional office of the DOE.)

Sefton and Stoke provide contrasting examples of local councillors not favouring area improvement policy for different ideological reasons. Conservative-controlled Sefton was unenthusiastic about a policy which would, in the main, benefit Labour wards and have revenue implications for the authority. A change in approach followed DOE pressure in the form of questions about the reliability of data on house condition, and about the rate of progress towards improvement. Officers were said to have been influential in changing the councillors' attitudes. Labour-controlled Stoke originally favoured clearance and new building, was not very sympathetic to the needs of owner-occupiers living in poor quality housing, and disliked the idea of housing associations having a large involvement in an improvement programme. 'This antipathy was evident at both the professional and member level' (p 109). The introduction of the HIP system in 1977, combined with a financial climate hostile to large-scale council building programmes, helped demonstrate the value of a wider approach to housing policy (Houlihan 1987). The early experience of the 1989 legislation suggests a similarly varied pattern. In a survey of a representative sample of 40 local authorities it was found that the level of enquiries in the first 10 months varied from less than 100 to over 3,000. Enquiries about mandatory grants made up 87 per cent of the total in one authority, and 14 per cent in another. They were handled far more quickly in some authorities than others — one had managed to apply the test of resources to only one per cent of enquirers. Policy differences in the generosity with which grants were made also existed. For example, some authorities did not provide minor works assistance. These variations could not be explained by the volume of enquiries, or by differential levels of housing in poor condition (Kirkham 1992, pp 38–40).

Some of the strongest reservations of local government officers about the 1989 provisions relate to their implications for area improvement. One senior officer of Bristol City Council estimates that it may cost £100,000 to carry out a neighbourhood renewal assessment of the type required. Administrative complexity, including the eligibility criteria for designation and for grant assistance, and lack of finance, made it difficult to persuade councillors to devote resources to this untried mechanism. For individual properties, the new fitness standard was revealing the extent of need and the inadequacy of resources. 'The new renovation grant system thus falls well short of what local authorities were seeking when the process of change and review began in the mid-1980s' (Samuel 1992, p 60).

Perhaps the strongest source of complaint in the first two years was from authorities who found it harder to make progress with area renewal and group repair schemes, because so many of their resources were consumed in mandatory improvement grants for individuals. Rochdale, for example, found 'having a renewal area tends to generate more applications from people who live just outside the boundary, and we cannot refuse them although clearly they are not within our strategic plan'. In Wales the situation was better, with additional allocations channelled to local authorities to enable area renewal and group repair projects to proceed, as in Ynys Mon (Bright 1992 pp 8–9; Battersby 1991).

The DoE launched a review of the 1989 legislation within months of its introduction. This led to proposals that housing authorities should not be required to pay mandatory grants outside areas involved in renewal or repair, and suggestions that mandatory grants should be abolished altogether. This would be an extraordinary development in the history of improvement policy, yet one which some hard-pressed housing authorities might welcome because of resource constraints.

HMOs

The worst housing conditions in Britain's towns and cities can often be found in housing in multiple occupation (HMOs). The problems can extend beyond lack of amenities and fire safety to management and maintenance issues, including harassment. They provide, therefore, something of a test of the enabling role of housing authorities in improving conditions, and are discussed here for that reason.

HMOs are defined in the 1985 Housing Act (s.345) as 'a house which is occupied by persons who do not form a single household'. This simple definition can be difficult to apply in practice, and the Institution of Environmental Health Officer's five-fold classification shows why:

(A) fully self catering flatlets and bedsitters;
(B) fully self catering shared houses normally occupied by students;
(C) houses let as lodgings;
(D) hostels and bed and breakfast establishments;
(E) buildings with self-contained flats.

The last two of these categories are disputed by many local authorities who will not use their powers in relation to HMOs in such cases.

The number of HMOs in England and Wales is estimated at 200,000 to 290,000, housing a population of two to 2.6 million (IEHO 1986, p 5; Thomas 1986, pp 97–100). They provide housing for those least well served by the social rented sector, and who cannot afford to buy their own housing, or who are seeking temporary housing, with easy access at a low cost.

The powers and duties of housing authorities in England were amended in the 1989 Local Government and Housing Act. Broadly, they provide for local authorities to ensure that standards of management and physical standards are adequate, but the only circumstances in which authorities are **required** to act remain limited to certain HMOs at least three storeys high. Enforcement of the regulations requires an authority to serve a notice, requiring compliance within a certain time. Previous provisions, including the possibility of a registration scheme, remain on the statute book. Other statutory provisions, such as the Environmental Protection Act, are also relevant to enforcing good conditions making HMOs one of the more esoteric areas of local government law. The complexity of the law may be a factor in the use made of it by local authorities. Since the 1989 provisions are not radically different from previous ones, it is possible to use earlier research to evaluate the condition of HMOs and the record of housing authorities in seeking to improve them.

A study carried out in the mid-1980s, found that around four-fifths of all HMOs surveyed were unsatisfactory in at least one respect — management, over-occupancy, or amenity provision —

and 'nearly a quarter were unsatisfactory on all three counts' (Thomas, with Hedges 1986, p 97). This is despite long-standing powers for local authorities to regulate conditions and management. Other studies in the 1980s have shown a similar picture, with the extent of deficiency varying with the category of HMO (Crook and Bryant 1982; Crook and Martin 1986; Kirby and Sopp 1986). Local housing authorities' powers to inspect and regulate HMOs have been criticised in the 1980s and 1990s on the grounds that they should be mandatory rather than discretionary, and strengthened to ensure more adequate enforcement. At least three Private Members' Bills have called for mandatory duties for housing authorities. In an unusual defence of local democracy, the government argued that local housing authorities should be left with the discretion to use their powers as they thought best (Crook 1989).

The administrative arrangements for dealing with HMOs in local government can be complex. Regulation of HMOs is usually the responsibility of Environmental Health Departments, but other departments have an important role. These include housing departments who may employ tenancy relations officers to advise HMO tenants about their rights, manage HMO property under control orders, and rehouse applicants from HMOs. Either department or some other department may be responsible for improvement grants, and the Planning Department may be involved over changes of use or access for escape. Fire services and social services may also be involved, and the DSS and the rent officers also have a role.

Despite the condition of many HMOs, four out of ten landlords said that their property had not been inspected in the last five years. Local authorities 'had served statutory notices on only 36 per cent of the sample. The greater the costs of disrepair, the less likely the property was to have received a notice'. It seems that whatever action local authorities have taken over HMOs is little known about by the tenants who stand to benefit. Less than a tenth of tenants had ever contacted the council about any problem relating to their house (Thomas, with Hedges 1986, p 106).

Some of the reasons for this inactivity are seen in the results of a study of 41 local housing authorities in the North and Midlands of England. First, most had very imperfect knowledge of the extent of HMOs in their area. Fewer than 10 per cent used house condition surveys or census data, and the one third who had registration schemes estimated that only one third of their HMOs were registered. However most authorities felt they had little difficulty locating HMOs, using Housing Benefit data, records of complaints, and other administrative records or local knowledge. Second, only a small majority (55 per cent) of authorities had a planned strategy for dealing with HMOs, the others choosing to react to complaints rather than actively seek contact with HMO landlords or tenants. Third, at times when improvement grants were available at a relatively high level, such as in the period from 1982 to 1984, authorities were favouring grant work, or responding to the demand, in a way which reduced the level of staff time available for HMO work. Fourth, some councils harbour doubts about the value for money represented by special grants for HMOs, which can be seen as unjustified subsidy for private landlords who may be seen as also benefiting from the Housing Benefit system (Crook 1989).

On the other hand, Crook found in 1987 evidence of more activity in relation to HMOs than the 1984 DoE study found. This was due to the growth of concern about single people and homelessness, as well as the activities of bodies such as the IEHO after a number of fatal fires in the late 1970s. The proactive authorities were found to follow a number of approaches, but most were more interested in retaining and improving HMOs than in converting them into a different sort of accommodation. However, fully one third of the proactive authorities sought to see HMOs converted into self-contained units. Many tried to protect management standards as well as improve physical conditions. They recognised the risk of harassment to tenants of HMO landlords seeking to avoid enforcement action, and so provided advice on tenancy rights and rents. However, overall the recent emphasis has been on 'physical standards rather than the acknowledged problems of mismanagement' (Crook 1989, p 48).

The value of the housing authority having a clear strategic view of its objectives and policies in relation to HMOs should be obvious. HMOs provide for a small but important section of the population, whose needs could probably otherwise only be met — for reasons of income — in the social rented sector. It is surely too complacent to question 'whether anything approaching a corporate approach can ever be envisaged' (Thomas, with Hedges 1986, p 107). This is no more than is expected of local government in relation to community care planning, for example, and other areas of their work. It should not be too ambitious to expect housing authorities themselves to co-ordinate their departments to a common set of objectives, and to put some effort into co-ordinating their activities with others. Thomas's suggestion that 'a more realistic approach' may be to designate some officers to act as advocates 'in protecting the rights of tenants and landlords' is useful but not likely to be sufficient, not least in resolving problems which arise from the conflict between landlords' and tenants' interests.

Council housing

Housing policy and legislation have been based on the assumption that public sector housing is in a fit condition and that what may be needed is some modernisation to take account of ageing fittings or major maintenance. Gradually, though since the 1970s, government and local authorities have shown a more far-reaching concern about the nature and attractiveness of certain council housing neighbourhoods, particularly those which are difficult to let (DoE 1981; Power 1987a). Over a quarter of a million dwellings were reported to be difficult to let by housing authorities in their HIP returns in 1981/2 (DOE 1982). This concern is wide ranging, and extends from the physical condition of the housing stock, the attractiveness of the neighbourhood, and the proximity of jobs and amenities, to the quality of management and maintenance services (Power 1987a; DoE 1980; CHR 1989).

Some recent evidence suggests that some areas of council housing may be in a worse physical condition than had previously been supposed by local authorities and central government (Glasgow District Council 1986; Malpass and Murie 1990; Public Accounts Committee 1991). The Association of Metropolitan Authorities has estimated that there are about two million dwellings which require £19 billion of investment to remedy defects. With government policy in the 1980s being geared to de-municipalisation, and with capital allocations constrained, local authorities have been encouraged to consider a number of ways of tackling the worst estates, sometimes involving forms of privatisation, sometimes management changes, and often some combination of approaches.

Housing authorities, on the whole, have been left to improve their own stock as best they can within the capital and revenue resources available to them. But special programmes have been used by central government to encourage particular approaches. Starting in 1979 the Priority Estates Project (PEP) provided advice and some practical management assistance to authorities tackling their worst estates. The PEP approach laid stress on 'ten key elements essential to the long-term success of an estate based management project' (Power 1987b, p vi): a local office; local repairs; localised lettings; local rent arrears control; an estate budget; resident care-taking (for flats); tenant participation; co-ordination and liaison with other services; performance monitoring; and training.

By 1986 PEP were working with 12 authorities on 25 estates, and a separate Welsh project involved six estates. The PEP approach has been promoted strongly by central government and the enthusiasm of its supporters, and there is evidence from PEP of significant improvements in the living conditions on estates included in the programme (Power 1987b) but little independent evaluation. The Project has become part of the 1980s orthodoxy about decentralised management, a rare example of agreement across the political divide and between politicians and professionals. The Project does not, however, provide additional capital resources for the sorts of improvements which might be necessary to remedy the defects on many council estates. This is part of the purpose of the Estate Action (EA) programme, introduced in 1985, which combines ear-marked allocations through the HIPs system with expectations about management improvements, tenure diversification, and private sector involvement. The aims are described by the government as:

— Diversifying tenure on estates by extending home ownership or passing management to co-ops, trusts or housing associations;
— Improving housing management and maintenance through the estate-based approach developed by the Priority Estates Project and similar measures such as concierge services;
— Revitalising run-down estates through resident involvement in estate-based initiatives such as Community Refurbishment Schemes, community enterprise and local employment initiatives;
— Attracting private sector resources and investment.

(DOE 1988b)

Pinto (1991) reports widespread scepticism by housing authorities about the government's claims that EA allocations are additional to HIPs allocations, and presents evidence in support of authorities' views. Nevertheless, 83 had taken part by 1988 (DOE 1988b) and their primary motive, not surprisingly, was to obtain additional capital resources, rather than to pursue the government's policy agenda of tenure diversification and private sector investment. However Pinto reports widespread dissatisfaction with the process of bidding which at its worst had involved allocations in July to November for spending in that financial year. Officers were also puzzled by the criteria for successful bids, claiming lack of clarity, inconsistency, and the danger of underspend. Few privatisation schemes had taken place. There was more consensus about the value of estate-based management initiatives, such as local repair teams and stronger management presence on estates. Progress towards tenant management has been much slower, with involvement in co-operatives and Estate Management Boards (see Chapter 6). Officers commented either that sufficient tenant consultation took place already, or that the timetabling of the bids and approvals process prevented fuller participation and carried the risk of raising expectations which could not always be fulfilled.

Estate Action represents a serious incursion into the freedom of housing authorities to determine their own priorities for capital spending and management arrangements which the HIPs system was intended to provide. On a smaller scale the arrangements which apply to the four partnership authorities in Scotland have a similar effect in requiring particular levels of expenditure on priority estates as a condition for the award of a certain capital allocation.

A more radical measure intended to improve conditions on council estates is the voluntary transfer of part or all of a housing authority's stock to a housing association. By early 1992, 18 transfers of the entire stock, ranging from around 4,500 to 12,000 in size, had gone ahead in England. No Labour controlled council has supported this development, and controversy rages about whether it represents in the short or long term an improvement for tenants and prospective tenants (Roberts 1992; Baker and Perry 1991; Fraser 1991). Fraser provides a balanced account of the procedures for large scale and partial transfers, and argues that the benefits can include:

- more resources for the repair and improvement of that housing
- more resources for the development of new housing
- the protection of rented housing from purchase under the Right to Buy.

(p 35)

Baker and Perry dispute some of these benefits and argue that most of the money received by authorities from associations has been used to reduce local taxes and borrowing, rather than being invested in new housing or housing improvement.

Partial voluntary transfers involving disposals to the private sector have taken place on a small scale, amounting to 0.1 per cent of the local authority stock in 1985 (Duncan 1988, p 6). Duncan reviews 11 such disposals, and reports considerable success in achieving better use of the stock, at less expense to the housing authorities, whose main reason for disposing of it was financial. Some would have preferred to retain the stock for rental, so for them disposal was the least bad, rather than the best option available.

Conclusion

This chapter has reviewed the evidence about the role of housing authorities in housing improvement. Surprisingly few have had adequate systematic information about local housing conditions, on which to base their approach. Without such information the nature of housing authorities' strategies cannot be entirely clear. Nationally, the evidence about slowly improving standards overall has to be set in the context of lower levels of public investment in the 1980s, evidence of declining standards for some, and the sheer scale of the needs revealed in recent house condition surveys.

The decline in the use of demolition as part of the means to improving conditions in the 1970s and 1980s is unlikely to continue indefinitely, if housing conditions do not improve significantly in the face of rising consumer standards and inadequate public and private investment. But it is not easy to see how a significant programme of clearance could be promoted against the resistance of residents, and in particular, owner-occupiers, without greater inducements being offered, probably involving higher public spending. The lack of emphasis on clearance at local level reflects a recognition that without greater resources and perhaps new powers, local authorities are not going to bring the wrath of local communities to bear on themselves, as happened in the 1960s and 1970s. Demolition of council housing is also problematic, unless local conditions make it easy to rehouse the residents in acceptable alternative housing. The prospects for large scale clearance of the worst council estates in the areas of greatest housing stress rely on a programme of public investment in new or modernised housing for rent.

The role of local authorities in housing improvement and repair has altered over time from the post-war concern to build new housing through the slum clearance activities of the 1950s, 1960s and early 1970s to the improvement and repair policies of the 1970s and 1980s. Throughout most of this period the implicit assumption has been that council housing itself generally provided satisfactory housing, and that the real problems lay with the private sector and in particular the private rented sector. As owner-occupation has grown and council housing has declined, the perception of where the serious problems lie has moved again to a more comprehensive concern with the improvement of conditions in all tenures and in particular with the problematic parts of the council sector and the dominant owner-occupied sector.

There is apparently contradictory evidence about the record of local authorities in improving housing conditions. In some cases enthusiastic authorities are constrained by inadequate resources and powers, in others little is tried let alone achieved. Some authorities, such as Birmingham, have pioneered new procedures and lobbied successfully for new powers. Other authorities have not seen the powers and resources available to them as relevant to their perceived needs. The case of houses in multiple occupation illustrates the apparent reluctance of some authorities to devise and carry out a strategy in relation to the poorest housing, sometimes occupied by the most disadvantaged people. When need is so great and resources so limited, it is inevitable that resources get concentrated on a limited number of problems, whether consciously or unconsciously.

Some local authorities have been reluctant to take an active role in relation to owner-occupied housing, but it will be increasingly difficult to ignore the needs of growing numbers of low income or disadvantaged owner-occupiers, especially in the context of community care policies, an ageing population, and the dominance of owner-occupation in the housing system.

The variety of experience of housing authorities is consistent with a genuine system of local government in the sense that autonomous local authorities should be free to be different from each other. However, at least part of the disparity is created by the resource constraints which hamper authorities and force them to concentrate on some activities, at the cost of others. The discretion authorities enjoy is a freedom to do little but not — to the regret of many — a licence to do enough to improve the housing stock.

It is likely that the resources available to operate the 1989 Act grant regime are not sufficient to cater for the level of need within a reasonable timescale. Other problems to do with administrative complexity, means testing, and project appraisal are significant, but less insuperable. If resource constraints lead to abandoning one type of grant in favour of another, some housing authorities may have to acknowledge the impossibility of achieving decent quality housing in their areas in a reasonable timescale.

Chapter 6
Influencing property management

Bringing about improvements to housing conditions can be done in a number of ways. The last chapter has been concerned mainly with improving the physical condition of housing, whether in the public or private sector. However, poor physical conditions may not be the only aspect of poor housing conditions. The quality and nature of housing management by all landlords may be as important in determining satisfactory housing conditions as the nature and quality of the housing stock itself. Even if in good physical condition there may be problems arising from the way in which housing is used or managed. Occupants of HMOs, for example, may suffer from harassment just as much as from poor physical standards. Satisfactory housing in the private sector may lie vacant while homelessness rises. Without a housing stock of its own, or with a diminishing supply, housing authorities are seriously curtailed in their capacity to assist in meeting need. Housing authorities have, therefore, increasingly sought to influence housing management by all landlords, and to assist the process of movement between tenures or types of housing. This chapter considers the scope and adequacy of their powers, using some current examples.

There are a number of ways in which housing authorities can influence the management of houses in the private and voluntary sectors, and the overall management of the housing stock of their area in addition to their role as managers of council housing. Broadly they fall under the headings of assisting access and influencing the quality and nature of management. They involve authorities in using powers to set standards and regulate other landlords, to act independently in the property market, to assist access and mobility with financial support, and to work together with others to achieve agreed objectives. They include:

- financial incentives or other inducements, such as the offer of a more suitable house, designed to release the beneficiaries' existing house for use by the housing authority. This can mean a switch from public renting to owner-occupation, or vice versa, or simply a move within the council rented sector.

- housing benefit which enables access to renting in the private sector for many who would otherwise be dependent on the council or housing association rented sector. Although there is little discretion available to authorities in the calculation of allowances, there is scope to publicise and administer benefits with more or less commitment. There is growing evidence that some authorities are failing to administer the scheme effectively (Audit Commission 1993). In their own defence, however, housing authorities have claimed they are amongst the victims of a scheme which has been described as the biggest 'administrative fiasco in the history of the welfare state' (Kemp 1985).
- local authority loans for house purchase. Finance for home loans has been a long-established feature of local authority powers, and remains an element in assisting some people to buy a home.
- management controls over HMOs, which allow housing authorities to regulate aspects of management as well as physical standards in certain circumstances, see Chapter 5 (DoE 1992c).

This is not an exhaustive list, but taken with the opportunities discussed below, they show that housing authorities have several means to improving access to decent housing and housing management for people the authority seeks to help.

This chapter concentrates on four ways in which housing authorities have attempted to make better use of the housing stock of their area, in co-operation with others. These are selected because of the relevance they are said to have for assisting housing authorities to play a part in meeting need. They are:

- nomination agreements
- leasing
- tenant participation
- establishing alternative landlords.

Nomination agreements

Access to rented housing in the housing association sector can be assisted directly by local authorities, through involvement in the allocation process. As the number of council houses declines overall, and as housing associations become the predominant providers of new social rented housing, they have assumed growing importance in assisting housing authorities to meet a variety of needs, including homelessness (Parker, Smith and Williams 1992).

Nomination agreements are seen by central and local government, and by housing associations and their funding bodies, as one means whereby local authorities can meet their obligations, particularly to homeless people. There is widespread consensus about the importance of nomination agreements in housing policy, and incentives on both sides to make the system operate smooothly. Housing Corporation, Scottish Homes and Tai Cymru circulars make it clear that housing associations are expected to assist local authorities. Legislation, unusually, allows housing authorities in England and Wales to require assistance in the case of homeless people.

As housing authorities have found it harder and harder to build new council housing they have shown more interest in the possibilities of using agreements with housing associations to achieve their objectives. It has not always been so. In the 1960s and 1970s housing associations were seen as complementary to the council sector. They were expected to provide for different needs and to specialise in types of property or types of tenant neglected by housing authorities. They were seen as adding a degree of pluralism to the rented sector, and were rebuffed or welcomed by housing authorities for that reason. Some authorities resented the ways in which housing asociations were funded to meet needs the authority did not see as a priority. Other authorities welcomed the additional contribution associations could make to meeting a variety of need in their area. The different purposes, financial frameworks and histories of housing authorities and housing associations led to different ways of working, and different organisational cultures. Increasingly, in the 1980s, housing associations were seen by central government as the preferred providers of rented housing. Instead of complementing housing authorities, associations were expected to replace them, or at least take on the major role of social housing providers for an increasingly poor and disadvantaged group of tenants. This policy background needs to be borne in mind as essential to an understanding of the current interest in the use of nomination agreements between housing authorities and housing associations, and the tensions that can arise.

The legitimacy of housing authorities in expecting associations to enter into agreements is open to question, but can be defended with reference to:

- the extent of public funding of housing associations, including although not exclusively, funding in the form of grants from local authorities;
- the role of housing authorities in representing the needs of the people of the area: no other body has the same

democratic legitimacy. This argument is often applied particularly to the role housing associations might play in housing homeless people, but there is a more general point to be made about the role housing associations can play in assisting housing authorities to meet their objectives, whatever form of housing need they are concerned with. This strategic role of the housing authority allows an overview of housing needs and provision to be taken into account at the local authority level. Housing associations do not necessarily have an overview of the whole area, and in any case, lack the legitimacy (and probably the resources) of the housing authority in examining the nature and extent of need;

- the effective use of the housing stock, based on the knowledge of conditions and needs which a strategic view provides, and which no other body is able to supply. This can have particular relevance, for example, where housing associations have a record of housing people with 'special needs' and housing authorities have relatively little such stock or management skills, or where housing associations have stock in a particular locality where the housing authority has no or little stock;
- in the particular case of housing authorities which have disposed of their stock to housing associations, there will be conditions about the continued access to that stock for homeless applicants to the housing authority.

Housing authorities have a number of levers, powers and resources to back up their role. Probably the strongest is the pressure which is placed on housing associations by their funding bodies. The Housing Corporation, Tai Cymru and Scottish Homes all expect at least 50 per cent nomination rights to be made available to housing authorities, and in particular circumstances even higher proportions, as in the case of local authorities providing land or Housing Association Grant. The 1985 Housing Act refers to the 'reasonable assistance' which authorities can require housing associations to provide to authorities in meeting their obligations under the homelessness legislation. Thirdly, the representative bodies of housing associations and local housing authorities have reached good practice agreements which they expect their members to observe. A survey of London Boroughs in 1992 found these to have been influential (National Federation of Housing Associations *et al.* 1989; Scottish Federation of Housing Associations and Scottish Homes 1989; Association of London Authorities *et al.* 1989; Association of London Authorities *et al.* 1992).

Despite these expectations, powers and exhortations the relationships between local authorities and housing associations have not always been trouble-free. While housing authorities have expressed scepticism about the record of housing associations in abiding by nomination agreements, housing associations have criticised local authorities for failing to make sufficient nominations of the type needed at the time needed. There are various reasons for this which can be summarised as:

- difficulties of definition
- difficulties of administration and management
- differences in values.

Definition

The crucial issue for definition is what makes up the 100 per cent from which housing authorities are entitled to have 50 per cent or whatever proportion is agreed. Fraser (1991) writes:

> In practice, the recommended method would work as follows.
> The first call on housing association vacancies would normally be decants, reciprocal transfers and "priority need" transfers. Of the remaining voids, 75 per cent of family sized dwellings and 50 per cent of smaller units would be made available to local authority nominees. Housing associations would then be able to use the remaining 25 per cent of family sized units and 50 per cent of smaller units to house special project nominees and people from their own waiting and transfer lists.
>
> (p 97).

The NFHA's Continuous Recording system (CORE) provides some information about the outcome of these types of policy. It collects information from all self-contained general needs new lettings, estimated at 76,000 in 1991. The proportion of lets made to local authority nominees rose from 34 to 39 per cent in 1991 (NFHA 1991, p 4). There were substantial regional variations, from 48 per cent in London to 20 per cent in Merseyside in the fourth quarter of 1991 (NFHA 1991, p 4). This upward trend was also observed in the most systematic study yet carried out into local authority and housing association lettings practices. In six case study areas the proportion of all lettings by associations which were the result of local authority nominations varied from 34 to 73 per cent in 1990–91. Five out of six authorities operated with a target of 50 per cent, but this was achieved in only one case. In the sixth authority (Camden) the target of 75 per cent was almost reached. Perhaps significantly, this was the authority with the most rigorous monitoring procedure (Parker, Smith and Williams 1992, pp 39–42). In Scotland, in the fourth quarter of 1991 local authorities (and new town development corporations) nominated a quarter (26.3 per cent) of new tenants of housing associations, about the same proportion as in previous quarters (SFHA 1992, p 3).

Differencees about administration and management

The issue of nominations has been at times fraught, with accusations from housing authorities of reluctance by housing associations to house nominees on the one hand, and accusations by housing associations of incompetence by housing authorities in making nominations on the other. It is clear that faults may lie on both sides and that close working relationships between housing authorities and associations provide the best chance of a remedy. More examples of such collaboration are being reported. For example, in Derby, Leeds and Exeter the councils have worked with housing associations to provide information about all the associations in the area for potential applicants (Parker, Smith and Williams 1992, p 18), and this study found that working relationships were generally felt to be good (p 47). However, in some cases improvements were possible, for example, in relation to the detailed running of a nominations system. 'It was fairly clear from the interviews with housing associations (apart from those in Camden) that the question of defining 'true' voids was not considered to be a major issue and it is doubtful whether many staff had a clear idea of what was involved' (p 47). And, housing association staff in three areas believed that the local authorities had difficulty in making nominations, while local authority staff felt no such difficulty (1992 p 42). This study found that there was a growing awareness by housing authorities about the importance of the nominations process, and this was reflected in a move away from 'pool' systems towards direct nominations at the point of a vacancy occurring (Parker, Smith and Williams 1992 p 48).

Fraser suggests a number of practical measures, such as:

- application forms should ask about the applicant's interest in being nominated to housing associations, so that time will not be subsequently wasted in approaching those who are not interested. Clearly, there is no point in including such a question in application forms unless steps are also taken to ensure that applicants are informed about housing associations.
- liaison arrangements between housing associations and local

authorities can assist in making nomination agreements run smoothly. Parker, Smith and Williams found liaison arrangements operating in all case study areas in their study.

Fraser claims that liaison officers can jointly monitor the agreements entered into and try to deal with problems as they emerge. Accusations that either side is not adhering to the spirit or the letter of the agreement can be examined and dealt with. Such accusations have in the past been difficult to refute or substantiate because of the absence of adequate data about who was being housed and how (CHR 1989). The introduction of new monitoring systems and requirements such as the CORE and SCORE monitoring systems operated by the NFHA and SFHA, and the tenants' reports requirement of the 1989 Local Government and Housing Act, should encourage better management information systems. The London Borough of Camden uses information supplied by associations to monitor their role in meeting need and to assist in devising housing strategies (Parker, Smith and Williams 1992, p 53). Without such information monitoring is impossible and liaison is potentially misdirected.

Finally, a remedy for some of the administrative difficulties can be found in the operation of a common applicants' register for all associations and the housing authority in an area. There are advantages for the applicant as well as the landlords in such a one door approach. However, the study by Parker et al. found that housing associations had reservations about this idea. Some feared the implications for associations' independence and capacity to take account of a diversity of need, some saw difficulties where they operated across the boundaries of more than one local authority, and some saw problems of maintaining confidence by themselves and applicants in a system operated by the local authority (Parker, Smith and Williams 1992, p 56). Wrekin District Council has set up a scheme with the five local housing associations which involves a common application form, a guide book and a computerised waiting list maintained by the District Council. The system is clearly the result of a process of bargaining in which housing authority and housing associations were willing to make concessions in order to reach agreement (Wincott 1992). Other attempts have not always been so successful, as in Exeter (Parker, Smith and Williams 1992, p 56).

Differences in values

Good administration and monitoring will not guarantee that nomination agreements always run smoothly. Housing associations are entitled to reject nominees and may do so for reasons which the local authority considers inadequate. Such circumstances may demonstrate clashes of organisational culture — differences of view about what the organisations' purposes and methods of working are — which no amount of liaison or co-ordination will overcome. Many nominees to housing associations in London are re-interviewed so that the associations' own allocation procedures can be applied, including sometimes more generous space criteria (ALA et al. 1992, p 6).

Anecdotal evidence suggests fears on the part of local authorities that housing associations are not willing to house the most problematic tenants. What exactly this means is not clearly defined — applicants from the lowest socio-economic groups, those most likely to incur rent arrears, those with the lowest house-keeping standards or those most likely to be involved in neighbour disputes are hinted at as possible factors. Local authorities in turn have been accused of failing to provide for the needs of special needs groups which housing associations have a tradition of assisting. Whether there is substance in these accusations cannot be entirely resolved with the available information about who is housed by associations and authorities.

The study by Parker et al. (1992) found that nominees were rarely rejected, but when they were this was usually for reasons to do with house type and size. The differences between stock types and sizes in housing associations and housing authorities is a recurring theme. In a 'very small number of interviews' housing association staff suggested that local authorities sometimes nominated people who were mentally ill without informing the association about this (p 51). There was some other evidence in this survey of a lack of trust between associations and authorities, and of associations seeking to maintain their independent role in assessing need. Another survey, of London Boroughs, found indications that a 'sizeable proportion of nominations were rejected by housing associations' (ALA et al. 1992, p 4). More information on these issues may need to be collected in the routine monitoring that takes place, or special studies carried out, to provide more insight into the respective roles of housing authorities and housing associations in housing those who pose the greatest challenge to the managers of the social rented sector.

There is little dispute that housing associations house people on low incomes. The CORE data showed average household incomes for new tenants of housing associations in the fourth quarter of 1991 at £96.31, with incomes for working households at £159.66 and for non-working households at £73.24 (NFHA 1991, p 5). The number of households eligible for housing benefit rose from

Influencing property management   111

56 per cent to 64 per cent in the year to the end of 1991 (NFHA 1991, p 3). In Scotland, over half the lets made in the quarter April to June 1991 were to people known to be eligible for housing benefit (SFHA 1991, p 1).

There is less agreement about the contribution housing associations make to housing homeless people. Making judgements about this is not easy. Account needs to be taken of the nature of the homelessness legislation and how it is administered, of the nature of the housing stock of individual housing associations, and the nature of the relationship between housing authorities and housing associations. If, for example, the only housing associations in a large town are special needs associations with a predominance of one-bedroom dwellings, and if the housing authority applies the homelessness legislation strictly to exclude most of the single people who apply, and if it then houses any priority homeless single people or couples in its own housing, then the number of nominations of homeless households to housing associations in that town is likely to be very low indeed. So crude figures showing the overall proportion of housing association lettings which go to homeless people have to be interpreted with caution, and do not necessarily reflect any reluctance on the part of housing associations to house homeless people.

That said, a growing proportion of housing association lettings are made to people defined as homeless, whether or not nominated by the housing authority. 'There has been a sharp rise in the proportion of homeless households accommodated from a year ago' (NFHA 1991, p 4). In London six boroughs were found which used all their nominations to two bed and larger accommodation for statutorily homeless applicants (ALA *et al.* 1992, p 5). In England in the last quarter of 1991 19 per cent of lets were made to applicants defined as statutorily homeless, a further 8 per cent to those 'non-statutorily homeless', and a further 7 per cent to people threatened with homelessness, a total of 33 per cent. There may, of course, be other lettings made to people who could be defined as homeless but who have not gone through the formal procedure of being so defined. The Housing Corporation's data, as reported by *Roof*, provide a different but perhaps out-of-date perspective. The percentage of lets going to statutorily homeless households in England is 11.5 per cent for 1990/91 (January/February 1992). Finally, it cannot be assumed that applicants will accept the offer of a housing association nomination. Thirteen London Boroughs report refusals to be nominated by statutorily homeless applicants (ALA *et al.* 1992, p 5).

Questions about the way in which local authority nominations to housing associations work in practice, and about who benefits, are increasingly important to housing authorities. Whether more

112 The Housing Authority as Enabler

housing authorities take the decision to divest themselves of their housing stock in favour of housing associations will depend partly on the answers. Only anecdotal evidence so far exists of how authorities with no stock of their own are proceeding. In two cases the investigation of homeless applicants is left to the housing associations which took over the stock — which raises questions about the nature of the approach taken and the monitoring which takes place, as well as about the housing authorities' view of its role (Stearn 1992).

Leasing

Despite periodic exhortations by government ministers to local authorities to do something about the scandal of vacant council housing at a time of growing homelessness, there is a higher proportion of vacant housing in the private sector (and in government-owned housing) than in the municipal sector. Since at least the 1970s local housing authorities have been involved in trying to make better use of the total housing stock by leasing such accommodation and making it available to homeless people, or others in need, on a temporary basis. Some of the earliest schemes were developed in rural areas where there were often small stocks of council housing, and relatively large proportions of vacant housing, some of it in the form of second homes which lay empty for significant periods of the year. More recently, attention has moved to the growth of leasing schemes in urban areas, where the growth of homelessness and dissatisfaction with the cost and quality of bed and breakfast accommodation has increased the level of interest in leasing. Leasing also grew because of the financial advantages it offered to local authorities, over bed and breakfast, until 1991.

Leasing involves local authorities taking a fixed-term lease on a property (not necessarily in their own area) and then making it available for rent to homeless households on a temporary, non-secure basis. For the household the temporary let represents a better quality of housing than that otherwise available to families waiting for permanent accommodation. For the local authority there is an additional advantage that the direct costs of leasing are less than those of using bed and breakfast accommodation. The London Research Centre estimates the annual cost of bed and breakfast accomodation at £15,000, compared with the average of £8,000 paid to landlords of leased houses (London Research Centre 1991b, p 6).

The recent growth of leasing started in the early 1980s with an experiment by the London Borough of Brent, to provide temporary accommodation for homeless people. By 1991 'over 15,800 properties in London were leased or licensed by local authorities from the private sector' (London Research Centre 1991b, p 7). (Licensing involves periodic use of a property, and payment only for the period involved. Leasing is for a set period, and payment must be made whether or not the property is occupied).

These developments have not been welcomed by central government, which has changed the financial framework for leasing to prevent long term leasing of properties, and to restrict the financial commitment by central government. Leasing now has to be considered alongside priorities for capital spending in the housing authority's work so that a decision to commit money to leasing means foregoing expenditure on other priorities such as renovation. However the revenue costs of leasing are accounted for in the authority's General Fund, rather than the Housing Revenue Account — an acknowledgement that the costs of providing for homeless people should be borne by the community as a whole and not just council tenants. The government is reluctant to see a 'build-up of privately owned property permanently ear-marked for leasing to local authorities. Ministers would not consider such an outcome desirable' (DoE 1991b).

Three research reports provide an evaluation of the use of leasing by housing authorities in England and Wales (London Research Centre 1989; London Research Centre 1991b; Evans 1991). Evans reports that by early 1990 a quarter of housing authorities in England and Wales leased some accommodation from the private sector, and a further 11 per cent planned to do so within a year (p 40). But most leased fewer than 30 properties. The largest concentrations of leasing are in London (85 per cent of local authorities) and the South East (54 per cent) (p 41), although some northern authorities such as Manchester, have well-established schemes. In London 15,827 properties were leased or licensed by March 1991, amounting to over 10 per cent of the private rented market in some parts of the city (London Research Centre 1991b, p 11).

Evaluation of leasing in the context of the housing authority as enabler needs to consider three different aspects. What are the costs and benefits of leasing in comparison with alternatives? Secondly, does leasing represent a net addition to the available housing stock? And thirdly, is leasing a temporary phenomenon which will fade away as the housing market returns to 'normal'?

First, leasing offers better quality accommodation for the short-term needs of homeless people than they would otherwise be able to obtain. The accommodation provided is clearly superior in quality than the alternatives available, either in bed and breakfast or privately-rented accommodation. Evans (1991) describes five types of temporary accommodation (apart from three types of leasing schemes, involving housing association and public bodies as well as private owners). The alternatives are local authority short-life accommodation, mobile homes and caravans, temporary use of local authority housing, local authority hostels, and other types of hostels. Virtually all the properties investigated in the London Research Centre (1991b) survey were self-contained, a stark contrast with the situation in most bed and breakfast accommodation. Other indicators of quality include the proportion of leased properties with central heating which, in Manchester, for example, was 57 per cent, compared with 32 per cent in the privately rented sector (London Research Centre 1991b, p 20). This study also showed that many landlords had been asked to carry out some improvements to their property by the council, before the lease was agreed (pp 23–24). Against this substantial advantage there are some costs, and in particular the capital work that must be foregone as a result of leasing. In the short term, and within the terms of the financial framework applying to local authorities, leasing appears to be advantageous. It is not clear, however, what a longer term view would be, taking account of all public spending considerations, and the social costs of different ways of providing accommodation for homeless people. But in the short term, and particularly when looked at from the perspective of homeless people, leasing probably offers more advantages and fewer disadvantages than the alternatives.

Secondly, the properties leased to the local authorities appear to represent a net addition to the housing available for occupation in the area, over and above what might have been available within the private sector. Over one quarter (28 per cent) of the owners involved in leasing who were surveyed in the London Research Centre's study were also acting as private landlords (1991b, p 34). About half the landlords reported buying the property specifically for leasing (p 36), and one third had considered private letting as an alternative to leasing. So there is evidence that some property is being diverted to leasing which would otherwise be available in the private rented sector. However, 45 per cent had considered no other alternative to leasing. In addition, the owners reported very high levels of satisfaction with leasing — 94 per cent were either very or fairly satisfied (pp 35–38). This all suggests that the addition to the stock available for occupation as a result of leasing is greater than any loss to the private rented sector. In addition, local authorities have been able to exercise their discretion in allocating the properties, rather than leaving their allocation to the vagaries of the private market. These represent two significant advantages to the enabling housing authority.

Thirdly, leasing has grown at a time of growing crisis in the housing market, with high levels of homelessness, and a stagnant owner-occupied market in many parts of the country. Local authorities fear that the popularity of leasing with landlords may diminish as the market recovers and this seems possible for some, given that 14 per cent of owners surveyed by the London Research Centre had considered selling as an alternative to leasing (1991b, p 36). However this does not necessarily diminish the value of leasing as a device for improving the efficiency of the housing market. If the supply of properties for leasing is reduced as a result of increased activity in the housing market, there may still be supplies of properties adequate for some of the needs of housing authorities. Leasing remains, in the short term, an imaginative and beneficial aspect of the housing authority's role. In the longer term it is a way of making better use of the housing stock as a whole in the interests of the most disadvantaged which may not be required on the same scale when housing conditions generally improve. It has the additional advantage of overcoming some of the resistance to letting an empty property which has apparently deterred some potential private landlords in the past. Even if housing associations took over as the principal agents in the management of leased housing, local authorities would still require to play a part through nominations and housing benefits, at least. The discouragement represented by recent changes to the financial framework within which it operates provides scant support for the view that the government is keen to develop the role of housing authorities as enablers.

Overall, private sector leasing measures up well against the other types of temporary accommodation available to homeless people. Its main advantages are the high physical standard and privacy of the accommodation, its relative cheapness, the flexibility it offers to local authorities, and its scope for efficient use of the housing stock. Disadvantages are vulnerability to changes in property market conditions and government policy changes, management problems if properties are scattered, and the difficulty of achieving low void rates especially in the last few months of a lease (Evans 1991, p 59).

Tenant participation

The quality and nature of housing management has been a persistent theme in debates about housing policy in the 1980s and 1990s.

Whoever the owner of rented housing in the social sector, the quality and effectiveness of management are under scrutiny. Local authorities, in particular, have been criticised for their management practices although the research evidence suggests much more equality in the performance of local authorities and housing associations than some commentary might appear to suggest (CHR 1989; Clinton et al. 1989). Increasingly good management has been interpreted as management which satisfies tenants and which allows them an explicit say over management decisions. In the context of the enabling housing authority, the case for seeing a role for community participation as an essential part of local governemnt is argued by the Association of Metropolitan Authorities:

> While the 'servicing' element of local government is certain to consume most of its resources, we ignore the 'enabling' element ... at our peril, for it is this which forges the link between local government and communities — links which are more and more required to protect the services local authorities provide. It is this role which has the potential to change the perception of local government from a paternalistic system run by the relatively privileged to a participatory system reflecting a cross-section of society.
>
> (AMA 1989, p 15)

From a right of centre political perspective tenant participation can be seen as another device for breaking down the traditional power of the municipal sector, and as one of a range of alternatives to traditional housing authority management. The 'Right to Buy', the tenant's right to choose an alternative landlord, Housing Action Trusts and compulsory competitive tendering for housing management are part of the same process of breaking up the power of the municipal landlord. Estate Action funds have been contingent on satisfactory arrangements for tenant participation, and the Department of the Environment has particularly favoured Estate Management Boards and tenant management co-operatives.

The criticism of housing management has not been restricted to the political Right. Measures such as decentralisation and participation have been promoted by Labour-controlled housing authorities, sometimes acting in advance of legislation, as a means of changing the image of public sector bureaucracies as uncaring, insensitive and inefficient, and of winning support from consumers for public services such as council housing. A Liberal administration was responsible for the development of housing co-operatives in Liverpool (McDonald 1986). Labour-controlled Glasgow and Islington have promoted more tenant management co-operatives than any other local authorities in Britain. Authorities of all or no party political complexion have used the 1988 legislation as a spur to develop tenant participation, in an attempt to ensure satisfied tenants who will not seek an alternative landlord. Parties of the Left, Centre or Right have agreed at times about the value of tenants managing their own housing in preference or in association with public landlords.

So from the perspectives of all the major parties, tenant participation has a place in housing management. Despite the differences in philosophy, what the parties have in common is a desire to create a relationship which gives more power to tenants over the nature and quality of management of their housing. How an enabling authority can assist tenants to acquire greater power is the subject of this section. Whether or not this is a first step to changing the ownership of the housing is largely irrelevant except to those who consider tenure to be the most important issue in housing policy.

Most forms of participation discussed here involve retaining council housing in the municipal sector. Other forms involve the tranfer of ownership to an alternative landlord, such as a housing association. Such transfers are discussed in the next section, and in any case are usually promoted for reasons other than the increased opportunities for tenant participation they usually involve. Here particular attention is given to tenant management co-operatives and Estate Management Boards. But first the meaning of participation is elaborated in a little more detail.

A concept which has the capacity to appeal to such a wide range of opinion is puzzling. The explanation lies in the complexity of the concept, and its use to mean different things by different people. Cairncross, Clapham and Goodlad (1989) identify three separate dimensions which feature in many accounts of participation. These are:

- objectives
- structures and methods
- forms or processes.

Objectives may vary from one participant to another. Tenants are likely to see concrete improvements to their living conditions as the primary motive for participation. Professionals and others may see less tangible advantages concerned with smoother administration or more satisfied consumers. Politicians may see wider or longer term benefits such as improved community spirit. It would be wrong to portray all supporters of tenant participation as seeking the break-up of municipal provision — the opposite may be the case. Enabling tenant participation will have very different meanings and intentions from one authority to another, and from one participant to another.

118 The Housing Authority as Enabler

Structures and methods of participation refer to the arrangements such as committees, newsletters or public meetings in or through which participation is intended to take place. Estate Management Boards and tenant management co-operatives are structures which give tenants a formal role in the decision making process, with the intention of reducing the power of the local authority, and possibly leading to collective tenant ownership through a co-operative. Other structures such as housing associations and co-operatives, may give tenants seats on the board or management committee.

Forms or processes of participation refer to what is actually going on when people participate. Exchanging information is possibly the most common form of 'participation' and some would argue it is not participation at all. Consultation is a familiar form. Dialogue is less common, but is supposed to take place in structures such as Estate Management Boards. There is great scope for misunderstandings and confusion about what form or process is to take place within any particular structure. A housing authority may invite tenants to set up a committee or other new structure to engage in a process of consultation while tenants expect that their views will determine — or control — the outcome. Processes of participation involving dialogue or negotiation are relatively rare, perhaps because landlords appreciate their unpredictability. The outcome will emerge from a process of bargaining in which both sides may concede some ground in order to win other ground, but the trade offs that emerge may not be clear at the beginning of the process.

The incidence of tenant participation is difficult to measure, since some aspects require detailed investigation of the processes at work. However, it is relatively easy to survey the incidence of different structures for participation, and this was done in the research carried out by Cairncross, Clapham and Goodlad (1989, 1990). Comparisons with an earlier survey (Richardson 1977) show a definite growth in the formal arrangements made for participation, in England and Wales. In 1977 only 12 per cent of housing authorities were reported as having a formal scheme for participation involving at least regular meetings between tenants and local authority. In 1986/87 this had grown to 44 per cent. When 'scheme for participation' is defined also to include irregular meetings between tenants and landlords the proportion of authorities with such schemes has grown from 44 per cent in 1977 to 80 per cent in 1986/87 (Cairncross *et al.* 1990, p 25).

What goes on within these structures is more difficult to judge. It is likely, as Kay, Legg and Foote (undated) reported in the early 1980s, that most authorities comply with the minimum levels of consultation required by the 1980 Housing Act, and relatively few take participation as far as negotiation and bargaining at the neighbourhood or authority-wide level. Difficult to let or problematic estates are the most likely focus for such attempts to work out solutions together, and this has been encouraged by the Priority Estates Project, and the requirements for tenant involvement in the Estate Action programme.

Tenant management co-operatives

Tenant management co-operatives are associations of tenants who take over from their landlord the responsibility for managing certain aspects of their housing themselves. They can be set up in local authority or housing association housing, and the Department of the Environment estimated only 41 such co-operatives in local authority housing in England and Wales in 1986/87, and a further 33 in housing association housing (McCafferty and Riley 1989, p 5). The rate of growth seems to have accelerated, however, and the Junior Housing Minister reported in January 1992 that, 'There are now 60 tenant management co-operatives in the housing association stock' and '30 tenant management co-operatives and estate management boards have been established since last April, compared with 15 in the previous year' (Official Report, Col.201, 22/1/92).

Tenant management co-operatives and landlords must agree the areas of responsibility of the co-operative, and the annual allocation of funds by the landlord. Management co-operatives vary in size from as small as 10 households or less to over 200 (McCafferty and Riley 1989, p 7). The largest usually employ their own staff on a full time or part-time basis. All depend on the voluntary efforts of their committee members who spend an average of one and a half hours per week helping run the co-operative. But this average masks a wide variation from nil to over 10 hours per week (McCafferty and Riley 1989, p 50).

As managers and landlords tenant management co-operatives in the local authority sector achieve high ratings from their members. At least 77 per cent of tenants surveyed by McCafferty and Riley were satisfied or very satisfied with repairs, upkeep of communal areas, accommodation, sense of community, and 'living in the co-op' (1989, p 70). When their performance was compared with mainstream local authority housing, the management co-ops 'spent significantly less than the corresponding local authorities on the management and maintenance of their dwellings to achieve higher tenant satisfaction and lower voids but had higher arrears and offer refusals' (McCafferty and Riley 1989, p 75).

In a more detailed account of the management performance of co-operatives, drawing on the same survey data, Satsangi and

Clapham report similar conclusions. However, until more research is carried out 'we will not know whether co-operatives are different because they are small or because they are co-operatives' (Satsangi and Clapham, 1990, p 29).

Estate management boards

Estate management boards are intended to provide a structure for joint management of an estate by tenants' representatives and local authority representatives. There are only about eight in operation in England, and they have developed largely out of the work of the Priority Estates Project. *Peptalk*, the newsletter of the Priority Estates Project provides the most accessible news of the development of this form of decentralised management. The issue of September 1990 (no. 25) announces ministerial approval of the first two estate management boards, at Bloomsbury Estate in Birmingham and Shadsworth Estate in Blackburn. By January 1991 four had been approved, with another 14 'in the pipeline' (*Peptalk* 26). By 1992 the number of Estate Management Boards was estimated at 12, with a similar number being formed (Scott et al. forthcoming).

Estate management boards (EMBs) are generally to be found in larger areas than the areas covered by tenant management co-operatives. They have developed out of the Priority Estates Project (PEP) which has worked in problem estates since 1980. The work of PEP has emphasised the value of local management, and of local estate offices with decentralised budgets, and discretion to make changes to the way estates are run. 'The local estate office is the vital base for running areas of rented housing' (Power 1991, p 5). Estate management boards are seen as a way of giving tenants and landlords a formal structure within which decisions about the management of the estate can be taken.

> The Estate Management Board is an independent, locally-based body, involving a partnership between the council and tenants of one estate or area. The Board becomes the management agent for the council in all day-to-day management and maintenance services .... The local authority delegates management and maintenance responsibility to a local organisation (in this case an EMB) .... Both the council and the tenants are represented on the Board, although the tenants are in the majority.
> (Power 1991, p 31)

Since all EMBs are very young, it is too soon to evaluate their achievements. Any evaluation would need to disentangle the effects of local management, a local budget, and any capital expenditure taking place at the same time, from the effects of the EMB *per se*. Many have been developed in areas which were the subject of capital spending projects, including estate action. Anecdotal evidence suggests a high level of enthusiasm and satisfaction on the part of tenant activists, but the views of the majority of tenants are not known.

Tenant management co-operatives and estate management boards are intended to give more influence to tenants at the local level. Housing authorities may also want to provide meaningful opportunites to tenants to influence their management policies at the authority-wide level. This may be attempted by bringing tenants representatives onto housing committees or sub-committees (as non-voting members, following the 1989 Local Government and Housing Act) but such structures do not guarantee the sharing of influence (Cairncross *et al.* 1989). The most ambitious attempts to share power at this level involve housing authorities in recognising and working with tenants' associations, including authority-wide federations of tenants' associations. A few authorities, including Sheffield and Glasgow, have collaborated in developing a levy system which involves tenants paying a voluntary levy of a few pennies per week with their rent. The proceeds are distributed to any local tenants' association and to the federation which has a role in assisting new tenants' associations to set up.

A larger number of authorities have provided encouragement for the development of a variety of forms of participation through the employment of specialist tenant liaison staff. In 1986/87 18 per cent of authorities in Britain employed such specialist staff, and the proportion has possibly grown since then (Cairncross, Clapham, and Goodlad 1990, p 42). Specialist staff often have a background in community development, or adopt community development ideas in their work.

> The community work and community development role is that of enabling people to achieve things for themselves — through suggestion, education, organisation-building, and providing information and advice.
>
> (AMA, 1989)

The most comprehensive recent study of tenant participation in council housing concludes, in relation to community development, that 'There is considerable evidence that tenant participation can aid a sense of community and that tenants' associations are the key to achieving this' (p 90) and there is 'Evidence that experience of tenant participation can radically change the lives of some tenants' (p 88). In relation to giving tenants more power:

The degree of power will differ considerably .... Therefore it is important for landlords to realise that the amount of power which can be exercised by tenants depends crucially on decisions made by the landlord and on the participation processes which they are willing to institute.

(Cairncross *et al.* 1989, p 94)

Alternative landlords

A variety of alternative forms of management involving transfer of ownership have been proposed to overcome the alleged weaknesses or difficulties of council ownership. These may be seen as complementary to tenant participation, which is usually stressed as an essential feature of all the alternative forms of ownership. There are a number of models, some of which have been inspired by a desire to liberate tenants from the oppression of a council landlord (Ward 1974; Clapham 1989; Henney 1985); others are more concerned to circumvent administrative and financial constraints within which housing authorities have had to operate in the 1980s and 1990s. The main models are:

- large scale voluntary transfers to housing associations;
- voluntary transfer of part of a housing authority's stock to a housing association or co-operative;
- 'trickle transfer' to housing associations, involving the transfer of houses which become vacant, rather than houses with sitting tenants;
- 'arms length companies'.

Large scale voluntary transfers are discussed in Chapter 5 in the context of securing improvements to the housing stock. Tenants have usually been represented on the management committee of the housing association which has taken over the stock. But since such transfers have so far taken place in smaller local authorities, where generally little tradition of tenants' associations exists, it is not clear who the tenants represent, apart from themselves, or how they are to carry out their role. An awareness of these issues has led one such housing association to employ a community development officer with a remit to assist the development of tenants' associations (Mason 1992). Large scale and smaller transfers are discussed and illustrated in Fraser (1991). Smaller transfers seem to be mainly inspired by the difficulty of rising rents and inadequate resources for improvement or repair. They are likely to become more common in the 1990s as the Treasury baulks at the implications of a large programme of disposals, and as the DoE seeks to prevent authorities from replacing one monopoly social landlord with another. In this context housing authorities may want to seek more diversity in the forms of management created, and may look to the Scottish experience of community ownership co-operatives set up by former council housing neighbourhoods. Although there are advantages to the tenants and housing authority in the Scottish experience, overall the scheme should be treated with some reservation — the authors of a systematic study conclude that community ownership is not an obvious choice for the improvement of social rented housing on financial grounds alone (p 213). This does not mean that community ownership is necessarily bad value for money. However, the study concludes that what is important is small-scale, locally-based, resident-controlled organisations, and 'that mechanisms other than Community Ownership have been very successful and should not be abandoned in favour of Community Ownership' (p 233). These include community-based housing associations and tenant management co-operatives (Clapham, Kintrea and Whitefield 1991).

There is growing interest in 'trickle transfer' and 'arms' length' companies. The latter have been enthusiastically promoted by Nick Raynsford, a housing consultant re-elected to Parliament as a Labour MP in 1992. He argues there are good management as well as financial investment reasons for his ideas, 'But the scope for expanding investment is likely to be the prime motive force in encouraging local authorities to consider this option' (p 26). He envisages the non-profit company being made up of one-third council nominees, one third elected tenants' representatives, and one third 'others' including 'financial and legal expertise' (Raynsford 1992, p 27). The transfer terms should involve a transfer of engagements, involving the company in taking over the assets and the liabilities of the local authority. Management benefits would accrue, Raynsford argues, from the 'single-minded focus' on housing, leading to more stream-lined decision making; from the freedom from 'corporate raiding' which has characterised many housing authorities' Housing Revenue Accounts in recent years; and from a separation of 'policy' and 'management' functions (Raynsford 1992, pp 27–28). These are not necessarily self-evident benefits — with the exception of the elimination of 'corporate raiding', which could be dealt with in other ways, if it were considered essential to prevent any transfers between housing and other accounts of a local authority.

The idea of 'arms length' companies has also been taken up by the Institute of Housing, in its policy statement *Housing — The First Priority*. The Institute is seeking to develop a model which would allow investment by 'local housing companies' to be outside the normal government controls, except in relation to any subsidy received from the housing authority. In addition, such companies would be a means to tenant 'empowerment' while allowing the housing authority a strong role (Institute of Housing 1992b, p 21).

Conclusion

This chapter has explored some of the ways in which local authorities can influence the management of the housing stock in their areas, without necessarily managing or owning it themselves. Central government has given sporadic encouragement to the measures discussed above, supporting those that are likely to diminish the direct housing management role of housing authorities, and discouraging those that provide a boost to the role of housing authorities as managers of property.

Access to housing association housing by local authority nomineees has been increasingly promoted by central government and housing authorities anxious to fulfil their statutory obligations to homeless people and others who are seen as a priority. Less than 50 per cent of allocations by housing associations are made to local authority nominees, but too little is known about whether this represents any great cause for concern that the housing association movement is not playing a reasonable part in providing for housing need. A growing proportion of housing association housing is being let to homeless people, especially in the South East, but the official statistics may not represent the only contribution of housing associations to the alleviation or prevention of homelessness. Tensions will continue in the relationship between housing authorities and housing associations, and it would be naive to expect them to be entirely removed even by the most carefully worked out agreements, but equally, without such agreements, tensions are going to be greater than they need to be. The role of housing associations as major providers of rented housing is evolving as well as the role of housing authorities as enablers. Housing associations must expect the outcome of their letting decisions to be open to the scrutiny of local authorities and the public, or they risk losing the confidence of both. There remains a tension between the view of housing associations as part of a pluralist rented sector, possibly providing for needs unnoticed, neglected or ignored by housing authorities, and the view of housing association housing as the alternative to council housing, able to provide for a range of needs many of which are statutorily defined or decreed by local authorities.

Leasing provides in some ways a more direct way for housing authorities to achieve some limited objectives. The costs have to be weighed against the costs of capital expenditure on the existing council stock. The policy debate has not been informed by considering whether the alternative many councils would seek of building new housing might prove the more effective use of public money. The benefits for homeless families are considerable — making their wait for permanent housing incomparably more satisfactory than bed and breakfast accommodation, and probably more satisfactory than the other alternatives to bed and breakfast accommodation. Landlords, on the whole, are satisfied too, and their relationships with local authorities have been good.

In the longer term housing authorities are entitled to wonder whether leasing and nomination agreements represent an adequate response to the need for an adequate supply of housing for rent at affordable prices, with security of tenure, and available to those the authority deems appropriate. Housing associations and the private rented sector provide for a degree of plurality in the rented housing market. Leasing and nomination agreements enhance authorities' capacity to ensure access for particular groups. This can be welcomed, while reservations remain about the adequacy of the overall supply of housing for rent.

The growth of tenant participation is a very different type of enabling activity, concerned with the nature and quality of housing management, and the balance of power between landlords and tenants. It has been welcomed not only by authorities seeking to secure funds for investment from central government, but also by a growing number of authorities who believe that in its own right tenant participation is likely to add to the quality of housing services and the quality of life of their citizens. There is perhaps more consensus about that than about the role of housing associations.

Participation can mean the development of a new status for tenants in the management of their homes. Enabling the social changes which participation represents is a possible role for housing authorities, working with its own tenants, with tenants of other landlords, or working with tenants in anticipation of tenure change. The concept can also be extended to owner-occupiers and private tenants, for example in a renewal area, whose housing circumstances could be improved more effectively with their active involvement. Here housing authorities can assist directly with advice and assistance. But housing authorities have very limited powers to assist the development of tenant participation in rented housing other than council housing.

Transfers of ownership, in contrast with participation, achieves little consensus, and is largely driven by the desire to avoid the financial consequencees for tenants of central government policy towards council housing. This is not an ideal context in which to consider the best form of management for a housing stock which is still measured in millions, and which has consistently shown both high levels of tenant satisfaction, and high levels of tenant loyalty.

The scope of local authority action in relation to property management is potentially wide, and growing in importance. But it is not well developed as a clear part of the administration of many housing authorities. Responsibilities are often split between housing and other departments such as environmental health. Poorly developed management procedures make it difficult to monitor the achievements of authorities. The resources required are often those of administrative and negotiating skills, community development skills, and housing management skills, only the last of which are likely to be readily available in many housing authorities. Fuller staffing has resource implications for the general revenue budgets of housing authorities.

Finally, the legislative basis for much housing authority activity involving regulating other providers is weak or unclear. Authorities have discretionary powers in some areas, and not in others. If housing authorities have a legitimacy in nominating applicants to housing associations, then they should also have a stronger role in regulating other aspects of the management of housing by other providers. The pleas for stronger powers from the Duke of Edinburgh's Inquiry to the Institute of Housing's 1992 policy statement have gone unheeded by the government.

Chapter 7
Reducing disadvantage

Inequalities in housing conditions between tenures, regions, neighbourhoods and house types are an important feature of earlier chapters of this book and in debates about housing policy generally. Such inequalities have been a focus of the work of housing authorities for over a century. But housing policy is not just concerned with the quality of the housing stock. Social inequalities of wealth, gender, race, and health, for example, have been addressed through housing policy as well as inequalities in the condition of the housing stock. This chapter is about the ways in which housing authorities can play a role in influencing the housing conditions of different groups of people, particularly those who are most disadvantaged. After an introduction which considers the nature of disadvantage in housing, including the crucial importance of poverty, the chapter goes on to examine the role of housing authorities in relation to community care, gender and race.

Housing authorities have been encouraged by governments of both major parties for many years to show particular concern for the 'quite large numbers of people who may face special difficulties in getting suitable housing' as the 1977 Green Paper *Housing Policy* put it (Cmnd 6851). After listing 10 groups, including homeless people, lower income households, physically disabled people, people with mental illnesses, and people with learning difficulties the Green Paper goes on:

> In the last analysis, the effectiveness of any national housing policy and local housing strategy is likely to be judged by how far it helps those facing the most pressing housing problems
>
> (p 108).

Instead of asking which **houses** are in poor condition, the concern sometimes expressed by local authorities themselves as well as pressure groups is with which groups of **people** suffer disadvantage in their housing conditions, and what can be done to alleviate their disadvantage.

> There is now a fairly good picture in Britain of who is disadvantaged by the quality and repair of their dwelling, by the property rights associated with their tenure, or by where they live in relation to services, jobs and other resources . . . . What

is most obvious from these accounts is that such inequalities are *structured*: some groups are consistently more likely than others to be in the worst parts of the stock, and in the worst (oldest, most run-down, least convenient and most poorly serviced) locations.
(Clapham, Kemp and Smith 1990, p 60).

The social groups who tend to do worst include black people, single parent families (usually headed by women), those on low incomes whether in work or not, and those who suffer disadvantages arising from poor health and disability. Whether the social disadvantage or the poor housing conditions came first is not always obvious, and may not matter. What matters is the inter-connections between different forms of disadvantage, and the role good housing and housing management can play in ameliorating other disadvantages.

The relationship between housing and inequality is complex. Inequalities in housing conditions or circumstances or chances can reflect inequalities of a different kind, such as gender, income, race and health. State, including local authority, action can alleviate housing inequality, for example by providing decent housing at an affordable price, possibly with the assistance of housing benefit, for people who would not otherwise have it. But if other forms of inequality are not also alleviated then housing policy at the local level can have the effect of compounding inequality. If a victim of domestic violence who is already disadvantaged by poverty and homelessness is rehoused in a peripheral estate with poor public transport, no child care facilities, few employment opportunities and located miles away from friends and family then the disadvantage is alleviated in one respect but compounded in others. The victim of a serious motor accident who is suddenly confined to a wheelchair is doubly disadvantaged if she owns a house unsuitable for wheelchair use.

Disadvantage in housing terms has a number of dimensions. It is possible to be disadvantaged in relation to:

- ability to pay, which will reduce choice for the poorest, and effectively prevent access to a large proportion of the housing stock;
- access through bureacratic mechanisms which do not take account of the ways the allocation process can compound existing disadvantages;
- condition;
- use;
- design;
- rights arising from tenure;
- location.

Reducing disadvantage 129

This is not to suggest that the alleviation of disadvantage is, for example, necessarily to be secured by equality of access, or by everyone living in the same design of housing, or in the same tenure. The objective of a housing authority might be more one of achieving equality of outcome so that peoples' lives are not made more disadvantaged because of their housing circumstances. In the case of people with certain physical disabilities this means a different design of house from the 'normal'. In the case of single parent families this could mean special attention to the allocation policy to allow rehousing close to the social support on which the mother relies for the quality of her life. In the case of people with learning difficulties this could mean ordinary housing but extraordinary forms of management and support. So reducing disadvantage may involve creating differences, of design or management, for example.

It is beyond the means of housing authorities to eliminate the major social divisions such as those of wealth and poverty even if they wanted to. But housing authorities should not imagine that their activities and policies are neutral with respect to these divisions. Housing authorities have a choice. They can attempt to make sure their policies do not compound existing disadvantages, and they can hope on occasions to remove them. Or they can pursue policies in a way which is blind to such divisions but which may act to compound them. Most housing authorities will wish to use their influence positively to the advantage of the social groups who are seen as a priority; but even if an authority chooses to concentrate on issues of house condition, they should be aware that their policies are likely to have differential effects on different social groups.

There is plenty of evidence that housing authorities and central government have pursued explicit policies in favour of certain social groups, from the 'working classes' of early housing legislation to the special needs groups of contemporary community care policy. But housing authorities have had some difficulties in achieving their social ends, finding sometimes that complex patterns of disadvantage result in unintended consequences. For example, the provision of state subsidy from 1919 was intended to ensure that reasonable housing could be provided at a price within the means of working class people. But there is plenty of evidence that it was not the worst-housed who benefited — only the better-off working class could afford the rent levels that resulted. Even where an authority seeks to prevent the compounding of disadvantage, for example by avoiding the concentration of the poorest families in the worst estates, it is not always easy to do so, given the favourable position of the better-off who can afford to wait for an offer that suits rather than be forced by circumstances to take the offer that is readily available. A common dilemma for housing policy at the local level has been the conflict between providing housing which is of a decent standard, and of providing housing which can be afforded by the poorest people in society.

Housing authorities do not, however, always seek to assist those groups who are most disadvantaged in the housing system. For example, the homelessness responsibilities of housing authorities were imposed upon an unwilling local government system in 1977; local authorities do not always appear to be willing to try to prevent the concentration of the poorest on the worst estates in the council sector; and it required legislation in the form of the 1976 Race Relations Act before housing authorities eliminated (indirectly discriminatory) residence requirements as a prerequisite for admission to council house waiting lists. Most housing authorities can, however, point to strategies which identify some disadvantaged groups as a focus of attention. By implication this may mean that other groups are ignored or neglected, or that councils feel they can only make effective progress on behalf of a few priority groups. The choice of priorities is a matter for local political debate and choice, but sometimes that choice has not been based on knowledge of the extent of need and how the housing system compounds it.

Tackling certain types of disadvantage has been a particular feature of the work of some housing authorities in the 1980s and 1990s and the rest of this chapter is concerned with discussing the role of housing authorities in relation to the housing needs of people with 'special' needs which cannot be met with general needs dwellings, women and black people.

'Special' needs

The phrase 'special needs' has been familiar in housing for many years, and has been used as an abbreviated way of referring to the housing needs of disadvantaged groups who require 'special' attention to be paid to the design, management or location of their housing. The development of 'special' needs housing has increasingly been seen as part of the development of community care policy, an important aspect of social policy in the last 20 years. The number of groups who may be covered by the term has expanded in the pages of housing authority strategies and community care plans to encompass as many as 15 or 20 groups. Legislation, such as the National Health Service and Community Care Act and the Children Act in the late 1980s and early 1990s has raised the profile of the issue. Demographic and social trends such as divorce and increasing numbers of older people have also been influential on some authorities. Growing awareness of the needs of those with health problems, including HIV and Aids, has resulted from pressure group activity.

The meaning and the origins of the policy of community care are obscure. The first use of the term is in a 1957 report on mental illness which calls for the expansion of local authority social services, and less reliance on institutional care. Bulmer (1987) traces the development of ideas about community care in the major reports, such as Seebohm (1968) and Barclay (1982) which created and influenced the development of social services departments from 1971 (1969 in Scotland). This leads Bulmer to assert that 'Policies for "community care" at the present time lie at the confluence of two streams, from the personal social services and from the mental health services' (1987, p 9). Equally it can be argued that the development of housing policy has seen increasing emphasis on 'community care' since the publication of Townsend's *The Last Refuge* in 1962, and the subsequent development of sheltered housing for older people, and other forms of supported accommodation for 'special needs' groups.

The reduction of institutional care for people with learning difficulties or mental health problems is the aspect of community care on which most agreement is obtained. Implicit in most accounts is the desirability of enabling a normal life to be pursued 'in the setting of ordinary life rather than in special institutions' (Bulmer 1986, p 13). The exact meaning of 'community' in community care is more contentious, and whatever definition is adopted it has important implications for housing authorities and other providers. It can be used to mean care by statutory social and health services. It can be used to mean care by the family of the individual in need of care, but if so, clearer definition is required of who constitutes the family and what exactly their obligations should be. It can be used to mean care by voluntary organisations such as the WRVS, with its 'Meals on Wheels' and other services, or care by volunteers, such as neighbours. Usually it is used to mean some combination of these, sometimes leaving unclear what the boundaries are between statutory, voluntary and family obligations. Accounts such as Bulmer's leave unstated the extent to which any definition of community care is dependent on the right type, size, tenure and quality of housing being available at the right time to house the recipients of community care, however delivered or administered.

The provision of housing and support services for people with 'special needs' is not necessarily the straightforward rational process it is sometimes portrayed as. There are some difficult questions to answer about motivation and definition for housing authorities who may think their task is to maximise provision for 'special needs' groups. There are dangers as well as opportunities in extending provision.

> Concentration on special needs may serve various purposes. It can set a verbal distance between "normal" people and those about whom they feel uneasy, whether through unfamiliarity, insecurity or fear. Or it can help to legitimate forms of provision which are not based on an acceptance of people in these groups as human beings with ordinary needs and rights. There are people whose jobs depend on special provision. Moreover, special provision is a tangible symbol of concern. Some people in central and local government will be glad to take credit for this, rather than emphasising wider problems of poverty, homelessness and powerless which they are unable or unwilling to remedy.
> (Purkis and Hodson 1982, p 26)

A number of writers have pointed to the way in which housing intended to assist people with 'special needs' can isolate them, or compound the stigma they already suffer from, or simply not live up to the claims made for the 'special' provision.

> Part of the case for sheltered housing addresses an exaggerated set of special needs rather than problems whose best resolution may in many cases be good quality, small, ordinary houses, and a wider range of support services linked to them.
> (Purkis and Hodson 1982, p 28)

This conclusion is broadly supported in a more recent review of the literature on sheltered housing for older people. 'The present standardised package only works if a substantial proportion of the older people allocated to sheltered housing do not need it' (p 182) and 'A variety of solutions needs to be found to meet the varied housing needs of older people' (Clapham, Kemp and Smith 1990, p 184). Increasingly the emphasis has been on cheaper, less disruptive remedies for poor quality housing or lack of support, such as 'staying put' or care and repair schemes (see Chapter 8), alarm systems and special management and support arrangements for mainstream housing.

After growing dissatisfaction about some of the difficulties — such as poor co-ordination, and insecure and complex funding arrangements — in implementing community care policies, the Secretary of State for Social Services appointed Sir Roy Griffiths in December 1986, 'To review the way in which public funds are used to support community care policy and to advise him on the options for action that would improve the use of these funds as a contribution to more effective community care' (Griffiths 1988, p 1).

The Griffiths Report is significant in the development of local government in the 1980s since it led to a new statutory responsibility for community care planning and development being given to social services departments, at a time when central government was resisting any expansion of the role of local government. The White Paper following the Griffiths Report placed rather more emphasis on the importance of housing to community care than the Griffiths Report had:

> The Government believes that housing is a vital component of community care and it is often the key to independent living. ... Social Services authorities will need to work closely with housing authorities, housing associations and other providers of housing of all types in developing plans for a full and flexible range of housing. Where necessary, housing needs should form part of the assessment of care needs and the occupational therapist may have a key role here.
> (Secretaries of State for Health, Social Security, Wales and Scotland, 1989, p 25)

This quote emphasises the two areas where housing authorities are most involved — community care planning, and needs assessment.

Following the 1990 National Health Service and Community Care Act social (work) services departments had, by April 1992, drawn up three year community care plans incorporating the authority's strategic plan for community care provision, including the role of statutory and voluntary organisations, informal care, housing agencies and the private sector. All these agencies should be involved in the Plan's development, since the Act requires housing authorities and other housing providers to be consulted. Housing authorities should at the same time incorporate community care policies into their HIPs, HSOPs and Housing Plan documents. Their assessment of needs could be crucial in identifying the shortfall of particular types of provision or management arrangements amongst housing providers. These points were stressed in the joint DoE and Department of Health Circular 10/92, with reference to the need for housing and other agencies to work together at strategic and individual level.

There is clearly a great deal to be gained from collaboration with other agencies whose information about the incidence of different 'special needs' groups is likely to be better than that of many housing authorities. This is a different but complementary sort of assessment from the assessment of individual care needs by social services authorities which the legislation required be in place by April 1993. Both types of authority have things to gain potentially from an exchange of data, for example, but traditional differences of perspective may delay good working relationships from being established quickly, even where housing and social services are part of the same tier of local government.

The final, but arguably most important part of the community care jigsaw, was the transfer of funds from the Department of Social Security to social services departments in April 1993. Social services departments are expected to operate in an enabling role to purchase the services needed for care in ordinary residential settings or in nursing homes, preferably by not providing them directly.

Most aspects of the new responsibilites of social services departments, including the new funding structure, were implemented by 1993, after a series of delays and postponements. It is, therefore, too soon to judge the effectiveness of the new approach, and criticisms of inadequate funding cast doubt on whether all the problems with community care have been resolved (Harrison and Means 1990). Better planning and co-ordination should be possible, although initially it may reveal that a policy which has important implications for housing, health, and social work services has developed within these separate sectors without necessarily meaning the same to everyone.

An increasingly common model for the development of housing and community care is the housing consortium. At least 50 of these exist in England and Wales (NFHA/ELHA 1991, p 1), and it is likely the number is growing. These are voluntary agencies, usually involving housing associations, health and social service authorities, voluntary bodies and sometimes housing authorities forming a charitable, umbrella organisation. A number of studies of housing consortia have taken place (Wertheimer 1988; Rochester 1989; Blakely 1990). A recent study of seven such consortia (NFHA/ELHA 1991) reports that the reasons for setting up the consortium vary from one to another, but most commonly are:

- to pool members' capital and revenue resources, including some examples of staffed houses or residential care homes being transferred to consortium management;
- to pool knowledge, expertise and skills;
- to define the respective roles of different agencies;
- to speed up the discharge of residents of long-stay institutions.

The seven consortia reported tangible benefits such as improved management, accelerated hospital resettlement, and some financial savings to consortium members. Given the variety of types of organisations involved, it is not surprising to find that the identity of consortia can be unclear, so that their participation in joint planning groups as a separate body, for example, was not always welcomed. With its close identification with statutory and voluntary agencies, the consortium 'ends up as neither fish nor fowl' (NFHA/ELHA 1991, p 18). With the continuing emphasis on local authorities as enablers it seems likely that consortia involving housing and social service authorities have a future.

The exact role of housing authorities, and the importance of housing to community care policy, has received less attention than the role of health and social services authorities. Fears have been expressed that housing is being neglected. The appearance of the DoE Circular on Housing and Community Care late in 1992, over a year after the equivalent one from the Scottish Office, confirmed some housing authorities' fears that the government was not prepared to accept the implications of community care policies for housing policy. Fraser argues:

> Clearly, the situation would be improved if one body took overall responsibility at a local level for developing and co-ordinating a special needs housing strategy. This co-ordinating role would have three primary facets — needs assessment, planning and finance. Local authorities are best placed to undertake this role.
> (1991, p 79)

This creates a challenge for housing and social work professionals to work together, with social workers having overall responsibility for community care planning and co-ordination, and housing professionals developing their role to take account of that.

The circulars from central departments to housing authorities about their role in community care stress the importance of housing strategies being consistent with community care plans. Housing authorities have a role not just at the level of broad stategic planning, but also in the delivery of services, such as in individual assessments of need. Issues such as repair needs, adaptations, and improvements will require a joint approach by social and housing workers. Where rehousing is required the government urges caution about assuming that new specialist or supported accommodation is required. General needs housing must play a role, and the allocation and management of it must be considered so that it assists rather than hinders community care objectives (Scottish Office 1991; Department of the Environment and Department of Health 1992).

Little systematic research has been done on recent experience of the community care role of housing authorities, and this is an important area for future research on the enabling role. One recent study carried out for the Association of District Council's Major Cities Group by Arnold and Page shows positive signs of progress, as well as signs of difficulties. Planning is the area where greatest difficulty appears to lie:

> ... there is clearly something wrong when major district councils and housing associations are excluded from the process of drafting community care plans, as has been claimed in some areas. The disappointing record of joint planning is not in dispute.
> (Arnold and Page 1992, p 10)

Another set of difficulties lies with the boundary between housing and social services expenditure at a time of public spending restraint.

> Popular, low cost but staff intensive schemes, such as Stoke's elderly and special needs team, are of clear, crisis-prevention benefit to vulnerable tenants, but such schemes are threatened by housing departments' reluctance to plug gaps which could be defined as social services' responsibility.
> (Arnold and Page 1992, p 10)

Despite these problems, the research identified a number of impressive examples of the sort of collaborative projects involving housing departments, housing associations, voluntary associations, and health and social services departments which the government clearly intended to encourage in its community care policy. The time they took to set up — up to ten years — is a source of concern, but Arnold and Page may be too pessimistic in not taking account of the prospect of much quicker developments arising from the cumulative experience of developing projects, and from the new funding and planning arrangements once they are properly in place. Not surprisingly, the housing authorities reported unequal progress between different client groups, reflecting the 'presence of dedicated individuals or the energies of a specialist housing association or voluntary organisation' (p 13). However, the prospects for some disadvantaged groups is not encouraging in the light of the study's findings that housing authorities are concerned about the way community care client groups have extended to include single homeless people, young people, people with HIV/Aids, and people with alcohol and drug-related problems.

Another review of the early experience of community care planning suggests, 'Many housing departments have allowed themselves to be marginalised so far in the community care planning process. This has resulted in most draft community care plans not addressing adequately the housing needs aspects of community care' (Warner 1992). This claim is supported by evidence from a small survey carried out in the North of England. Only five out of fifteen council working groups preparing community care plans had included a representative from the housing department; 'only three of the plans included more than a cursory discussion of the role of housing'; and 'only six authorities presented any detailed information about their intentions to resettle people in the community on leaving residential care' (Brown 1992, p 33).

Suggested remedies for this neglect are that more attention should be given to information collection and analysis, which housing authorities are uniquely qualified to do given their status as housing and planning authorities. Secondly, joint local planning forums are required which can relate effectively to the timescales and formats of the different resource allocation processes involved.

This generally pessimistic view is disputed by one Director of Housing in Hampshire, who argues 'The only housing authorities I know of which have been allocated a bit-part role are those which have simply not devoted the necessary time, effort and expertise to joint planning' (Smith 1992, p 9). He describes the Hampshire experience which involves the chief housing officers' group drawn from all 13 districts taking the lead in agreeing overall principles with social and health services.

Some authorities have made significant progress with such developments. There has, however, been a tendency for planning activity to concentrate on traditional, capital intensive forms of provision of housing, rather than on a more wide ranging analysis of options. It is understandable that authorities seek to achieve sheltered housing, for example, where there is a prospect of funding being available to a housing association to build it. Other options may be more revenue intensive at a time when revenue budgets are under even more pressure. But the danger is that opportunities to develop appropriate forms of support are being missed.

Gender

Women are disadvantaged in the housing system, mainly because of their lower incomes, and their role as carers (Baker 1992; Munro and Smith 1989; Watson 1988). Lower incomes, on average around two-thirds those of men, affect access to owner-occupation and the private rented sector — and women who work part-time earn less.

At different stages in their life cycle, and in different types of family circumstances, women can suffer disadvantages. Lower incomes remain a feature throughout most of their lives. While young and single, women are less likely than men to become owner-occupiers. During child-bearing years, women tend to spend longer in the home and suffer disproportionately from any problems of poor design, location and repair. Relationship breakdown poses particular problems whether women have children or not. Their relative lack of financial independence makes them more reliant on the social sector. Women with children receive priority under homelessness legislation, because of the children. Women with no dependents are less fortunate, and less able than men to cater for themselves in the market. Single women are more likely than men to live in 'concealed' households. One study in London reported six times the number of female to male-headed 'concealed' households (reported in Watson 1988). As they get older, women who have remained or become single are disadvantaged relative to men, and married women, who benefit from the easier access to housing which couples enjoy because of men's higher earning power, or the effects of two incomes for one household. In old age the associations betweens age, poverty, poor health and poor housing are strongly associated also with women.

Women are therefore more reliant on the council and housing association rented sector than men. But they are likely to have a long wait for a let from a housing authority or association — small households are the largest group on most waiting lists, and small houses are in short supply. Lone parent families (90 per cent of which are headed by women) are concentrated relatively in the local authority and housing association sectors, and owner-occupation houses a higher proportion of two-parent families with dependent children (General Household Survey 1989, reported in Baker 1992).

Housing authorities could not be expected to use housing policy to overcome the multiplicity of disadvantages women suffer in our society. But they might be expected to work to ensure that housing policy at the local level does not compound them. There is little evidence of any such effort, with two exceptions. First, many councils fund voluntary agencies or work with housing associations that provide services particularly for women. These include Women's Aid and other groups working with particularly vulnerable women.

Secondly, a number of authorities have tried to make equal opportunities policies an intrinsic part of their everyday operation. The best known illustrations of this approach include the setting up of women's committees and women's units in the 1980s. The work of these committees included researching ways in which housing as well as other services were delivered in a 'gender blind' way which obscured their discriminatory effects on women.

> A study in Southwark, for example, revealed that single parents were disproportionately allocated flats on the least desirable council estates. Single women with one small child were only allocated bedsitting rooms, which they had to share with their children, while couples with children were automatically entitled to two bedrooms.
>
> (Lansley, Goss and Wolmar 1989, p 147)

The normal pattern was for issues like this to be referred to the relevant service committee with a recommendation for action. These committees did not always share the same priorities, although some advances have been made in housing. Most attention has been devoted to direct service provision and support for voluntary groups. Most aspects of the role of housing authorities — improvement grants, area renewal, nominations to housing associations, partnerships with the private sector, and so on — are apparently carried out in a gender blind way in most housing authorities. In the late 1980s several women's committees and units were disbanded, or merged into general equal opportunities committees and units.

Race

The disadvantage of black people and other minority groups in the housing system have been documented over many years. In the private sector, several studies in the 1960s, 1970s and 1980s showed discrimination by private landlords, accommodation agencies, estate agents, building societies, and vendors (reviewed in Henderson and Karn 1987). The quality of housing occupied by black people is also disproportionately poor, with concentrations of 'minority' groups in segregated neighbourhoods containing the worst housing, and so mitigating any advantage of segregation such as mutual support against racial harassment. In addition, 'black tenants and buyers have on average to pay more for equivalent accommodation' (Henderson and Karn 1987, p 4).

The record of housing authorities as landlords also provides cause for concern, showing that it is not simply the operation of a market process in the private sector which leads to exclusion and discrimination. Bureaucratic systems of allocation are just as likely to lead to discriminatory outcomes. Since the pioneering studies of Rex and Moore (1967) the restrictions on access to council housing have been well documented. Problems of access were seen as due initially to residential qualifications, and later to the weight attached to waiting time on the list. Exclusion of owner-occupiers, even those in the worst conditions, also acted as a discriminatory device. As in the private sector, black people tended to receive the worst housing.

As these findings emerged some housing authorities conducted their own research into their allocation procedures. Until the mid-1970s few authorities had made any attempt to monitor the administration or outcome of their allocation policies, and 'even those who kept a record of racial origins had signally failed to use them for this purpose' (Henderson and Karn 1987, p 7). In the late 1970s and 1980s several studies confirmed earlier findings about housing disadvantage and race in local authority housing, and a few studies of housing associations showed a similar picture (reviewed by Henderson and Karn 1987).

> The sum product of all these studies, then, is that racial concentrations are happening, particularly in areas close to the main concentrations of black people in the private sector . . . . The causes suggested have been the nature of the choices blacks make, and assumptions about black choice; white prejudice, and assumptions about white prejudice; the necessity to let the worst dwellings to someone; the desperation of black applicants in poor housing conditions who are more likely to accept a poor offer; and ignorance of wider opportunities.
> (Henderson and Karn 1987, p 11)

Further confirmation of direct and indirect discrimination in housing authorities has come in the form of a series of reports on formal investigations by the Commission for Racial Equality. The first of these, for Hackney (CRE 1984), resulted in a non-discrimination notice in 1983. The response to such investigations and research has been the introduction of ethnic monitoring which has become more commonplace in local authority housing departments and housing associations, encouraged by a number of good practice reports (Commission for Racial Equality 1991a, 1991b; NFHA 1985; 1990; Housing Corporation 1989; Institute of Housing 1985; 1991; Local Authority Housing and Racial Equality Working Party 1988). The Commission's survey of 1990 found that 55 housing authorities had a policy to keep ethnic records of housing services (CRE 1991a, p 10).

Much attention has, therefore, focused on the allocations process of individual local authorities, and less on the role of housing authorities as enabling greater equality in other parts of the housing system. This is understandable and necessary — council housing is a substantial part of the housing stock, and equality of access to it must be an important part of any strategy for enabling greater equality for black people. And apart from the intrinsic benefits in achieving greater justice for black people, it is hard to see how a housing authority could hope to influence other housing providers if it did not adopt the best practices itself.

In a number of authorities, especially Labour controlled London Boroughs, racial equality became an important issue in the 1980s. Units and committees examined services and employment practices, and tried to make changes, such as Lambeth's introduction of a target of 30 per cent of lets to black people (Lansley *et al.* 1989, p 123). Other authorities, such as Brent, Newham and Bradford, concentrated on policies for dealing with racial harassment (p 125). Overall, these policies 'have been implemented fairly and progressively, contributing, albeit slowly, to fairer recruitment policies and delivery of services: 'There is an emerging consensus of (*sic*) the importance of such policies for the promotion of greater racial equality' (Lansley *et al.* 1989, p 141).

The emerging consensus seen by writers in London is less easily seen in other parts of Britain. Inasfar as it exists it concerns two aspects of the housing authority's role — the allocations process, and harassment. With only 55 authorities claiming in 1990 that they monitored their housing service, doubts must be raised about how far racial equality has become an issue in the general housing work of authorities. However, a number of local authorities — mainly large urban authorities — have mapped out the task they see. A report from the Local Authority Housing and Racial Equality Working Party, which included representatives of local authority associations in England and Scotland, in 1988 suggested the issues authorities should address in their housing strategies. These included:

— the geographical distribution of investment and the use of area improvement powers to tackle the concentrations of black people in the worst areas of housing;
— the mix between new building and rehabilitation, to maximise the availability of housing for homeless families, who contain a disproportionately large proportion of black households;
— the size mix in new and rehabilitation schemes, to take account of some concentrations of larger household sizes in minority ethnic populations;
— the relative emphasis in special needs and general needs housing, to take account of the smaller proportion of black people who are elderly now — but to be aware of how this is changing;
— security considerations, which are relevant to reducing harassment;
— the number and type of offers of accommodation to homeless people compared with other access channels, which may

142 The Housing Authority as Enabler

discriminate against groups such as black people (and women) who are likely to form a higher proportion of homeless applicants than of applicants to other channels. (In London, members of ethnic minorities are four times more likely than white people to be homeless (CRE 1991a, p 76);
— recruitment of staff, either into general posts or as specialist workers to further the racial equality policy (Local Authority Housing and Racial Equality Working Party 1988).

Another prescription for action — which is largely being implemented — was provided in a report on ethnic minority housing problems in Glasgow. Apart from a series of recommendations on monitoring the allocations process, the report recommended:

— improved monitoring of the repairs and improvement grants systems to ensure take up by ethnic minority groups;
— translated material to be readily available, including in the council's newspaper, particularly in relation to allocations, grants, mortgage services, sheltered housing, new legislation, and housing benefit;
— translation services in relation to debt recovery following repair and improvement grants;
— continuing dialogue with ethnic minority groups, and their representation on area committees;
— greater publicity for the system of nominations to housing associations;
— improved communication with local advice agencies;
— monitoring of racial abuse and harassment by all housing offices, and an agreed procedure for follow up and any necessary repairs to be treated as emergencies;
— compensation for victims who are forced to move;
— use of existing community development staff to foster good community relations;
— staff training;
— recruitment of bilingual staff.
(Bowes, McCluskey and Sim 1989)

Finally, the Commission for Racial Equality has set down guidance for housing authorities in their work including allocations to their own stock, but also in the other services they provide. This covers homelessness, nominations to housing associations, housing advice, repairs and sales. Advice about monitoring in these areas is given, and it is suggested that other services which could be usefully monitored are housing benefit, arrears and court actions, participation in tenants' associations and tenant management, complaints and ombudsman cases (CRE 1991a).

The complex web of racial disadvantage existing in the housing system is one of the greatest challenges facing local housing authorities. They are important potential actors on the local race relations scene, with the capacity to support agencies such as racial equality councils and advice centres, as well as seeking to influence good practice in the private and voluntary sectors. Their role in regulating housing in multiple occupation, for example, may in some neighbourhoods have a racial dimension, as might their role in area renewal programmes. Their capacity to influence private sector agencies may be limited by a lack of levers — powers and resources — to use to gain compliance. It might be argued this is less of a problem in the housing association sector, where nomination arrangements and other safeguards may ensure disadvantage is reduced. But this will not be the case if the authority itself is not able to operate in a non-discriminatory way. The fact that in 1990 only 55 authorities in Britain had a policy of ethnic monitoring provides little evidence that this is an aspect of the enabling role that authorities have yet taken very seriously.

Conclusion

Although local authorities have for many decades sought to use the powers and resources of local government to assist the disadvantaged, in practice many of the social groups identified as most disadvantaged are apparently invisible to many housing authorities. This paradox is partly explained by the ability of council housing to cater in the past for a significant proportion of the most disadvantaged, in a fairly undifferentiated way. But even when (and to some extent, especially when) council house building was at its height, the type of housing stock created, its cost, and the allocations policies and processes regulating entry prevented it serving the needs of significant social groups. This was a reflection, and a consequence, of the tendency of housing authorities to reflect the prejudices of wider society.

The development of community care policies have been favoured where they are directed at older people and others who are seen as deserving, but some authorities fear the alleged proliferation of special needs groups requiring attention. This is understandable if linked to a concern about assisting larger and larger groups of people to improve their housing circumstances without adequate resources and levers over other agencies. But housing authorities also have a role in the assessment of needs which should precede action. The early experience of community care planning suggests that housing authorities have a greater role to play in strategic planning of community care services than has so far been achieved. As Chapter 3 showed many authorities are not well placed to make such a contribution. There is also a tendency for assumptions to be made about the type of action which should be taken to meet needs, rather than a full consideration of all options, including those which are less capital intensive than sheltered housing, for example. The housing disadvantage suffered by black people and women has been recognised explicitly in the policies and activities of relatively few housing authorities. And even fewer have extended their concern from their role as landlord to other ways in which they might influence the practices of other providers or other parts of their housing services. The extent to which the most disadvantaged groups in our society are assisted or hindered by the activities of housing authorities might be one measure of the success of the enabling role. This is a view apparently held by many people in local government, but their commitment has not been matched by adequate monitoring arrangements, or possibly by adequate policies. Housing authorities have discretion about the extent to which they attempt to use their resources to reduce disadvantage amongst particular social groups. Ultimately their record will be judged by the electorate. Unfortunately many of the people suffering housing disadvantage are in as weak a position to influence the local and national policy process as they are to influence their housing conditions.

Chapter 8
Providing information and advice

The provision of information and advice has been seen by commentators, professionals and governments as an important role for housing authorities since the 1960s. In the 1990s it has received new attention because of its alleged relevance to the new role of housing authorities.

> If, as the Government plans, authorities are increasingly to have an enabling role in carrying out their housing responsibilities rather than to be direct providers of housing, then housing advice is likely to be of growing importance in carrying out this function.
> (Audit Commission 1989, p 31)

In addition the Audit Commission claimed in 1992 that:

> 'Housing advice can help to resolve housing problems and prevent homelessness without the need to provide a local authority tenancy.
> (Audit Commission 1989, p 52)

Yet very little is known about this part of the work of housing authorities, and the scope of housing authority powers and duties remains uncertain:

- What is the purpose of information and advice work?
- What role should housing authorities play? Is it a direct role, or one of ensuring others make provision?
- How should housing authorities complement the role of other statutory and voluntary agencies?
- What sort of information and advice is required or requested? Are general or specialist services required?
- What skills and knowledge are required by information and advice workers?

This chapter reviews the role of housing authorities in relation to information and advice, drawing where possible on the sparse literature and considering the questions asked above. The chapter starts with an outline of the development of the housing authority role in information and advice, considers alternative and complementary services, and goes on to examine the role in relation to homelessness, mortgage arrears and housing improvement in the private sector.

A new role?

A possible role for housing authorities in providing information and advice services grew out of the role of housing authorities as housing providers. Tenants and prospective tenants require information about allocations policies, and tenancy conditions, for example. Increasingly, as housing authorities have had less prospect of easily meeting housing need through direct provision, and as the needs of those such as elderly owner-occupiers and private sector tenants have been brought to the attention of housing authorities, there has been a growth of interest in the idea of housing authorities guiding and assisting people to improve their housing circumstances without moving into the public sector. But two other strands can be detected in the origins of this role. First, housing authorities have a longstanding duty to assess housing conditions throughout their area, and this more general and strategic concern with housing conditions and opportunities has been seen as the starting point for a more explicit role as provider of information and advice to assist in meeting housing needs. Second, the idea of housing as a social service involves the notion of attention to the housing needs of individuals and families irrespective of tenure. This view of information and advice would place some emphasis on the rights of citizens to receive assistance, irrespective of wealth, disability, race or gender. Information and advice work would therefore be partly about exercising rights, and partly about achieving the desirable outcome of improved housing conditions. These two strands are related by the notion that providing information and advice can reveal needs that are not already known or fully understood. Information and advice giving can therefore play a part in strategic analysis and planning, although it is not a substitute for it.

Given this background, housing authorities have been seen as the natural providers of information and advice to those who were unlikely to have their needs met directly through housing authority provision as well as those who might. Private sector tenants, those in need of social support, those new to an area, and increasingly those in difficulties with a mortgage have all been suggested as possible beneficiaries of housing authority information and advice. In the early 1970s, in the wake of the Seebohm, Cullingworth and other reports, several housing authorities set up housing advice centres intended to provide assistance to people in housing difficulty whatever tenure they were in or aspired to be in. Some housing

Providing information and advice 147

authorities also gave grants to voluntary agencies which aimed to provide advice services, sometimes to people with a grievance against the local housing authority itself. Writing in 1977, Smith reviewed their progress:

> Many housing aid centres were initially very successful in advising, guiding and even motivating people towards house purchase as a method of solving housing needs, but unfortunately market conditions are denying this solution to many people. The centres, especially in areas of housing stress, are finding that an increasing proportion of time is taken up with guidance in tenancy problems, both to landlord and tenant, which often prevents hardship and possible evictions.
> (Smith 1977, p 82)

Over the years since then, some authorities have appointed specialist tenancy relations officers to assist private sector tenants with problems faced in the private sector.

In 1992 the number of local authority housing aid centres in England was estimated to be at least 100 (42 per cent of authorities) in one survey (London Research Centre 1992, p 26), which means that more than half do not have such specialist provision. In the same year the Audit Commission reported that in inner London all housing authorities provided housing advice — not necessarily the same thing as having an aid centre — falling to 36 per cent in Northern shire districts. Two thirds (69 per cent) of outer London Boroughs, half (50 per cent) of Southern shire districts, and just over one third of northern shire districts provided advice (Audit Commission 1992, p 53).

In the 20 years from the early 1970s to the early 1990s several developments in policy and legislation have increased the role of housing authorities in relation to information and advice. In 1977 housing authorities were given an explicit role in providing advice and assistance to homeless people or anyone threatened with homelessness, whether or not the authority was required to find accommodation for the recipient of the advice. In 1980 public sector tenants were given new rights to information. The development of tenant participation has gone hand in hand with calls for tenants and tenants' organisations to be provided with more information about housing management matters. The growth of voluntary transfers and tenant management organisations such as tenant management co-operatives and estate management boards has been accompanied in England by government funds for training tenants intending to take over the management of their housing. In Scotland, Scottish Homes funds independent advice for tenants considering voluntary transfer to a new landlord. The emphasis in policy on choice has been accompanied by some concern to see that consumers are able to exercise an informed choice about their prospects and rights under alternative landlords or management arrangements. The development of concern about the quality of housing management and the introduction of the Citizens' Charter has meant a new emphasis on information, including the requirement to publish information for tenants on housing management performance in England and Wales under the provisions of the 1989 Local Government and Housing Act. And the new renewal areas to be established under the same Act will require agencies to be set up to advise and assist people in the areas affected. In Scotland concern about the situation of public sector tenants involved in discussions about transfers led to a review of housing information and advice (Scottish Homes 1992).

Despite these specific developments, the legal basis for a general role in providing information and advice remains relatively unclear. Housing authorities have a number of powers which allow them to give information or advice directly or by assisting other organisations to do so. These powers relate to homelessness, the rights and duties of landlords and tenants, renewal, and assistance with rents. Loughlin (1991) argues that these powers, taken together with more general powers in the Local Government Acts, allow housing authorities to provide as comprehensive an information and advice service as they wish. However, the legal basis for a service that goes beyond information and advice to representation relies on the existence of a power which allows local authorities to spend a small proportion of their budget on anything which they consider beneficial to the area or its inhabitants. 'Here, it would seem, that a Housing Advisory Service (even one which takes up claims on behalf of its clients) can be justified under this discretionary expenditure power' (Loughlin 1991, p 23). While this provides grounds for rejecting a solicitor's call of *ultra vires*, the absence of explicit general powers may help explain why many authorities have not developed information and advice services, despite being advised to do so for many years. This discussion raises the issue of the purpose and nature of information and advice services.

Defining housing information and advice

Providing information and advice is not the same thing as meeting housing need. Information about alternatives and options will not compensate for lack of skills, money or other resources required to exercise choice. For that reason some information and advice services have gone beyond the provision of information and advice to acting on behalf of people who need assistance in dealing with the law or with grant application forms, for example. Even then, advocacy cannot create additional affordable housing, and the work of housing advisers may help one needy group of people while preventing another group from gaining access to housing. For this reason housing advice work is difficult to evaluate. It may or may not result in any reduction in the need for social housing.

The wide possible range of different types of advice work creates difficulties in defining information and advice work, and in considering who should carry it out. Housing information and advice services extend from providing an address or telephone number on request to providing an advocacy service involving representation at a court hearing, for example. The wide range of information and advice services have been defined as:

— straightforward information;
— explanation, for example explaining technical or legal terms;
— advice, for example setting out a course of action;
— practical aid, such as helping with letter writing or form filling;
— referral to another source of help;
— mediation with another party on behalf of someone;
— counselling by listening and helping someone clarify their feelings;
— advocacy, for example preparing and presenting a case at court.

(Scottish Homes 1992, p 10)

These services can be provided to individuals or to groups such as tenants' associations. The characteristics of the person or group may help determine the nature of the service required. People with poor literacy skills or particular types of disability will require assistance as well as information when filling in an application form, for example. Some tenants' groups will require more advice than others about alternative forms of tenant management, for example. Traditionally much emphasis in housing information and advice work has been placed on enabling people to exercise their rights, for example of redress against a private landlord. However, some people will require assistance with confronting an alleged injustice perpetrated by the local authority itself. It is not obvious that housing authorities should or can be the provider of information and advice in all cases. Some place their advice centre outside the control of the housing department, as in Cardiff, where it is responsible to the Chief Executive. But there will still be times

150 The Housing Authority as Enabler

when natural justice requires that people are able to call on advice from independent sources.

Apart from illustrating the varying depth of the information and advice that might be necessary, this discussion also demonstrates that a variety of skills and knowledge will be required to provide for all the possible needs. The demands on staffing for a fully comprehensive service would extend from a well-informed receptionist to a fully-experienced lawyer, from a knowledgable housing practitioner to a trained counsellor. Few housing authorities would attempt such comprehensive provision directly, although some could point to the availability of a wide range of information and advice by other agencies in their area.

The demands of a comprehensive housing information and advice service are complicated by the subject matter of housing. At its simplest, what is required is information and advice on *access* and *use*. But this covers a wide range of topics from rights in relation to noisy neighbours to living in a conservation area; from advice about benefits to mortgage finance; from improvement grants to advice about how to influence a landlord's management policies. Given the complexity of the legal, technical and administrative aspects of some of these topics, it is not surprising that some specialist information and advice services have grown up, within or outside local authorities.

Alternative and complementary provision

Housing information and advice is provided by a wide range of bodies apart from the housing authority, in most localities. One review found over 50 agencies providing housing information and advice services in one city, Edinburgh (Scottish Homes 1992). The list, unlikely to be comprehensive, includes six CABx, a citizens rights office, a local council of social service, a council for the single homeless, several housing associations, a social service welfare rights team, several national voluntary organisations, and the District Council. The pattern of provision varies from one locality to another, but a useful starting point for any housing authority concerned about its own role in housing advice would be to consider the availability of different types of service, and what might be needed to complement or assist existing provision. The providers tend to fall into one of five categories.

1. Statutory agencies include public bodies such as urban development corporations, new town development corporations, the Housing Corporation, the Department of Social Security, health authorities, and social services departments. Social workers, in particular, are seen to play an important role in giving information, advice and support to clients with housing and financial problems. They, and health workers, have a developing role in relation to community care. Social work assistance may prevent the emergence of a housing problem, by for example enabling someone to stay in their home after illness or disability. Social workers may identify design, management or location needs.

Contact between social workers and housing authorities in the past has mainly related to the role of housing authorities as providers. Social workers who are trained in some of the skills of advice work, such as counselling and advocacy, may encounter conflict in their relationships with housing authorities as providers. Their concern to serve the needs of individual clients can appear to conflict with the administrative procedures of housing authorities, which are intended to categorise and treat similar cases in the same way. For the future, housing authorities could be a valuable source of expert information for social workers about housing opportunities throughout their area. New legislative requirements such as the 1991 Children Act and community care add to the need for close working. This could enable better relationships to develop than have sometimes characterised the housing/social work professional relationship. But social workers are able to see the wider picture too, and their individual case work is relevant to the identification of need which is part of the housing authority's role, whether or not it has a housing stock of its own. Conflict will occur, though, as long as local authorities have any housing role, since the priorities of housing professionals will not always coincide with the priorities of social workers, even when both are employed by the same local authority.

2. Many *voluntary agencies* employ their own professional staff to provide information and advice services, or to manage and co-ordinate the activities of voluntary advisers. The best known in the housing field are the Citizen's Advice Bureaux (CABx), Shelter, whose network of Housing Advice Centres feed into Shelter's policy and campaigning work, Women's Aid, the Tenant Participation Advisory Services in all three parts of Britain, and the growing number of home improvement agencies usually known as Care and Repair, or Staying Put. Another recent growth area over the last decade is that of money advice centres whose work includes advice on housing debt. There were an estimated 300 such units in Britain in 1990, many based in Citizens' Advice Bureaux, and some within local government. Apart from these, few voluntary advice centres specialising in housing exist, but legal and technical advice

centres do a lot of housing-related work, some of it for groups rather than individuals. Most advice agencies are concentrated in the urban areas of Britain, with large cities usually with several CABx. In rural areas, and in some urban areas, there are significant gaps in the nature and type of provision. Relationships between voluntary advice centres and housing authorities vary from excellent to poor, and usually arise in relation to the authority's roles as provider and as the body responsible for homelessness. Voluntary agencies have a special role to play as independent and alternative sources to the local authority. Many are very dependent on the local authority for the funds that keep them going.

3. Private bodies such as housing consultants, banks, building societies, estate agents, solicitors' property centres, mortgage advice centres, and other property and finance professionals provide specialist advice about housing and housing finance. These services are largely, though not exclusively aimed at home owners and potential home owners, and not at people interested in other tenures, or in need of advice arising from problems with their tenure as owner-occupiers. Some lawyers develop an expertise in all aspects of housing, but most do not. In contrast, housing consultants are experts in most housing issues, but are not accessible to most consumers. Some have experience of working with tenants' groups, and are paid for by the housing authority, particularly those faced with management or development changes.

4. Housing associations, private landlords and other *housing providers* are primarily concerned to fulfil their duties to their own tenants or potential tenants. This may extend to the wider community of owner-occupiers or shopkeepers, for example, in the case of neighbourhood based associations. Housing associations are considered by their tenants to keep them informed — in one survey, four out of five said so, and nine out of ten said that housing officers were easy to contact (Centre for Housing Research 1989, p 88). Some social landlords may go beyond immediate tenancy matters to give advice about alternative housing options, for example. In contrast, many private landlords are considered by their tenants to be uninterested in providing even the minimum information required by law.

5. Tenants' organisations can be particularly well-placed to provide information and advice to their members. Local tenants' associations are, on the whole, trusted by their members. They are accessible, and have an understanding of tenants' concerns. Yet providing information to tenants emerged as a very minor activity in a survey of tenants' associations carried out in five areas (Cairncross, Clapham and Goodlad 1992). The reasons for this are probably concerned with the lack of resources, including information, which tenants' associations suffer from. As a consequence, the tenants' organisations which have developed most effectively as information providers are the better resourced federations of tenants' associations, and other specialist tenants' resource centres, such as the Tenants' Information Service (Scotland) and the Tenants' Resource and Information Service (Newcastle). These agencies provide services mainly to tenants groups rather than individual tenants, and use their resources to employ their own expert staff, as well as using the skills and knowledge of volunteers.

What housing authorities do

Little is known systematically about the information and advice role of housing authorities. Although over one hundred provide housing aid centres (London Research Centre 1992, p 26) and the proportion providing advice in different regions varies from 36 to 100 per cent, the nature of what these authorities provide is not clear, nor is its effectiveness. Nor is it clear whether authorities which do not have a centre and do not provide advice fund voluntary agencies to operate independent centres. Writing in 1989 about all types of centres Smith says that:

> Restrictions on public expenditure have led to a reduction in the number of such centres, although several bodies have drawn attention to the changing emphasis in the nature of the work of centres and the urgent need for help and advice in the housing field.
>
> (Smith 1989, p 95)

Within housing authorities the information role is hard to disentangle from the work of managing the stock, but a survey in Scotland found that 'of the District and Islands councils included in the research, only about half give advice to housing consumers about access to accommodation across all the different forms of tenure ... few District and Islands councils offer help on topics outside their role as public sector landlords' (Scottish Homes 1992, p 16).

This research also reports the views of a varied group of consumers about housing information and advice services. Housing authorities were seen as the obvious first source of information and advice. The council is well known and considered impartial and accurate. People wanted to be able to approach the council for all the housing information they needed. As one respondent said, 'You should get all your information from them . . . they should tell you all in a oner' (Scottish Homes 1992, p 20). But council staff were also criticised as being unfriendly or ineffective. 'I've never come out of the Town Hall ever feeling that I've achieved anything', one council tenant said (Scottish Homes 1992, p 18). Another criticism was of councils' lack of interest in the problems of home owners, or the availability of alternative housing options such as housing association housing. This may, of course, reflect a judgement by the council about the poor prospects of achieving alternatives. The report concludes, 'Three major gaps in existing provision frequently emerged' (Scottish Homes 1992, p 19) — inadequate information from councils about their own allocations process, the lack of information on housing options other than the council, and the absence of co-ordinated information for people in difficulties with house purchase. Even if councils were to provide a comprehensive information and advice service the Scottish Homes report suggests a need for alternative, independent sources of guidance. This is particularly, but not only, compelling in relation to the council's own role as provider — it should be an essential but not exclusive source of information about its own housing services.

Another Scottish survey of tenants in rent arrears found the major sources of advice were the Citizens' Advice Bureaux (37 per cent), DSS (26 per cent), the housing authority (23 per cent), and the social work department (18 per cent). More than one in five tenants who consulted the housing authority found it unhelpful (Scott and Kintrea 1992).

These surveys are small in scale; further research would be useful. Other surveys have sought to throw light on the role of housing authorities in relation to specialist housing advice services. Before going on to review their findings it is necessary to consider how advice services should be evaluated.

There are broadly two approaches that might be taken to this problem. The first is to consider the outcome of cases handled by advice services, and the extent to which the provision of advice made a difference to the outcome. This is not necessarily easy to judge. Any evaluation would require to separate advice from other influences — would the problem have been solved anyway, for example? Did the advice make a difference to the nature of need that was met? Did the advice lead to any net reduction in the needs remaining unmet? These questions are not easily answered, and few have attempted to develop appropriate research methods to tackle them. The Audit Commission (1989, 1992), for example, shows no awareness of the complexity of the task of evaluating homelessness or other advice work by housing authorities. Their apparent assumption that successful outcomes are a result of advice rather than other factors, and that advice leads to an automatic net reduction in overall housing need is gratifying to those who provide advice, but less than convincing to others.

The second approach to evaluation is to examine the advice provided in particular cases to see how appropriate, well delivered and well received it was, irrespective of outcome. This form of evaluation starts from the perception of housing advice as an entitlement, or as a social service. The Audit Commission makes no attempt to evaluate housing advice from this perspective, seeing it only as a way of reducing demand for social rented housing.

The remainder of this chapter considers the information and advice work of housing authorities in three areas — homelessness, mortgage arrears, and housing renewal in the private sector. These show the pattern of provision in relation to a statutory duty (homelessness), a growing problem in owner occupation (mortgage arrears), and in a field (housing renewal) where advice has been increasingly provided by the voluntary sector, often in collaboration with housing authorities. These do not provide a comprehensive account of the nature of housing advice and the role of housing authorities, but illustrate different approaches and purposes.

1. Homelessness advice and assistance
There are two specific areas of the homelessness legislation where housing authorities must give information, advice or assistance to applicants. The first is in preventing homelessness, whether or not the applicant is in priority need. However if the applicant is threatened with homelessness intentionally the duty is only to those in priority need (Departments of the Environment and Health, Welsh Office 1991, p 29). Secondly, housing authorities have a duty to give advice and assistance to anyone who is homeless but not in priority need.

The government's Code of Guidance (DoE, DoH, Welsh Office 1991; Scottish Office 1990) stresses the role that specialist advice centres can play in the prevention of homelessness, and of the importance of liaising with voluntary and statutory agencies in seeking to avoid homelessness in particular cases. In relation to private sector tenants, the guidance is fairly explicit, that, 'Authorities should always be ready to offer advice and guidance' (DoE *et al.* 1991, p 30). For owner-occupiers in difficulty with their mortgage the Code does not encourage an active role for authorities, suggesting that people are told to contact their lender 'at an early stage'. For other social groups, such as young people and hospital patients, the Code is not explicit about the nature of the advice and assistance required, other than pointing to some of the entitlements people may have, for example to housing benefit. Elsewhere, in a section entitled *Advice and Assistance* the nature of what authorities should do is addressed:

> The nature of the advice given is likely to vary from case to case. Authorities should interview everyone for whom it has a duty to provide advice and should counsel them on the local accommodation options open to them, where appropriate referring them to other specialist agencies. Authorities should give active help to assist applicants to secure their own accommodation taking account of the local housing situation and individual needs. Authorities should ensure that the information provided is accurate and up-to-date.
>
> (DoE *et al.* 1991, p 43)

As a means to achieving this, authorities are asked to consider providing or funding housing aid centres, and to maintain close contact with voluntary agencies which provide advice or accommodation in the area.

This does not provide a clear prescription of how far authorities should go in assisting people. Does it, for example, encourage practical aid, advocacy, or mediation? The Code provides a good deal of scope for authorities to interpret the nature of advice and assistance as they wish and several studies of the homelessness policies and practices of housing authorities have found very different procedures operating.

One survey found that 'the number of advice cases . . . in the year to 31 March 1988 varied from nil to 2,809. Caseloads varied widely from two to 397 per advisory officer per month' (p 29). 'Housing advisory officers' were more optimistic about the potential of advice and assistance than homelessness officers — perhaps because the purpose of their jobs was to attempt to prevent homelessness rather than deal with it when it arose. In one authority an increase in the effort devoted to advice and assistance had resulted in lower rates of acceptances as homeless in categories such as mortgage arrears and insecure private renting, but not in relation to eviction by friends or relatives.

There was little monitoring of the effectiveness of advice and assistance given. Over two-thirds of the authorities could provide only estimates of the outcome of the assistance given, and one in five could provide no information at all. However, in 58 per cent of the cases the outcome was known. In only eight per cent of cases was no solution possible. In 28 per cent of cases the home was retained. In 14 per cent of cases a new home was found. And in the remaining nine per cent of cases other housing was found. The Audit Commission claims that, 'In just over half of all cases, the provision of housing advice and assistance led to a solution to the client's housing problems' (p 30), without giving any evidence to show that the effects of other factors — such as assistance from elsewhere — had been accounted for. The Commission cites one survey carried out of the clients of a debt counselling agency in which 50 per cent of clients said that they had been helped to keep their home (p 31). However they acknowledge elsewhere that the exact impact of housing advice is uncertain, and call for more research (Audit Commission 1989).

In another study the homelessness policies and procedures of nine housing authorities in England and Wales were examined for the Department of the Environment. A similar picture of variations in practice is painted. One of the case studies, Birmingham, stood out as going further than the others in seeking vacancies in its own stock for non-priority applicants. In general advice and assistance took the form of 'verbal advice, lists of bed and breakfast accommodation, housing associations, hostels, etc, other advisory leaflets and sometimes more direct action towards finding a vacancy in B&B or a hostel' (Niner 1989, p 40). Very few were helped through referral to housing associations (which does not necessarily mean that very few homeless people are housed by housing associations). Westminster offered the most comprehensive range of leaflets, and Cardiff was planning to do so. Two of the nine authorities, Cardiff and Hillingdon, provided advice and assistance from a housing advice centre, rather than from the homelessness unit.

In relation to the prevention of homelessness the study also found that some of the case study authorities were more active than others. 'Many authorities, while firmly in favour of prevention of homelessness in theory, appeared rather more doubtful in practice' (Niner 1989, p 41). In their defence these authorities said that it was found that many applicants turned for help too late for it to be given effectively. Also, preventative action can be resisted by the applicant, creating dilemmas for the housing adviser given the policy emphasis on choice and preferences. And for many applicants the prevention of homelessness may be better described as the postponement of homelessness, it was felt.

These factors were perceived by authorities as sufficient to justify the low priority given to the prevention of homelessness. Three issues of importance to the information and advice role of housing authorities emerged from the research:

- The open-ended nature of their statutory duties meant that staff were doing as much as they could on the particular day the applicant appeared, so that those who called on a

busy day received less help than those who happened to call during a slack period. Even in Birmingham the help given to find permanent accommodation was limited by the availability of suitable vacancies.
- Staff reported frustration at the unavailability of alternative accommodation. They felt that most of the options were likely to be ineffective because of cost or other considerations.
- The effectiveness of the service was largely unknown. Few people returned and there was little if any feedback on the outcome or the applicants' satisfaction with the service provided.

In a third study, carried out by the Scottish Office in 1987/88, a familiar picture of variation between authorities emerged. Only 13 authorities (25 per cent) had information leaflets on homelessness rights available to enquirers, and none had any in minority languages, although two had interpreting facilities. In general, in housing offices where no homelessness officer was present the normal procedure was to refer an enquirer to a designated officer straightaway, rather than make a preliminary assessment. In one quarter of such offices, however, there was a possibility or a certainty that an assessment to see whether an enquirer could qualify as homeless would be carried out by the receptionist (p 13), and in only a small minority of such offices were the reception staff given more than induction or on-the-job training (p 9). In specialist homelessness offices there was a greater chance that the reception staff would conduct an assessment, with over one-third (36 per cent) reporting that reception staff were instructed to conduct a preliminary assessment. However, although reception staff in these offices were more likely to have had special training in procedures, only 31 per cent of such offices reported doing so (p 9). In a small number of offices (six out of 35 and four out of 53 respectively) applicants would be interviewed by the receptionist or the designated homelessness officer in an open, semi-open or screened off section of a public office (pp 13–15). In relation to the prevention of homelessness most authorities (94 per cent) would advise applicants of their rights in relation to security of tenure, and the same number would liaise with the social work department, DSS, and other relevant agencies. Slightly fewer (77 per cent) tried to help in domestic disputes, two-thirds (65 per cent) would liaise with building societies, and the same number with private landlords (p 31). Six out of ten (60 per cent) would liaise with other agencies, and two out of ten (19 per cent) would take other sorts of action (Duguid 1990, pp 30–31).

Unusually this study included interviews with applicants to five local authorities. A large majority (86 per cent) reported receiving some advice and assistance from the homelessness officer. The advice included joining the council's waiting list, being aided to find alternative accommodation and being helped to retain existing accommodation. But variations between district councils existed, for example in the proportions of applicants referred to social workers, or in the proportions told to wait for court orders for eviction, or advised to go and stay with relatives (Duguid 1990, pp 58–60).

These studies paint a picture of great variations in procedures and approaches between different authorities, and of inadequate evaluation of services provided. Some of the differences may reflect legitimate differences of policy between authorities which are entirely justified in a system of local government, but others seem to stem from factors such as inadequate training or uncertainty about the purpose and effectiveness of advice-giving. This could explain the uncertainty felt by many authorities, and others, in responding to the growth of mortgage arrears in the 1980s and 1990s.

2. Mortgage arrears

The most publicised cause of homelessness in the 1990s has been mortgage arrears, as the figures for repossessions rose to 75,000 in 1991 (London Research Centre 1992, p 1), and the proportion of homeless acceptances in England in which mortgage arrears was the main cause of homelessness rose from 6 per cent in 1989 to 12 per cent in 1991 (p 16). This major housing problem provides a test of the role of housing authorities. If those who are in difficulty with the predominant tenure cannot be helped by housing authorities, then what meaning has the enabling role got? Have authorities the skills, resources and will to get involved in this issue? How have they responded to the growth of mortgage arrears as a housing problem in the 1980s and 1990s?

The role played by local authorities, including the part played by advice, is examined in a report largely based on a postal survey of housing authorities in England carried out early in 1992 which achieved a 67 per cent response rate (London Research Centre 1992). The report suggests there are four main ways in which local authorities can play a role in relation to mortgage default:

- 'playing a strategic role' by pressing lenders, housing associations and advice agencies to act, and by ensuring co-ordination between them
- providing or funding advice services

- by taking up individual arrears cases with lenders
- by operating or funding mortgage rescue schemes

Despite the advice contained in the Council of Mortgage Lenders' Code of Guidance (1992) that housing authorities should be given advance warning about specific cases, homelessness applications were the main way that most local authorities heard about mortgage arrears cases. Having had notification, there are a number of possible ways of helping. Only one in five authorities (21 per cent) had produced any written information aimed at people in mortgage arrears, whereas almost two-thirds (64 per cent) had funded other debt counselling agencies. One hundred authorities (42 per cent) said they had their own internal housing advice service, two-thirds of which offered debt counselling and one quarter of which intended to expand their provision. Overall, four out of five authorities said they either had their own housing advice service, or had staff trained in debt counselling, or had funded other agencies to provide debt counselling. However some expressed reservations about the adequacy of their services. One officer wrote, 'Unless you have the time to work out people's budgets, look at their debts in more detail, and try to show them how they should organise things better, and then help them in the first few months to establish a regular routine of budgeting, you are lost' (p 28). Nine out of ten authorities (90 per cent) had taken up cases with lenders, but only one quarter of those always did it, and the rest did it mostly, sometimes or very little. Three out of ten reported that they got no response from lenders approached in this way, others (43 per cent of authorities) reported that a delay in repossession to allow other accommodation to be found was the most common outcome. Three-quarters of authorities thought their intervention was not very successful or unsuccessful (pp 19–33). Only 22 authorities (9 per cent) ran mortgage rescue schemes by 1991/92, and by then only 105 households had been rescued (p 42). The rescue schemes are expensive in capital and staff resources, and 'pale into insignificance compared with the 76,000 repossessions that took place in 1991' (London Research Centre 1992, p 45). Clackmannan District Council's scheme has prevented 14 repossessions at high capital cost, and required a full time housing officer to operate.

The London Research Centre's report deals with three of the four measures that authorities might use to assist with mortgage default. The fourth — encouraging and co-ordinating the work of others — is less well researched. Anecdotal evidence suggests a familiar picture of variation in the approach taken by housing authorities, with some doing nothing and others innovating actively. For example, Colchester Borough Council's Housing Advice Centre produced a series of seven mortgage advice booklets, and organised arrears workshops for local banks and building societies at a time in the early 1990s when banks and building societies were the subject of growing criticism for their arrears procedures (*Adviser*, No. 30 1992, p 12).

3. Home improvement agencies

The involvement of local authorities in the improvement and repair of private sector housing, especially since 1974, has been accompanied by a growing concern about the information and advice needs of residents of renewal areas, where the population is sometimes disproportionately disadvantaged in ways that make it more difficult for residents to find their way through the rules and procedures. A second strand in the growth of improvement advice and assistance is the development of community care, and in particular the growing desire of policy makers to allow older owner-occupiers the choice of staying in their home, by providing sensitive advice and assistance in improving, adapting or repairing it. The development of home improvement agencies as a means to tackling these issues has been a notable feature of developments in approaches to community care and housing renewal since the 1970s. Home improvement agencies therefore provide a case study of specialist housing information and advice services and the possible role of housing authorities.

> Home improvement agencies provide practical help and support to people requiring assistance with repairs, improvements and adaptations to their properties. Some of these schemes are run by housing associations or the voluntary sector but others are run directly by the housing authorities themselves. Many are known as Care and Repair and Staying Put projects
> (Mackintosh and Leather 1992, p 89)

The first home improvement agencies were set up by local authorities or voluntary organisations supported by Anchor Housing Trust, Shelter, and the Housing Associations' Charitable Trust. Local authority schemes concentrated on helping people to apply for and take up improvement grants, whereas the voluntary agencies concentrated on assisting older people to meet their needs, not necessarily to the highest possible standard. Some voluntary sector schemes were funded by local authorities. In 1984 Neighbourhood Revitalisation Services (NRS) was launched by an umbrella group representing private sector construction interests to promote more and better improvement work, initially in four areas, Sheffield, Oldham, Gloucester and Bedford. NRS's work was targeted on owner-occupiers in local areas, not on particular target groups. In 1985 Shelter and the Housing Association's Charitable Trust set up Care and Repair to promote and assist local projects, usually run by housing associations, and aimed at older people. Limited funds made progress slow. In 1986 the government made a major expansion of these projects possible with grants for 50 new projects, 25 Care and Repair and 25 NRS. In 1987 the Welsh Office funded six further Care and Repair projects in Wales. A number of other projects were funded from other sources, allowing a total of 74 projects to be evaluated by Leather and Mackintosh (1990), in an unusually thorough examination of a major housing policy innovation. (There are also several such projects in Scotland.)

Projects were set up where local conditions, including local authority support, make it possible. Most covered the area of a local authority, but some, including all NRS projects, concentrated on a smaller area. Most Care and Repair and Anchor (Staying Put) schemes employed few staff — an average of 2.5 of which 0.6 was technical staff (p 17). NRS projects employed more staff, including the services of a surveyor's or architect's firm to provide technical expertise (p 19). The importance of good working relationships with housing authorities is stressed by Leather and Mackintosh:

> It is essential for projects to have good working relationships with local authority staff to ensure that grant cases proceed smoothly and it is advantageous to have some priority for certain clients ... in most areas schemes dealing with older people or other specific client groups are seen as a valuable complement to local authority services (pp 89–90).

This applies particularly to the Staying Put and Care and Repair projects. The majority of the NRS projects had an allocation of improvement grants in 1988/89 and 1989/90. After the government, local authorities were the second most significant funder of local projects, and contributions varied from generous to nil. Very few Staying Put and Care and Repair agencies charged any fees, and NRS projects charged only the fees of the building agency used for technical support.

The projects were evaluated against a range of performance criteria including volume of improvement work generated, and clients' views of the service. Performance varied across a wide range, but about half of the Care and Repair and Staying Put clients said they would not have carried out the work without the help received, and the extent of attention to the needs and wishes of clients was a particular strength. Over two thirds of the NRS clients would not have carried out the work without the help received from

Providing information and advice 163

NRS. Leather and Mackintosh conclude that the agencies played an important role in tackling poor housing. Although the services of the improvement agencies were valued by the clients, housing authorities and others, some housing authorities did not value it enough to fund it. For the future, they argue, local authorities should be the main funding agency, although they are concerned that some authorities will not take on this responsibility. In these circumstances, a second source of funding should be available.

Agencies are expected to have an important role in renewal areas and in the delivery of minor works grants under the 1989 Act provisions for renewal and repair (see Chapter 5). The early experience is variable. Some housing authorities have devolved a 'great deal of this work to home improvement agencies, whereas others have made only limited use of agencies or have not made any resources available for minor works assistance'. Involvement has extended as far as allocating a sum of money to a Care and Repair agency in Bristol to administer the scheme, with suitable safeguards to ensure acccountability. Elsewhere authorities have 'nominally' given control to an improvement agency, but have then duplicated the work of assessing applicants, scrutinising specifications, and so on. Minor works assistance was found to be a growing and significant part of the work of agencies (Mackintosh and Leather 1992, pp 90–91).

Conclusion

This chapter has discussed the development of housing information and advice as a role for housing authorities, and considered some experience of the advice work of housing authorities and of other agencies. Little is known systematically about the housing aid work of housing authorities, and little guidance is available about what sort of advice work is necessary or effective, or what skills are required to do it. With some exceptions, notably the work of Leather and Mackintosh (1991) there is little appreciation of the difficulty and complexity of evaluating advice work. The process of advice giving as well as the outcome should be evaluated, but there was little sign of systematic evaluation of either by authorities themselves. In addition, the growth of interest in the enabling role has not been accompanied by any clarification of the legal powers available to authorities.

From the evidence about advice and assistance in relation to homelessness, mortgage arrears and home improvement it is clear that intensive counselling and advocacy is required in some situations as well as less time-consuming information provision, but that some authorities are not well equipped to provide it. Housing authorities take very different approaches to their advice work.

164 The Housing Authority as Enabler

Even where authorities have a statutory role, as in the case of threatened homelessness, there can be no guarantee that a housing authority will ensure a trained member of staff is deployed to provide counselling in a private room for the amount of time that may be necessary to explore the nature of the problem and any potential remedies. In contrast, some authorities provide specialist units and staff, and in addition fund other agencies, such as CABx to carry out debt counselling, and improvement agencies to help the take up of improvement grants. Independent advice should be available for those who are aggrieved by housing authorities' own activities, but the extent of provision is not clear.

Housing information and advice work should be concerned with two aspects of housing conditions in a locality. First, it is concerned to ensure that people, individually or jointly, can exercise their rights to whatever quality and type of housing service they are entitled to. But there is a limit to this type of work. Rights cannot be divorced from the context in which they are exercised. Some rights can only be exercised at the cost of other people's misfortune, and some rights cannot be exercised at all without the resources to make them effective. Housing information and advice work is therefore, secondly, concerned with the policies which have led to the housing difficulties and problems which people face, including the conflicts which arise between the needs, aspirations and rights of different groups in a locality. Attention to one without attention to the other is to neglect the best prospects for improving housing conditions for individuals and for the community as whole. For this reason alone it is arguable that housing authorities should be involved in advice work directly and indirectly if they want to be well informed about the nature of housing conditions in their area.

Chapter 9
Managing the enabling role

The task of managing a housing authority today is very different from the traditional tasks of local government management, concerned as they have been with running services within a policy framework determined by the council. The management of service delivery is not easy. It is complicated by the political nature of local government, and the complexity of decision making and implementation processes. But the task for the enabling authority is even more complex, as it involves working through others in an attempt to achieve objectives. This chapter is intended to raise questions and sketch in some of the background to the organisation and management of the enabling role in local government.

- How should housing authorities organise themselves to carry out the varied tasks involved in enabling?
- What is the nature of the management tasks associated with the enabling role? What resources, skills and knowledge are required and how should they be used?
- Are housing managers trained to take on the new tasks associated with the enabling role?

The chapter traces the way in which management concerns about internal co-ordination and administration of the policy process have given way to concerns about the impact of local government on the consumers of services, the capacity of local government to influence others on the local housing scene, and the effectiveness of service provision in meeting housing needs and demands. The discussion concludes with an examination of the capacity of housing authorities to manage the enabling role, with reference to staff, other resources, and the relationship between authorities and central government.

Styles of management in local government

Five broad styles of management can be detected in the recent history of local government in Britain. Chronologically these are professionalism, corporate management, accountability, performance measurement, and networking. The last of these is most closely associated with the enabling role, but there are strong elements of the others reflected in the organisation and administration of local government today, and which therefore need to be understood if the management of enabling is to be understood.

1. Professionalism

The post-war growth of local government was also a growth of new professional groups such as town planners and social workers, who developed their own culture and style of working, as well as a body of knowledge in which they claimed exclusive insight. Older professional groups such as lawyers, environmental health officers and engineers were already entrenched in the local government structure. Housing work was not so easily established as a separately defined set of activities, perhaps because it grew from a close association with work already claimed as the province of an established professional group such as planning, social work, environmental health, or architecture (Power 1987a). When housing workers established a single professional association in 1965 the professional qualification of that Institute was a long way from being accepted as a necessary qualification to engage in housing work. The term 'housing manager' is associated with a definition of housing work which puts the emphasis on the management of the rented stock, with the tasks — such as rent collection, ordering repairs and resolving neighbour disputes — of managing social rented housing, and not with the tasks of negotiation, co-ordination, monitoring and development associated with the enabling concept (Kemp and Williams 1990).

2. Corporate management

Housing work was, therefore, in the post-war period, a weakly professionalised area of local government work, in contrast with others. This has implications for the status of housing workers, but also for the influence they may exercise in the local government structure and in the overall management of the housing authority's work. Even so, housing had become established by the 1980s as an area of activity which usually was thought to merit a separate local government department. One study of the organisation of council housing management in England reports, 'In almost all there was a separate Housing Department' (Kirby, Finch and Wood 1988, p 9), but 'traditionally, housing has involved using the skills

Managing the enabling role

of a number of different departments. Some councils have tried to bring many of these skills within the Housing Department. But even the most comprehensive Housing Departments rely on other parts of the council for some services' (Kirby, Finch and Wood 1988, p 4). Commonly important aspects of a housing authority's work will be traditionally the responsibility of departments such as environmental health, architecture and planning. Another study confirms, 'The comprehensive housing service is still far from the norm. In particular, environmental health aspects are not the responsibility of the Main Housing Department in the majority of authorities' (Davies and Niner 1987, p 1). And another study found that two thirds of English housing authorities (67 per cent) reported housing benefit payments to private sector tenants being administered by departments other than housing, and one third (31 per cent) reported rent collection as the responsibility of departments other than housing (Centre for Housing Research 1989, p 14). This sort of organisational structure raises questions about the capacity of professional staff to develop and monitor housing strategies.

A variety of arrangements also apply at the committee level in local government with aspects of housing inevitably being discussed on a number of committees such as those concerned with planning, building control, environmental health, social work services, and direct labour. Housing, and any of these other local government functions, may or may not appear in the name of a committee. Often, in practice, housing is the main responsibility of one or two committees, with discussions about housing issues which take place elsewhere being referred to the main housing committee or committees. Housing committees are sometimes restricted in their remit to matters concerned with the management of the authority's own stock. Matters such as HMOs, repair grants and Housing Action Areas may be discussed elsewhere. So at the committee level as well as the officer level, there may be little opportunity to develop an overall housing strategy. In many parts of Britain a two-tier system of local government acts for the time being to complicate the situation, particularly in relation to land-use planning issues, and social work services.

It is clear that effective implementation of the enabling roles is, at times, unlikely to be assisted by some of the departmental divisions and jealousies which arise from differences of professional orientation, or from differing departmental loyalties and objectives, but it would be naive to suggest that there should be one all-encompassing housing department in all housing authorities. There are two reasons why this is the case, both related to the intrinsic complexity of housing as a commodity, as a service and as an occupational category. First, even in the most comprehensive of housing departments there will be occasions when the work requires relationships to be built with other departments and external agencies. The most comprehensive department would still require links with other departments whose mainstream work (dealing with planning applications, for example) had a housing dimension. It seems foolish, therefore, to see the comprehensive housing authority as the panacea for the ills of local government departmentalism. Second, housing impinges on the legitimate professional areas of those such as social workers, town and country planners and architects in the public sector, and estate agents, builders, and building society managers in the private sector. Professional as well as departmental jealousies are involved. This means that bringing together in one department all the housing related activities in local government is unlikely, given the established hold that occupational groups such as environmental health and planning officers have. The challenge is to find ways of developing productive working relationships so that housing strategies can be developed and policy objectives pursued, and accepting that other professional and departmental interests may have a role in the complex bargaining process which is so characteristic of housing work in local government.

In the 1960s a growing critique of local government management developed, as local authorities came under attack for the way in which they managed their programmes of urban renewal, for example. The post-war growth in the scale and impact of local government on people's lives may have made such comment inevitable, and the growth of a better educated electorate may have led to less quiescence, but whatever the reason, one of the strongest strands in the debates about the reform of local government in the late 1960s and early 1970s was the need to achieve improvements to the quality of local government management.

As the 1970s began, the critique of local government had broadened into a concern with the alleged lack of co-ordination in council services and activities, and the alleged lack of a cohesive management structure through which corporate objectives could be pursued. Local government was accused of not managing its affairs towards the achievement of objectives. Professionalism, and its close relation, departmentalism, were seen as the twin enemies of effective management.

Corporate management, as it developed in the 1970s, was essentially about internal cohesion within local government. It had the potential to strengthen the power of elected members to have their key objectives pursued through a policy making, implementation and review process. However, in many authorities the process of corporate planning, based on private sector management techniques, was alienating for all but officers trained in the traditions of strategic analysis (Hampton 1991).

In most accounts of corporate planning in local government, objectives were to be pursued through a number of programme areas, of which housing was invariably one. This notion of a housing programme coincided closely with the ideas about comprehensive housing services being developed in the 1970s. A housing programme was intended to be as comprehensive as the housing service, although not necessarily located in one department. The new-style Chief Executive was given the role of ensuring that all relevant departments co-ordinated their efforts to achieve the objectives of the programme area. The corporate planning techniques of the 1970s were influential on local government, although never as widely practised as their most enthusiastic exponents wished. However, corporate management ideas have left a mark on the management of many local authorities. Policy and Resources committees, management teams, and matrix structures, for example, are direct legacies of the attempt to co-ordinate the activities of local government to a set of common, key, objectives. Housing strategies which specify the contributions of different departments and professional perspectives to the achievement of housing objectives, and which set out a programme of action, can also be seen as descendants of the corporate planning tradition.

3. Accountability

Corporate management, as practised, was often an example of a 'top down' approach to planning. The rational model of decision making on which it was based was increasingly subjected to criticism, not only because it failed to take account of the realities of negotiation and bargaining in the public policy process, but because it failed to address the need to create management structures which allowed for citizen and consumer participation.

The critique of local authority management which emerged in the 1970s was concerned with how local authorities could be more accountable to the citizens and consumers of local services. The interest in decentralisation and participation which characterised the early 1980s was partly a response to criticisms of the way in which local government had become remote from those it served, and partly a response by Labour authorities in an attempt to build an alliance with local people against central government. This remains a significant factor in the development of the role of housing authorities.

4. Performance measurement

In the 1980s the application of public choice theory by central government was intended to make the public sector more economical, efficient and effective, while reducing it in size. The government attempted to inculcate a performance culture through the introduction of measures such as competitive tendering, and tenant's choice. In response some local authorities welcomed the opportunity to demonstrate the quality of their services. Housing authorities are now faced with potential competition from other landlords, and alternative property managers; the Right to Buy and other measures have reduced the scale of the housing task of local government; and cuts in public spending have put pressure on all aspects of housing authorities' work. The work of the Audit Commission has emphasised the unit cost of services as a measure of performance, while arguably neglecting the more difficult measurement of quality in service delivery. Housing management has been a particular focus of the moves to establish performance measurement (Audit Commission 1986; 1992). The DoE's requirement to publish information for tenants about performance on a number of specified aspects of housing management has been criticised as not providing a full enough picture of the nature of the task, but has been carried out with enthusiasm by some authorities. Although less has been heard about the performance of housing authorities in relation to other activities, that too is the subject of performance measurement in the 1990s. Housing authorities which cannot demonstrate that they are effective (preferably at achieving the government's objectives, see Chapter 2) will be penalised. Accountability to central government, as well as accountability to consumers, has become one of the challenges of managing in local government.

5. Networking

A housing authority which cannot achieve its objectives directly must do so through others. Some of the regulatory activities of local government, such as in the fields of public health, building control and planning, provide one model of how to do that based largely on legal powers of enforcement. A combination of carrots and sticks should achieve the authority's objectives. But the legal powers of housing authorities are insufficient to assist the housing authority seeking to influence independent agencies, over whom the authority has little effective sanction. As an additional model, several writers have suggested the idea of enabling authorities as networkers — members of a network of agencies seeking to pursue objectives to the mutual satisfaction of all, with negotiation and bargaining characterising relationshiops (Brooke 1989; Stewart 1989; Stoker 1991).

> Under the network model organisations learn to cooperate by recognising their mutual dependency; through discussion, negotiation and open communication; and by the development of shared knowledge and experience which encourages a long-term commitment to one another.
>
> (Stoker 1991, pp 265–66)

These commitments may be entered into voluntarily, or because some third party requires it. There are examples of both types of relationships in housing authority dealings with other agencies today. Such relationships can be formalised through a written statement or agreement, perhaps signed in the presence of the press, and taking on symbolic significance. Examples include nomination agreements between housing associations and housing authorities, strategic agreements between Scottish Homes and housing authorities in Scotland, and similar strategic agreements between housing authorities, housing associations and Housing for Wales. Several other examples have been referred to in earlier chapters, such as agreements between housing authorities and health or social services departments in relation to community care, or agreements between housing authorities and home improvement agencies about the delivery of grants and advice services. A diagrammatic representation of a housing authority as part of a network is shown in Figure 9.1.

This account does not necessarily suggest an appealing picture of happy cooperation. Stoker identifies three factors which might mar the prospects of housing authorities achieving their objectives. These are concerned with resources, skills and the autonomy of action open to local authorities.

Resources of one sort or another will play a crucial role in achieving the housing authority's objectives in negotiation with another agency. The main resources of an enabling housing authority are likely to be land and property, including the housing stock of a housing authority, grants or loans of money, co-ordinating skills, information, and purchasing power in relation to its own work. There are also less tangible resources derived from the legitimacy the authority has as a directly elected body. In the networking model these are used as levers, to assist another agency to improve housing conditions in some way, in return for which the authority achieves some desired outcome. But the process is not usually so mechanistic. Independent agencies are not obliged

172 The Housing Authority as Enabler

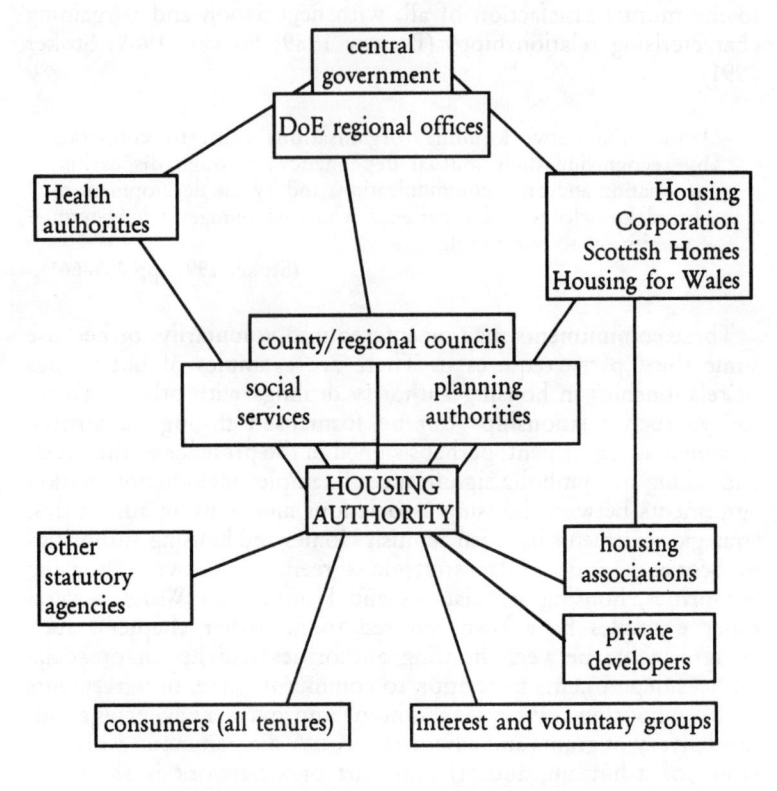

```
                    central
                  government
              DoE regional offices
    Health                              Housing
   authorities                         Corporation
                                      Scottish Homes
                                     Housing for Wales
              county/regional councils
                social      planning
               services    authorities
                   HOUSING
                   AUTHORITY
    other                               housing
   statutory                          associations
   agencies
                                        private
                                       developers
   consumers (all tenures)    interest and voluntary groups
```

Figure 9.1: The Enabling Network

to respond to the offer of some land or dilapidated council housing, for example. In a voluntary relationship there must be some overlap in the objectives and purposes of the parties before any kind of agreement will be reached. For example, a housing association seeking to develop new housing in one of two neighbouring authorities will be more likely to agree to work with the authority that offers land at a low price or at no cost, if all else is equal. In return the authority would achieve a favourable nominations arrangement.

In some circumstances — such as in the development of community care projects — a housing authority may do no more than bring the right people together to the mutual benefit of all concerned, or may persuade someone with resources, such as a landowner, to use them for the benefit of the community, using information about housing need. But even in these circumstances housing authorities are using resources such as knowledge, and the legitimacy that comes from their position as elected local bodies, speaking and acting on behalf of their area.

Implicit in the model is the notion of bargaining and negotiation, with the authority and other agencies involved in using their own levers to achieve something. One of the characteristics of bargaining is its unpredictability (Richardson 1983). The probability of adjustments in negotiating position is implicit, leaving open the possibility that the authority will not achieve all its objectives in any particular case. This is the reason why some councillors and officers are reluctant to rely on this indirect means to achieving housing objectives — they consider that direct use of the authority's resources for service delivery is more likely to achieve the authority's objectives, and to do so more efficiently. The networking model is based on the assumption that local government in the 1990s cannot achieve its objectives through traditional service provision, and that networking is an essential complement or alternative.

This networking model has costs attached to it, which have received little attention. The costs are in skilled staff time, and in the work which would otherwise have been done, as well as in the direct grants, land or other resources used as levers. It may or may not be more effective to spend resources in funding, developing and supporting a housing co-operative, for example, than to spend the money on building some traditional council housing (if that choice were available). The costs and benefits of different enabling strategies are little researched, although housing authorities are expected to consider them in adopting a strategy (Audit Commission 1992). Intuitively, officers and elected members have developed their own views about which strategies are effective, but this is an area which would benefit from further research and advice to housing authorities.

Resources lie at the heart of the effectiveness of this sort of local government. 'An enabling authority needs leverage and leverage implies powers and resources' (Stewart 1989). Reducing the extent of local government's resources has been part of the purpose of central government in recent years. People in local government are naturally suspicious that the resources required for their work are not protected from the general approach to reducing the scope and extent of the public sector. Ministerial statements about the importance of the enabling role are no substitute for resources. An authority cannot enable anything if it has nothing to offer. This leads to the second of the factors which determine the effectiveness of the enabling role: the autonomy of local government.

A housing authority which is free to use a wide range of powers and which can decide for itself the extent of resources to be committed to its priorities, is better able to achieve its objectives than one without such freedom. An autonomous authority is not dependent on others for initiating action, and is free to use its resources as an independent participant in a network. If central government constrains the nature of local government action by financial, legislative or administrative measures, local authorities will be more dependent on central government and other agents to achieve objectives. The 1980s have seen the autonomy of housing authorities reduced, but this does not necessarily remove the capacity of local authorities to create and use networks. It does though influence the nature of the housing authorities' involvement.

> Things would still 'get done', but the choice of policy arena and options would reflect local government's dependence on central government agencies or powerful business interests with the resources and powers to drive the network. For example, when Conservative ministers and private builders call for partnership in urban renewal it could be argued that it is the dependent networker role that they envisage for local authorities.
> (Stoker 1991, p 267)

Similarly in relation to housing associations it could be argued that the Right to Buy, tenant's choice, capital funding constraints, and the virtual prohibition on council building have weakened the bargaining position of housing authorities; and in relation to council tenants, the tenant's choice and tenant's charter provisions, and the 1989 financial regime for council housing similarly weaken the housing authority's position.

The third factor determining the effectiveness of housing authorities is the skill of those involved in managing them. The nature of the task has to be considered in order to demonstrate the importance of skills.

Taking the widest and most interventionist possible view of the role, it is seen as one which may vary from the task of managing the housing stock to the task of persuading a potential developer or landowner to make provision for social needs in a housing development. At its narrowest and most non-interventionist a housing authority is restricted to carrying out in a minimal way its statutory responsibilities, concentrating on duties rather than powers, and leaving as much as possible to the market. But even this minimal role involves a wide range of tasks associated with influencing the design, management, and provision of housing in the private and housing association sectors, the management of

HMOs, the allocation of housing association dwellings, and the co-ordination of community care policies, for example.

Management of housing authorities in the 1990s

This book has depicted the tasks of housing authorities as falling broadly into four areas. First is the intelligence function, wider than collecting information on housing conditions and needs, and encompassing knowledge of demands, of other providers, of levers available to the authority, and other opportunities for development. Second, the housing authority needs to be able to monitor and appraise existing and possible strategies and project proposals, including monitoring the management practices of other providers. Third, skills in development are required, taking strategy forward in agreement with others such as providers and consumers. Fourth, skills in administering services are required, whether that be the management of a council stock or the disbursal of renovation grants.

Many weaknesses in the capacity of some housing authorities to engage in these activities have been commented on in earlier chapters. At least part of the reason for this lies in the educational backgrounds of housing managers, many of whom have no particular qualifications or training for their jobs. Even the small minority who have gained membership of the Institute of Housing in the past have gained a qualification which emphasised the housing manager as knowledgeable and caring property manager. A critique of this syllabus is implied in a DoE review of housing education (DoE 1990d).

Certainly, some experience gained in the field of housing management has wider relevance for the other work of housing authorities. For example, the experience of developing working relationships with tenants' associations is relatively easily transferable to working with other voluntary groups; the financial and management packages put together in some innovative community care projects involve skills which are equally transferable; and the negotiation skills involved in relationships with departments or agencies supplying services to housing departments may be applicable to other situations.

But arguably this training did not provide a good grounding for alternative ways of meeting need. It provided little understanding of market processes of production and consumption; it neglected the politics of housing, and the skills, such as communication and negotiation, involved in acting as a player on the stage of local housing policy; it paid little attention to the techniques of appraisal which are used to evaluate alternative policy options and to review performance; it disregarded the financial institutions which had not traditionally been involved in public housing; and it failed to address the complexities of public involvement in meeting aspirations and demand as well as officially-defined need. Arguably no course of study could hope to develop such a large range of skills and knowledge, but, in contrast, the Institute's 1991 syllabus for the professional diploma places much stronger emphasis on the study of organisational management issues, and strategic planning and review.

The information and research role of housing authorities is crucial to the thoughtful monitoring of performance and to understanding the nature of the local housing system and how it is changing. Housing professionals should be as familiar as planners or accountants with the use of information technology for a variety of data collecting and analysis purposes.

Developments in the syllabus for the Institute of Housing's professional qualification, and other developments such as the launch of new courses in management development, are echoed in the types of appointment increasingly being made by housing authorities. Growing numbers appear to be seeking to employ staff with research, appraisal, and development and negotiating skills, if an unsystematic survey of the housing press can be relied on. Some authorities have established enabling divisions or sections, or less ambitiously appointed staff with new job titles such as 'research and development officer', 'enabling officer', or 'chief officer (strategy and review)'. Posts such as these are surely required if housing authorities are to be able to develop their role as council housing stocks decline.

Part of the government's case for reducing the local authority's role as provider is that housing authorities will be more able to devote time and attention to the other ways in which they can influence housing conditions. The introduction of compulsory competitive tendering for housing management in the mid-1990s, and the transfer of complete holdings of council housing to specially-created housing associations, is likely to emphasise the division between the providing and other aspects of housing work. The creation of 'arm's length' companies, or the 'trickle transfer' of vacant housing to housing associations would have the same effect. The housing authority will be required either to ensure the effective management of its own stock, if it has any, at the distance created by CCT, or to influence the management of companies or housing associations involved in managing former council-managed stock. The traditional tasks of housing management will be carried out by agencies with a number of different institutional forms, and staffed by people who will have the task of managing housing as their primary role. In contrast, the housing professional employed in local government will be involved in activities intended to influence, monitor, and appraise the condition and management of housing in all tenures. The emphasis on monitoring and appraisal suggests that housing professionals will require high levels of analytical skills. The proposal for a Master's degree in Public Administration (DoE 1990d) reflects this concern. The emphasis on influence suggests that housing professionals will require a range of development skills, including community development, finance, project co-ordination and negotiating skills.

The importance of these organisational and professional skills can be illustrated with reference to the situation in two housing authorities. In Authority A the council has decided to do whatever it can to improve housing conditions in the area, and senior councillors and officers have a good working relationship through which contentious issues such as stock disposal have been discussed and agreed. Relationships between departments are not perfect, but are good enough for the Housing, Planning and Technical Services Departments to have collaborated in the production of a new strategy based on house condition, land availability, house price, demographic and other information about the housing situation and needs. A working group of officers is co-ordinating this effort, and the council has appointed a development officer to service the group and work on implementing the strategy. In contrast, in Authority B, the statement of the housing authority's strategy is out of date, and even when produced was based on poor information about housing needs, land availability, and housing conditions. The housing department is principally concerned with managing the council housing, rather than with wider issues, and senior staff have little time to do more. Although these are fictional characterisations, it would be credible to suggest that Authority A is Labour controlled and that Authority B is Conservative controlled. It is easy to see that Authority A will be able to respond more effectively and quickly to an approach from a housing association seeking to extend its development programme. Indeed the approach may come from Authority A, rather than from the housing association. In the unlikely event that Authority A disposed of its own housing stock, there would remain an identifiable housing function, perhaps spread across several departments, but providing an overview of the housing situation, and actively seeking ways to improve it. If Authority B disposed of its stock, there would be little sign of a housing strategy, or of staff consciously seeking to further it. Some anecdotal evidence suggests that the authorities which have disposed of their stock are more like Authority B than A.

Conclusion

This chapter has considered the management styles which have influenced the way in which local authorities have carried out their tasks since the 1960s, and considered their relevance to the housing authority today. The emphasis on objective setting, options appraisal, monitoring, performance review, and citizen participation which characterised the 1970s and 1980s have echoes with the tasks of 'enabling'. The more recent emphasis on networking raises issues about the effectiveness of local government which is not able to rely on direct service delivery to achieve its aims. Networking will achieve the best results if authorities are autonomous enough to pursue their own policy objectives, with adequate resources and skills. The traditional skills and approaches of housing managers require to be supplemented with high level analytical skills in relation to research, appraisal and monitoring, and wide ranging development skills involving the harnessing of resources and agencies to achieve objectives.

In summary:

> A well-resourced local authority, with competent organisational and professional skills and autonomy from central direction would be able to act as an independent networker, developing its own local strategic vision to select and guide the networks it assembled.
> (Stoker 1991, p 267).

It would be able to act, but freedom to act does not guarantee action. An autonomous housing authority would not acquire the resources or use the necessary skills to the end of improving housing conditions unless the political will to do so existed. There appear to be more authorities with some political will to achieve improvements in housing conditions than those without such a will. A growing number have at least some of the skills and knowledge. Unfortunately, in practice, housing authorities which have the skills and political will are unable to apply them fully because of the resource and other constraints faced by local government. It is these constraints the final chapter considers.

Chapter 10
Performance and prospects

This book has discussed the role of housing authorities in the last decade of the twentieth century. This final chapter reflects on the evidence available on how housing authorities are performing, and looks ahead at the prospects for the role of housing authorities into the twenty-first century. It does so first by examining the difficulties involved in evaluating housing authorities as enablers. Then it considers whether general conclusions about performance by housing authorities can be drawn (individual chapters have drawn conclusions about specific aspects of housing authorities' work). It goes on to a wider consideration of enabling as part of government housing policy. And it concludes with an examination of the future prospects for housing authorities.

Evaluating enabling

Evaluating the activities of housing authorities involves answering questions like:

- What is the record of housing authorities in improving housing conditions?
- Is the present framework of powers and resources adequate?
- What place do housing authorities play in relation to others in improving housing conditions?
- Have housing authorities adequate staff, skills and knowledge to carry out their role?

Answering these questions, however, is not straightforward. Little consensus exists about the objectives of housing authorities. Housing authorities operate in very different circumstances, under a variety of party political control, or none. And much of their work depends partly on the contributions of others who are not under the direct control of the authority.

Objectives in the arena of public policy tend to be complex and competing. But even if agreement could be reached about what they are, measuring performance against them would be problematic, for two reasons. First, in a situation where success depends partly on external circumstances and the actions of those other than the authority itself, it is necessary to account for these factors before making judgements about the effectiveness of what a housing authority is doing. Secondly, authorities will vary in the effectiveness of their management, as well as in what they achieve in new or improved housing, for example. Evaluation of the process and management of enabling is as important as evaluation of the outcomes.

These points can be illustrated with the example of two authorities seeking to secure new rented housing. Authority A is well staffed, has a clear strategy for enabling new housing, and actively seeks housing association and private development. But no association or developer is able to build due to market conditions or the absence of development funds. Authority B has no research and development staff, no clear strategy, no list of development sites, and depends on housing associations to make the first approach. Despite this, a housing association receives a gift of development land from a private landowner in the area, Authority B grants planning permission and new housing is achieved. A superficial analysis might judge Authority B as more effective than Authority A, and only a more detailed evaluation would distiguish between effective management of enabling, and effectiveness in outcomes.

The evaluation of housing authorities as enablers needs to take account of their dependence on others, and of the intrinsic difficulty of the tasks involved. Different authorities will have different opportunities and constraints — to judge all as if they are operating in the same environment would be unfair. A well organised and managed housing authority which performs well the management tasks associated with enabling may achieve little in improved housing conditions. Evaluation is therefore problematic, involving consideration of multiple and sometimes competing objectives, and a complex process of 'implementation' in which the housing authority is in no position to impose its will (Ham and Hill 1993).

The task of evaluation is, however, assisted by the body of knowledge which has been built up over the last few years about the performance of housing authorities in relation to specific aspects of their role. This book draws on a large and disparate literature, much of which is based on research carried out in the last 15 years, reflecting a rapid growth in the amount and nature of housing research. This made the task of synthesis more productive than it would have been 10 years ago, for example. But little research has been done into many aspects of the role of housing authorities. Too little is known about the way housing authorities organise themselves to carry out their role; little is known about the attitudes of councillors and officers towards some aspects of their role; the use of the planning system to achieve social housing requires further careful monitoring, as do the new provisions for area renewal and individual house renewal; little is known about the involvement of housing authorities in community care and equal opportunites work; and too little is known about the effectiveness of housing authorities in influencing the management of the housing stock across all tenures.

The performance of authorities in relation to a range of powers has been examined in several chapters, taking account of objectives set by authorities themselves. But there has been little consideration of whether assessments of performance in relation to different activities can be usefully combined into an overall evaluation. It might be argued that is neither necessary nor desirable. Housing authorities and their electorates could be left to reach their own views about how well the authority is performing, and to make any adjustments as a result.

Yet there are reasons why more systematic knowledge is necessary. Three main reasons can be identified. First, the capacity of housing authorities to act is increasingly subject to their convincing central departments (DoE, Welsh Office or Scottish Office) that they are efficient and effective at carrying out their role. They cannot do so without a better means of demonstrating their overall performance than appears to be available to most. And central departments cannot make sensible resource decisions — whether within the terms of their Ministers' policy objectives, or in response to authorities' claims about need — without fuller information and clearer criteria for judging performance. What, for example, should civil servants and ministers do to separate the effects of how well authorities manage their role, from the outcomes they achieve? In the absence of clear evaluation criteria, ministers will have no defence against the accusation that favour is shown only to those who support the government's policy objectives.

Second, the possibilities and opportunities of the role of housing authorities is insufficiently understood by authorities themselves. Authorities can learn how to improve their performance from the experience of others. The management of council housing has been subjected to a rigorous scrutiny in recent years, but little such debate has taken place in relation to the many other management tasks associated with the role of housing authorities. Little is known about what if any performance targets authorities set for themselves, or of how they monitor their progress. There is little guidance available about the indicators that might be used. Practice in relation to assessing needs and demands, new provision, improvement, influencing management of the non-council stock, equal opportunities, housing advice and community care could all benefit from the wider dissemination of knowledge, and from more attention to the criteria for evaluation. Housing authorities would gain directly from understanding the effects of their activities better, and more generally from assisting research into the potential of their role.

Third, more research is required into enabling as an instrument of central government housing policy. The current role of housing authorities is very largely of central government's creation. The administrative and financial framework within which housing authorities act is largely controlled by central government. The powers and duties available to housing authorities are set down by Parliament. Whether housing authorities are performing well cannot be answered without reference to the adequacy of the framework within which they operate. So any evaluation of the enabling role of housing authorities is to some extent an evaluation of central government commitment to creating an appropriate framework. Whatever housing authorities achieve is therefore one measure of the ability of government policy to achieve a decent home for every household at a price within their means. Experience from other countries with similar democratic traditions may also be instructive, especially given the convergence which appears to be taking place in housing policy across many European countries.

In summary, some of these issues are not easily researched. The complexity of enabling, and the disparate nature of the objectives held for it make 'success' difficult to define let alone measure. Even if 'success' and 'failure' can be defined it is not easy to attribute them to housing authorities themselves, central government, or the multiplicity of agencies which play some role in influencing local housing conditions. With these comments in mind, this chapter goes on to consider what general conclusions can be drawn about British housing authorities' experience of the enabling role.

The performance of housing authorities

The evidence points to a great degree of diversity in the attitudes and experiences of housing authorities. Some have not attempted the use of certain powers, some have a poor record in analysing need, some have made half-hearted attempts to survey housing conditions, some do nothing to recognise the impact of housing policy on different social groups, some concentrate on one aspect of need or provision to the neglect of others. Others are innovative and pragmatic, wide ranging and well organised and committed to developing their enabling network as widely as possible to take advantage of any opportunities that arise. In the absence of a systematic survey it is hard to generalise, but a tentative categorisation of the approach and record of housing authorities sees them falling into three groups. In practice, many authorities will not fall neatly into any one of these categories, and without further research, it is impossible to know how adequate is the typology they present.

The first group — likely to be a significant number of larger authorities, but a minority overall — feel a sense of frustration that the wide range of powers available to them cannot be used as effectively as they would like. These authorities may be controlled by any or no political party, but many are Labour-controlled. They are pragmatic in being willing to consider any means to improve housing conditions, and are well-placed to consider policy options because of their commitment to research, analysis, strategic planning and review. They have for many years been involved in working with other agencies, such as housing associations, tenants' associations, independent advice agencies and private developers, some of which will receive funding. Relationships with social welfare agencies will be well-developed if not always very good. The councillors and officers primarily concerned with housing will have a sense of urgency about the seriousness of housing problems and the need to work hard at creating solutions, alone and with others. Research, analysis and development work will be recognised in the authority's staffing structure, and staff concerned will probably be based in the housing department. A strategy will have been developed over several years, and will be well-known to staff and councillors. The frustration felt by these authorities will stem from some inadequacies in the legal framework for enabling, resource constraints, and lack of sufficiently effective levers in relationships with other agencies.

A second, large, group of authorities may suffer the same sense of frustration, but will be much less active in seeking innovative solutions. Less will be heard from these authorities about the inadequacies of the enabling framework since some measures will not have been attempted. This group of authorities might also be controlled by any political party, but will often be Labour. A tradition of building council housing as the main response to poor housing will have ended, but the management of the remaining stock will be seen as the essential role of the housing department. Enquiries from developers and housing associations will be dealt with by the planning department, possibly involving the Director of Housing. There will be no research officer in the housing department, but there may be a development officer who works mainly on the capital programme for council housing, with little time to do more than cope with that and the regular filling in of statistical returns required for central government and other purposes. Relationships with voluntary groups, and statutory agencies will not be very good or productive, with some mutual suspicions and contact largely restricted to formal meetings. Some limited experience may have been gained of partnership with a housing association or a developer in dealing with a rundown council estate now no longer in council ownership. Councillors will have judged it the mark of central government policy failure that the council was not itself allowed to increase borrowing to deal with the estate. These authorities will have a statement of strategy which might look at first sight similar to the first group, but which, on closer examination, will contain less information about housing conditions, perhaps more complaints about lack of resources, and fewer commitments to innovation.

The third, and final, group of councils will mainly be small relatively rural authorities, rarely Labour-controlled. They will not feel such an urgency about housing problems, but may feel some sense of frustration at their inability to provide new council housing, and at the recent growth in homelessness applications. These authorities are likely to have the least comprehensive housing departments, and will have neither research nor development staff — functions which fall, in theory, within the remit of the Director's deputy. Staff will have difficulty recalling the content of the authority's strategy statements, which are usually written in a rush by the deputy in collaboration with the planning department. There will be little housing association activity in the area, and relationships with the voluntary and private sectors will be distant, except in the case of authorities which sell their entire stock to a housing association. These authorities see solutions such as leasing as the province of larger, more urban authorities with a more serious housing problem. The planning department may be looking at the possible use of the rural exceptions policy, and the environmental health department may be considering the use of the new renewal procedures in the Local Government and Housing Act 1989, for example, but progress is slow with such innovative work.

Although it is being suggested that most authorities will fall into one or other of these three groups, it might be argued that some authorities may fall into one group for some purposes, and another for other purposes. Many of the specific aspects of enabling which have been examined have shown a variation in practice which corresponds with the three categories, but no systematic evidence exists about how consistent is the approach of authorities across the whole range of their potential work. Variation within and between authorities is not necessarily a problem — it might be seen as a positive aspect of the relative freedom of local authorities to act or not, depending on local circumstances and perceptions of need.

However, there are three reasons why such variation may occur, which are worth examining.

First, the least active authorities may ignore or neglect problems because of the ideological dispositions of the leading councillors. The authorities that take advantage of this autonomy to fail to address problems that could be dealt with should be free to do so in a system of local government as distinct from local administration. Their inaction is a matter of public concern to the electorate of the areas concerned, and to the groups whose housing circumstances might have been improved. In some circumstance, however, central governments have felt justified in legislating to enforce action by reluctant authorities, but there has been little sign of such an approach by recent governments. Some trade off is required between central direction and local autonomy. In this the price of local autonomy for some people is to have their poor housing circumstances ignored, but, the price of uniformity would be the establishment of a network of local offices of a central government department, instead of a network of local authorities.

Tne second possible reason why variation in the work of housing authorities occurs is that it may indicate a lack of skill and knowledge at the local level. The type of skills required were discussed in Chapter 9. Better training, guidance and more experience will bring improvements, but more could have been done to assist the learning process.

The third reason for the apparently uneven performance of different housing authorities is that it may illuminate weaknesses and difficulties in the enabling framework and resources provided by central government. Authorities differ in the character of the problems they face, and the enabling framework and resources available may be more appropriate in some areas than in others.

Leaving aside their role as provider, housing authorities have duties or powers in relation to:

— the schemes for rent rebates and rent allowances (Housing Benefit);
— the condition of housing in their area;
— enforcement action against unfit properties;
— slum clearance;
— declaring renewal areas;
— administering renovation grants and group renewal schemes;
— financing housing associations and private landlords;
— financing individuals for house purchase and improvements;
— homelessness;
— overcrowding in privately rented housing; conditions in HMOs and common lodging houses;

- compulsory purchase in support of housing functions;
- travelling people.

In addition, planning powers can be used to achieve housing policy objectives, and public health provisions for new building remain in place.

Recent housing legislation is largely concerned with the council stock — its management, financing, and disposal. The Local Government and Housing Act 1989 is widely seen as providing an enabling framework (House Builders Federation 1990; Northern Consortium 1991). If so, this is a temporary framework, useless after the authority's assets have been disposed of and all the benefits derived. The authority then would have to fall back on the powers listed above, most of which had their origins well before the 1980s. Taken together these do not add up to a clear set of guidelines for an active role for housing authorities. Most of these statutory provisions were framed long ago for circumstances that are no longer relevant. They have little or nothing to say about the role of the housing authority in influencing property management across all tenures; the achievement of social rented housing depends significantly on a strange manipulation of a planning system designed for other purposes (see Chapter 4); and there is a weak statutory basis for providing housing advice. They are strongest in relation to the role of the housing authority in renewal and repair, but this area of activity illustrates that legal powers are only part of the framework required. The level of resources is arguably more important than the legislative framework. There are few, if any, housing authorities satisfied with the resources available. This may be seen as special pleading, and merely what could be expected. However there are indications that insufficient resources are being devoted to the renewal and repair of the housing stock. The growth of homelessness is another example, coupled with the discouragement of local authority leasing of private sector properties as a means of improving effective use of the housing stock (see Chapter 6).

In summary, it seems that the variations in performance between authorities are explained by:

- the differences in approach and commitment to their role which different authorities display, which may or may not be related to objective differences in the level and nature of need;
- difficulties and unevenness in the availability of staff skills and expertise which may reflect a lack of political will, or simply a lack of awareness of the possible scope of the role;

— weaknesses and inadequacies in the financial and legislative framework within which housing authorities operate. This framework is the creation of central government more than local government. It is an expression of the government's housing policy at the local level, and it is to this aspect we now turn.

Enabling as government policy

The housing authority as enabler has antecedents in post-war attempts to widen the role of housing authorities from clearance and construction of new council dwellings to a concern with all tenures and all social groups who may be in housing need. But the enabling role of the 1990s is different in its emphasis on private provision of housing, and in its association with a government view of local authorities as minimal actors on the local housing scene. Enabling housing authorities are part of a wider housing policy which, at its most general, aims to provide a decent home within the reach of every family, as all governments have sought to do for decades. The difference is that state action at the local level is intended to be as a last resort, and aimed only at those who cannot operate in the market.

Despite this, the role of housing authorities in housing policy remains important, whether measured by spending, or by the range of the activities of housing authorities, from dispenser of improvement grants to owner-occupiers, to securer of accommodation for the homeless. The housing authority's role as landlord also remains highly significant in most areas. Unlike housing associations, builders and building societies, for example, housing authorities have a presence throughout the country. Arguably, housing authorities are the principal agents, along with the tax system, and the housing association movement, for the delivery of national housing policy. Any evaluation of housing policy generally must take them into account. If housing policy is in difficulty, as it appears to be, then one possibility to be explored is that the policy of housing authorities as enablers is not working as well as it might. The possible reasons for any failure of enabling would include the weaknesses of implementation by housing authorities themselves; the failure of implementation by central government; and the intrinsic inadequacy of the policy to address the causes of housing problems. The first of these has already been considered and found to have some limited value.

The second possible reason — that of a failure of implementation by central government — is supported by the discussion of enabling powers and resources above. The level of resources made available to housing authorities are inadequate for the scale of the tasks they face. The legislative framework is out-of-date or limited to a concern with disposal of the council stock. But these are not necessarily fatal flaws in the policy itself. They could be rectified, and any such attempt would be supported by local government as well.

The question which remains is whether the overall policy objective of relying to the utmost extent on the private provision of housing is likely to achieve decent housing conditions in a reasonable timescale. The government's judgement about when market provision should be supplemented is not the same as most housing authorities'. The present balance between public provision and private enterprise is not achieving enough rented housing at prices those on low incomes can afford (see Chapter 4). It may not be the policy of 'enabling' that is flawed, but the level of reliance on the market to supply decent housing for everyone.

In summary, housing authorities as enablers are hampered by the reluctance or inability of some authorites to act; by the weakness of authorities' powers, levers and resources in carrying out their role; and by the ability of government to impose a limit on public sector action, restricting it to a role which most authorities consider ineffective at meeting need.

Prospects for the future

The future role of housing authorities is bound up more generally with the future of local government. The period since 1979 provides a contrast with previous periods because the autonomy of local government has been so curtailed as to make it virtually impossible to resist the national policy imperative. The autonomy of local government to determine its own role has been severely constrained, especially when authorities seek to play a larger role on the local housing scene. The future relationship of local government to central government is likely to be the most important factor in determining the role of housing authorities in the 1990s as it was in the 1980s. Also significant will be the future shape and structure of local government.

The reorganisation of local government will have some implications for the conduct of the housing authority's work, and for the nature of the network of agencies within which housing authorities will work. The most immediate effects will be to assist the conduct of relationships between departments of local government which were formerly operating at different geographical levels, although it would be naive to imagine that this would remove inter-departmental rivalries. Housing work in local government could benefit from the bringing into one unitary authority of the departments and committees responsible for social services, education, town and country planning, and local employment issues. Other agencies may find it easier to deal with a unitary authority in relation to planning or funding issues, for example.

Other effects will depend on the exact nature of the local government system which emerges from the rather unsystematic process of reorganisation which is being conducted. If very small unitary authorities emerge, they are unlikely to retain all the present powers and functions of local government. Any benefits of a 'unitary' system may be lost in a new and complex web of joint boards or committees, or of new non-elected bodies. If large unitary authorities emerge, they will be a lot less local than the housing authorities created in the mid-1970s. These authorities may have more influence in the relationship with central government, but a lot will depend on how the relationship with central government develops. The future prospects for the role of housing authorities depend to a greater extent on the scope and nature of that relationship, and the autonomy it grants housing authorities.

Two dimensions can be detected in debates about the nature of the enabling role and its relationship to central government. First, the scope of the role of the state is seen by some as minimalist. This is a view often associated with the Right Wing of the Conservative Party. At the other extreme is a maximalist position often associated with the Left in British politics. Broadly, minimalists want to leave to the market-place decisions about the distribution of resources, and want to restrict the role of government to the minimum compatible with ensuring basic standards are observed. This view sees the provision of direct state funding for housing as possibly unnecessary, and certainly undesirable. Maximalists, in contrast, see no limit to the action government should take, with direct provision and management being amongst the range of measures available.

This typology takes no account of which level of government should control state action, so the second dimension is concerned with alternative views about the extent to which local authorities should be free to determine their own role. On one side are those who might be termed localists who support local autonomy, and on the other are those, centralists, who support central control. In practice, most debates are about the position on the continuum to occupy, with most national politicians claiming a localist stance, sometimes in spite of their record in government.

The criterion against which central government's attitude to the role of housing authorities would be measured by a localist is not whether they hold a narrow or wide view of the role of the state in housing policy. Rather it would be whether they allow housing authorities freedom to answer that question themselves. That housing authorities should be able to define their role for themselves would be seen as marking a commitment to local government, even when an authority chose to interpret their role narrowly.

The Conservative governments of the 1980s tended to favour a minimalist role for local government combined with increasing central control as a means to achieving their objectives. Conservative-controlled authorities which supported the broad objectives of minimal intervention and provision of services, nevertheless complained about the tighter controls exercised over local authorities, some of which prevented them from doing what they had no desire to do anyway. In Labour-controlled local authorities the resistance to central government was on the grounds of incursion into local autonomy as well as on the grounds of reducing the scope of local government's role. However the two dimensions show that it is possible to be a 'centralist maximalist', as was the case arguably in the period immediately after 1945. The four positions these two dimensions delineate are shown on Figure 10.1

Using these two dimensions two contrasting futures for housing authorities can be set down. These are called the minimalist/centralist and maximalist/localist views.

The minimalist/centralist view of housing authorities

The top right quadrant of Figure 10.1 shows a view of local authorities not free to decide their own role — central government would set the framework for the work of housing authorities, and that would be restricted to assisting the market to run smoothly, with minimal intervention.

It might be argued that this is the view taken by government in the 1980s and early 1990s. Recent developments suggest a continuation of the trend to diminishing the autonomy of local government, and its capacity to pursue policy objectives independently of central government. As the redistributive services — such as education and council housing — provided by local government are reduced through privatisation, and consumer control, and as the services that remain are increasingly managed at a distance by private contractors, so the capacity of local authorities to influence the provision and co-ordination of local services is reduced. This

```
                centralist view —
                  authorities as
                agents of government
                        ▲
                        │
maximalist view ◄───────┼───────► minimalist view —
of state action         │         maximise market mechanisms
                        │
                        ▼
              localist view — authorities
              with power of general competence
```

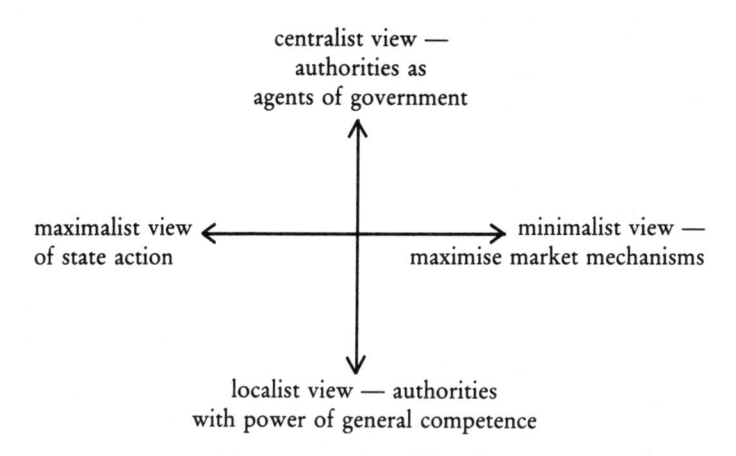

Figure 10.1: Alternative visions of the enabling role within the central-local government relationship

view sees a limited role for housing authorities in overall housing policy. The government's overriding commitments are to expanding owner-occupation and reducing public investment and intervention in housing, except where the worst conditions and circumstances require public involvement. The role seen for housing authorities is therefore a supportive role, assisting the smooth running of the private market, monitoring and maintaining minimum standards, and assisting the voluntary sector to make provision for the most needy. Government policies are pursued from the centre, through tax benefits, and direction of capital and revenue support to the agencies, including local authorities, which show most willingness and ability to further central policy objectives. Local authorities have no special place amongst the multiplicity of agencies operating at the local level. They have no more legitimacy than any other local agency, and the issue of the extent to which their objectives are achieved is of less importance than the extent to which private developers or housing associations, for example, can achieve their objectives.

The maximalist/localist view of housing authorities

The second possible future, shown in the bottom left quadrant (Figure 10.1), sees housing authorities — and local government more generally — as at the heart of creating the urban living conditions of the future. The most far-going, maximalist and localist account of the meaning of 'housing authority as enabler' puts no limit on the scope of the role, and leaves local authorities free to decide their own role, including whether to be providers or not. Such local authorities would have a power of general competence giving them freedom to do whatever seemed appropriate to further their aims, unless it had been proscribed in law. The place of other local agencies is either as supporters of the objectives of the municipality, or as independent agents, providing for a degree of pluralism in as far as they are able to pursue their own objectives independently. Central government is seen as also supporting the attempts of local government to meet needs, in a partnership involving some tensions when the objectives of the two do not coincide, but which leaves local authorities with some capacity to pursue their own agenda. This view of the role of housing authorities sees them as having greater freedom than now to determine the nature of their role. If they wanted to continue as providers of housing, for example, this would be tolerated.

What is not clear from this elaboration is the limits of central government tolerance. Are the financial controls that bind local authorities to be removed, leaving them accountable only to the local electorate? If so, how is local government to be financed? And if local authorities use their freedom to do nothing to improve housing conditions, what minimum duties will be placed on them by Parliament?

Neither of these futures is likely to happen, but the first is the more likely in the light of what is known of current trends. The future role of housing authorities will be as dynamic as in the past in the sense that it will change in the light of changes in the balance of power between local and central government, and between the multiplicity of agencies who determine the role of the state in housing policy. There is no objective answer to the question of what local authorities' role should be. The view taken is ultimately based on values, beliefs and opinions rather than facts or arguments. The best that housing authorities may be able to hope for is a centralist maximalist rather than a centralist minimalist government. It is a measure of the disenchantment with central-local relations that many Conservative local authorities would favour that to the present minimalist attitude of government.

This chapter has considered the role of housing authorities as enablers and suggested that there are significant difficulties in evaluating it, arising from the difficulties of defining objectives, and in separating the effects of housing authority performance from that of others, including central government. There is some evidence, however, of a reluctance by some housing authorities to use certain powers, or to carry out some of their duties with much enthusiasm.

There is also evidence that central government's commitment to enabling is more limited than most housing authorities'. The role of housing authorities in helping to improve housing conditions could be enhanced in ways that many authorities would support. Even if housing authorities have no future role as large scale landlords, they will have a role in the improvement of housing conditions and in supporting the provision of new affordable housing. Whether they are able to play the part most would like to will depend on the future relationship between central and local government. Within the present policy framework that would require housing authorities having greater freedom and resources to pursue the solutions to housing problems they see in their communities. Within a different policy framework there may yet be a better match in future between the role seen for housing authorities by central government and the role they see for themselves.

References

Arnold P and Page D (1992) 'A Caring Community' *Housing* 28:2, pp 9–13.
Arnold P and Page D (1992) *Housing and Community Care: Bricks and Mortar or Foundation for Action?*: a report to the major City Councils housing group, Hull: School of Social and Professional Studies, Humberside Polytechnic.
Ascher K (1987) *The Politics of Privatisation* London: Macmillan.
Association of London Authorities, London Boroughs Association, National Federation of Housing Associations (1992) *Nominations and Statutory Homeless Households – A Survey of London Boroughs* London: ALA, LBA, NFHA.
Association of London Authorities, London Housing Associations Council, London Boroughs Association (1989) *Partners in Meeting Housing Need: Good Practice Guide* London: NFHA.
Association of Metropolitan Authorities *Community Development: the local authority role* London: AMA.
Audit Commission (1986) *Managing the Crisis in Council Housing* London: Audit Commission.
Audit Commission (1989) *Housing the Homeless: The Local Authority Role* London: HMSO.
Audit Commission (1993) *Developing Local Housing Strategies* London: HMSO.
Audit Commission (1992) *Remote Control: the National Administration of Housing Benefit* London: HMSO.
Baker L (1991) 'A Wasted Opportunity' *Housing* November, pp 14–17.
Baker L (1992) 'Women at the Bottom' *Housing* Vol. 28, No. 4, p. 36.
Baker L and Perry J (1991) 'A Wasted Opportunity' *Housing* 27:9, pp 14–17.
Barclay P M (Chairman) (1982) *Social Workers: their Role and Tasks* Report of a Working Party, London: Bedford Square Press.
Barlow J and Chambers D (1992a) *Planning Agreements and Affordable Housing Provision* Brighton: Centre for Urban Regional Research, University of Sussex.
Barlow J and Chambers D (1992b) 'Planning Agreements and Social Housing "Quotas"' *Town and Country Planning* Vol. 61, No. 5, pp 136–142.

Barlow J (1989) 'Planning the London Conversions Boom' *The Planner* January, pp 18–21.
Battersby S (1991) 'Repair Grants – an Improvement on the Past' *Housing* 17:3, pp 13–17.
Bayley R (1992) 'Gainers and Losers' *Housing* 28:1, pp 9–11.
Bishop K and Hooper A (1991) *Planning for Social Housing* London: Association of District Councils.
Blake J (1992) 'A Man of Discretion' *Inside Housing* 9:36, pp 8–9.
Blakely J (1990) *Housing Consortia for Community Care – a viable working model?* Unpublished dissertation, Sheffield: Postgraduate Diploma in Housing Administration, Sheffield City Polytechnic.
Blincoe B (1987) 'Demand Attention – Why Development Plans need to take account of market demand' *The Planner* November.
Bowes A, McCluskey J and Sim D (1989) *Ethnic Minority Housing Problems in Glasgow* Stirling: University of Stirling.
Bramley G (1989) 'The Demand for Social Housing in England in the 1980s' *Housing Studies* 4:1, pp 18–35.
Bramley G, Leather P and Murie A (1980) *Housing Strategies and Investment Programmes* WP7, Bristol: School for Advanced Urban Studies, University of Bristol.
Bright J (1992) 'Doing the hokey cokey' *Inside Housing* 9:27, pp 8–9.
Brooke R (1989) *Managing the Enabling Authority* Harlow: Longman.
Brown T (1992) 'On the Edge of Community Care' *Housing* 28:7, p. 33.
Bulmer M (1987) *The Social Basis of Community Care* London: Allen & Unwin.
Cairncross L, Clapham D and Goodlad R (1989) *Tenant Participation in Housing Management* Coventry and Salford: Institute of Housing and Tenant Participation Advisory Service.
Cairncross L, Clapham D and Goodlad R (1990) *The Pattern of Tenant Participation in Council Housing Management* Discussion Paper No. 31, Glasgow: Centre for Housing Research, University of Glasgow.
Carter N and Brown T (1991) 'Local Housing Policies and Plans in England' *Local Government Policy Making* Vol. 17, No. 4, pp 44–50.
Centre for Housing Research (1989) *The Nature and Effectiveness of Housing Management in England* London: HMSO.
CHAC (Central Housing Advisory Committee) (1969) *Council Housing: Purposes', Procedures and Priorities* (the Cullingworth Report) London: HMSO.
Charles S and Webb A (1986) *The Economic Approach to Social Policy* Brighton: Wheatsheaf.

Clapham D (1989) *Goodbye Council Housing?* London: Unwin.
Clapham D, Kemp P and Smith S J (1990) *Housing and Social Policy* London: Macmillan.
Clapham D, Kintrea K and Whitefield L (1991) *Community Ownership in Glasgow: an Evaluation* Edinburgh: Scottish Office.
Clark D M (1990) *Affordable Rural Housing – A National Survey of Needs and Supply* Cirencester: Action with Communities in Rural England.
Clinton A et al (1989) *The Relative Effectiveness of Different Forms of Housing Management in Wales* Cardiff: Welsh Office.
Commission for Racial Equality (1984) *Race and Council Housing in Hackney: Report of a formal Investigation* London: CRE.
Commission for Racial Equality (1990) *Out of Order – Report of a Formal Investigation* into the London Borough of Southwark, London: Commission for Racial Equality.
Commission for Racial Equality (1991a) *Accounting for Equality: A Handbook on Ethnic Monitoring in Housing* London: Commission for Racial Equality.
Commission for Racial Equality (1991b) *Achieving Racial Equality in Housing Co-ops* London: Commission for Racial Equality.
Committee on Local Authority and Allied Personal Social Services (1968) *Report* (Chairman: Seebohm), Cmnd. 3703, London: HMSO.
Cooke M E (1987) 'The Improvement of Houses in Multiple Occupation, Hostels and Bed and Breakfast Establishments' *Housing Review* 36:2, pp 48–51.
Council of Mortgage Lenders (1992) *Code of Guidance* London: CML.
Crook A D H (1989) 'Multi-occupied Housing Standards: the application of discretionary powers by local authorities' *Policy and Politics* 17:1, pp 41–58.
Crook A D H and Bryant C L (1982) '*Local Authorities and Private Landlords: a case study*' Sheffield: Sheffield Centre for Environmental Research.
Crook A D H and Martin G J (1986) *Decline and Change, investment and disinvestment: patterns of change in private rented housing in inner Sheffield since 1979* Paper TRP67, Sheffield: Department of Town and Regional Planning, University of Sheffield.
Cullingworth J B (1966) *Housing and Local Government* London: Geo. Allen & Unwin.
Cullingworth J M (1979) *Essays on Housing Policy* London: Geo. Allen & Unwin.
Davies M and Niner P (1987) *Housing Work, Housing Workers and*

Education and Training for the Housing Service: A Report to the Institute of Housing Birmingham: University of Birmingham.
Department of the Environment (1981) *An Investigation into difficult to let housing* 3 vols. London: HMSO.
Department of the Environment (1982) *Improvement of Older Housing: Enveloping* circular 29/82 London: HMSO.
Department of the Environment (1983) *English House Condition Survey 1981 Part 2: Report of the Interviews and Local Authority Survey* London: HMSO.
Department of the Environment (1988a) *English House Condition Survey 1986* London: HMSO.
Department of the Environment (1988b) *Estate Action 3rd Annual Report 1987–88* London: DoE.
Department of the Environment (1989a) *Planning Policy Guidance Note 9: Regional Guidance for the South East* London: Department of the Environment.
Department of the Environment (1989b) *Tackling Racial Violence and Harassment in Local Authority Housing: A Guide to Good Practice for Local Authorities* London: HMSO.
Department of the Environment (1990a) *Local Authorities' Housing Role: 1990 Housing Investment Programme Round* London: Department of the Environment.
Department of the Environment (1990b) *Local Government and Housing Act 1989: Area Renewal, Unfitness, Slum Clearance and Enforcement Action (circular 6/90)* London: Department of the Environment.
Department of the Environment (1990c) *Local Government and Housing Act 1989: House Renovation Grants (circular 12/90)* London: Department of the Environment.
Department of the Environment (1990d) *Training Education and Performance in Housing Management: Efficiency Report and Action Plan* London: Department of the Environment.
Department of the Environment (1991a) *Circular 7/1991: Planning and Affordable Housing* London: Department of the Environment.
Department of the Environment (1991b) *Local Authorities' Housing Role: 1991 Housing Investment Programme Round* London: Department of the Environment.
Department of the Environment (1992) *Circular 10/92: Housing and Community Care* London: Department of the Environment.
Department of the Environment (1992a) *Housing Investment Programme Round 1992: Guidance to Local Authorities* London: Department of the Environment.
Department of the Environment (1992b) *Planning Policy Guidance Note 3: Housing* London: Department of the Environment.

Department of the Environment (1992c) *Management Guide for Houses in Multiple Occupation: draft* London: Department of the Environment.

Department of the Environment and Department of Health (1992) *Housing and Community Care (Circular 10/1992)* London: DoE/DoH.

Department of the Environment, Department of Health, Welsh Office (1991) *Homelessness Code of Guidance for Local Authorities* London: HMSO.

Duguid G (1990) *Homelessness in Scotland: A Study of Policy and Practice* Edinburgh: Central Research Unit, Scottish Office.

Duncan S (1988) *Public Problems, Private Solutions* London: HMSO.

Dunmore K (1992a) 'Opening the Door to Social Housing' *Housing* Vol. 28, No. 4, pp 21–22.

Dunmore K (1992b) *Planning for Affordable Housing* Coventry/London: Institute of Housing/House Builders Federation.

Englander D (1983) *Landlord and Tenant in Urban Britain 1938–1918* Oxford: Oxford University Press.

Ermisch J (1990) *Modelling the Income–Household Formation Relationship* Edinburgh: Scottish Homes.

Ermisch J (1991) 'An Ageing Population, Household Formation and Housing' *Housing Studies* 6:4, pp 230–239.

Evans A (1991) *Alternatives to Bed and Breakfast: Temporary Housing Solutions for homeless people* London: National Housing and Town Planning Council.

Forder A (1974) *Concepts in Social Administration: A Framework for Analysis* London: Routledge & Kegan Paul.

Forrest R and Murie A (1988) *Selling the Welfare State: The Privatisation of Public Housing* London: Routledge.

Fraser R (1991) *Working Together in the 1990s* Coventry: Institute of Housing.

Gauldie E (1974) *Cruel Habitations* London: Geo. Allen & Unwin.

Gibb K and Munro M (1991) *Housing Finance in the UK: An Introduction* London: Macmillan.

Glasgow District Council (1986) *Inquiry into Housing in Glasgow* Chairman: Professor Sir Robert Grieve, Glasgow: Glasgow District Council.

Griffiths R (1988) *Community Care: Agenda for Action: A Report to the Secretary of State for Social Services* London: HMSO.

Grimley J R Eve incorporating Vigers in association with Thames Polytechnic School of Land and Construction Management and Alsop Wilkinson, Solicitors (1992) *The Use of Planning Agreements* London: HMSO.

Gyford J (1991) 'The Enabling Council – A Third Model' *Local Government Studies* 17:1, pp 1–5.
Ham C and Hill M (1993) *The Policy Process in the Modern Capitalist State* (2nd edition) London: Harvester Wheatsheaf.
Hambleton R (1986) *Rethinking Policy Planning* Bristol: School for Advanced Urban Studies, University of Bristol.
Hampton W A (1991) *Local Government and Urban Politics* (2nd edition) Harlow: Longman.
Hancock K E and Maclennan D (1989) *House Price Monitoring systems and Housing Planning in Scotland: A Feasibility Study* Edinburgh: Scottish Office.
Harrison L and Means R (1990) *Housing: The Essential Element in Community Care* Oxford: Anchor Housing Trust.
Heap D and Ward A J (1980) 'Planning Bargaining: The Pros and the Cons: or How Much Can the System Stand?' *Journal of Planning and Environment Law*, pp. 631–637.
Henderson J and Karn V (1987) *Race, Class and State Housing: Inequality and the Allocation of Public Housing in Britain* Aldershot: Gower.
Henney A (1985) *Trust the Tenant: Devolving Municipal Housing* London: Centre for Policy Studies.
Hogwood B W and Gunn L A (1984) *Policy Analysis for the Real World* Oxford: Oxford University Press.
Hole W V and Brindley T S (1983) 'Housing Strategies in Practice – problems and possibilities' *Local Government Studies* 9:3, pp 31–44.
Holmans A E (1987) *Housing Policy in Britain* London: Croom Helm.
Home R K (1991) 'Deregulating U.K. Planning Control in the 1980s' *Cities – the International Journal of Urban Policy and Planning* Vol. 8, No. 4, pp 292–300.
Houlihan B (1987) 'Policy Implementation and Central – Local Government Relations in England: The Examples of the Sale of Council Houses and Area Improvement' *Housing Studies* 2:2, pp 99–111.
House Builders' Federation (1990) *Partnership Housing and the Local Government and Housing Act* London: House Builders' Federation.
House of Commons (1975) *Parliamentary Debates (Hansard)* 5th ser., Vol. 899, 10 November, cols 425–54.
Housing Corporation (1989) *Performance Expectations: A Housing Association Guide to self-monitoring* London: Housing Corporation.
Hunter D (1991) *Housing Practice and Information Technology* Coventry and Harlow: IoH/Longman.

HSAG (1977) *The Assessment of Housing Requirements* London: Department of the Environment.
HSAG (1978) *Organising a Comprehensive Housing Service* London: Department of the Environment.
Inquiry into British Housing (Chairman HRH The Duke of Edinburgh) (1985) *Report* London: NFHA.
Inquiry into British Housing (Chairman HRH The Duke of Edinburgh) (1991) *Second Report* York: Joseph Rowntree Foundation.
Institute of Housing (1985) *Race and Housing: Monitoring* Professional Practice Series No. 2 London: IoH.
Institute of Housing (1991) *Housing Services to Homeless People: Performance Standards Guide* Coventry: IoH.
Institute of Housing (1992a) *A Radical Consensus – New Ideas for Housing in the 1990s. A Green Paper on Housing Policy* Coventry: Institute of Housing.
Institute of Housing (1992b) *Housing – the first Priority* Coventry: Institute of Housing.
Institute of Housing Managers (1972) *A Comprehensive Housing Service* London: IoH.
Jowell J (1977) 'Bargaining in Development Control' *Journal of Planning and Environment Law*, pp 414–433.
Kay A, Legg C and Foote J (undated) *The 1980 Tenants' Rights Act in Practice* London: Housing Research Group, The City University.
Kellas J (1984) *The Scottish Political System* (3rd edition) Cambridge: Cambridge University Press.
Kemp P (1985) *The Housing Benefit Review: An Evaluation* Discussion Paper 6 Glasgow: Centre for Housing Research, University of Glasgow.
Kemp P and Williams P (1990) 'Housing management: an historical perspective' *A New Century of Social Housing* (eds) S Lowe and D Hughes, Leicester: Leicester University Press.
Keogh G and Evans A W 'The Private and Social Costs of Planning Delay' *Urban Studies* 29:5, pp 687–699.
Kirby K, Finch H and Wood D (1988) *The Organisation of Housing Management in English Local Authorities* London: HMSO.
Kirby K and Sopp L (1986) *Houses in Multiple Occupation: Report of a postal survey of local authorities* London: HMSO.
Kirkham A (1992) 'First Results from the New System' *Home Improvement Under the New Regime* (eds) S Mackintosh and P Leather, Bristol: School for Advanced Urban Studies, University of Bristol.
Lansley S, Goss S and Wolmar C (1989) *Councils in Conflict: The Rise and Fall of the Municipal Left* Basingstoke: Macmillan.

Leather P (1983) 'Housing (dis?)investment programmes' *Policy and Politics* 11:2, pp 215–229.
Leather P and Mackintosh S (1990) *Monitoring Assisted Agency Services, Part I Home Improvement Agencies – An Evaluation of Performance* London: HMSO.
Leather P and Mackintosh S (1991) 'Home Improvement Agencies in Wales' *Welsh Housing Quarterly* Summer, pp 16–18.
Leather P and Murie A (1989) 'A Housing Strategy for the 1990s' Municipal Journal No. 29, July, pp. 18–19.
Local Authority Housing and Racial Equality Working Party (1988) 'Local Housing Strategies' *A Strategy for Racial Equality in Housing – a policy and good practice guide for LAs* London: AMA.
Local Authority Housing Division (1992) *Local Authority Housing Investment Programme Process: A Consultation Paper* London: Department of the Environment.
London Research Centre (1989) *Private Sector Leasing* London: London Research Centre.
London Research Centre (1991a) *Much Ado About Nothing* London: London Research Centre.
London Research Centre (1991b) *The Local Impact of Private Sector Leasing* London: London Research Centre.
London Research Centre (1992) *Tackling Mortgage Default: the Local Authority Role* London: London Research Centre.
Loughlin M (1986) *Local Government in the Modern State* London: Sweet and Maxwell.
Loughlin M (1991) 'Housing Advice, Local Government Law and the Enabling role' *Scottish Housing Law News* 14, pp 21–5.
Malpass P and Murie A (1990) *Housing Policy and Practice* London: Macmillan.
Mason P (1992) 'Pilgrims' progress' *Housing* February, pp 19–21.
Merrett S (1986) *Local Housing Plans: Process and Product* London: Haringey Council.
Midwinter A, Keating M and Taylor P (1984) 'The Politics of Scottish Housing Plans' *Policy and Politics* 12:2, pp 145–166.
Morris J (1992) 'New Approaches to Clearance and Rebuilding' *Home Improvement Under the New Regime* (eds) S Mackintosh and P Leather, Bristol: School for Advanced Urban Studies, University of Bristol.
Munro M and Smith S J (1989) 'Gender and Housing: broadening the debate' *Housing Studies* 4:1, pp 3–17.
McCafferty P and Riley D (1989) *A Study of Co-operative Housing* London: HMSO.
McDonald A (1986) *The Weller Way* London: Faber and Faber.
Mackintosh S and Leather P (1992) 'Home Improvement Under the

New Regime' *Occasional Paper 38* Bristol: School for Advanced Urban Studies.

Maclennan D (1991) 'Extending the Strategic Role' *The Housing Service of the Future* (eds) D Donnison and D Maclennan, Coventry and Harlow: Institute of Housing and Longman.

Maclennan D (1986) *The Demand for Housing: Economic Perspectives and Planning Practices* Edinburgh: SDD.

McKay D H and Cox A (1979) *The Politics of Urban Change* London: Croom Helm.

National Federation of Housing Associations, Association of Metropolitan Authorities, Association of District Councils (1989) *Joint Statement on Local Authority Nominations to Housing Associations* London: NFHA/AMA/ADC.

National Federation of Housing Associations (1985) *Race and Housing: Ethnic Record Keeping and Monitoring* London: National Federation of Housing Associations.

National Federation of Housing Associations (1990) *Target Setting and Equal Opportunities in Housing Associations* London: NFHA.

National Federation of Housing Associations and East London Housing Association Limited (1991) *Housing Consortia for Community Care: a study of seven housing consortia* London: NFHA.

National Housing Forum (1989) *Housing Needs in the 1990s: An interim assessment* London: National Federation of Housing Associations.

NFHA (1991) Core Quarterly Bulletin No. 9.

Niner P (1989) *Homelessness in Nine Local Authorities: Case Studies of Policy and Practice* London: HMSO.

Niner P and Forrest R (1982) *Housing Action Area Policy and Progress: The Residents' Perspective* Research Memorandum No. 91 Birmingham: Centre for Urban and Regional Studies, University of Birmingham.

Northern Consortium of Housing Authorities (1991) *The Enabling Role and New Initiatives in the North* Chester-le-Street: NCHA.

Parker J, Smith R and Williams P (1992) *Access, Allocations and Nominations: The role of Housing Associations* London: HMSO.

Pateman C (1970) *Participation and Democratic Theory* Cambridge: Cambridge University Press.

Perry J (1991) 'The Case for Clearance' *Housing* June/July, pp 28–9.

Pinto R R (1991) 'Central/Local Interaction in Renovating Run-Down Estates – The View of Housing Authorities on the Estate Action Initiative' *Local Government Studies* January/February, pp 45–62.

Power A (1987a) *Property Before People* London: Allen & Unwin.

Power A (1987b) *The PEP Guide to Local Housing Management: 1 The PEP Model* London: DoE.

Power A (1991) *Housing Management: A Guide to Quality and Creativity* London: Longman.
Prescott-Clarke P, Allen P and Morrissey D (1988) *Queuing for Housing: A Study of Council Housing Waiting Lists*, London: HMSO.
Purkis A and Hodson P (1982) *Housing and Community Care* London: Bedford Square Press.
Raynsford N (1992) 'Arm's Length Companies: An option for Local Authority Housing' *Housing Review* Vol. 41, No. 2, pp 26–28.
Rex J and Moore R (1967) *Race, Community and Conflict* London: Oxford University Press.
Richardson A (1983) *Participation* London: Routledge and Kegan Paul.
Richardson A (1977) *Tenant Participation in Council Housing Management* HDD Occasional Paper 2/77 London: Department of the Environment.
Ridley N (1988) *The Local Right – Enabling not Providing* London: Centre for Policy Studies.
Roberts T (1992) 'The Money Monster' *Roof* January/February, pp 27–29.
Robertson, Douglas (1992) 'Scottish Home Improvement Policy, 1945–75: Coming to Terms with the Tenement' *Urban Studies* 29:7, pp 1115–1136.
Robson W A (1954) *The Development of Local Government* 3rd edition, London: Geo. Allen & Unwin.
Rochester C (1989) *Southwark Consortium 1984-1987: Organisation and Action in the Local Development of Services for People with Learning Difficulties* London: King's Fund College.
Rowan-Robinson J and Young E (1989) *Planning by Agreement in Scotland* Glasgow: The Planning Exchange.
Royal Town Planning Institute (1992) *Planning Policy and Social Housing: A Discussion Paper* London: Royal Town Planning Institute.
Samuel R (1992) 'Implementing the New system: the local authority experience' *Home Improvement Under the New Regime* (eds) S Mackintosh and P Leather, Bristol: School for Advanced Urban Studies, University of Bristol.
Satsangi M and Clapham D (1990) *Management Performance in Housing Co-operatives: A Report to the Department of the Environment* London: HMSO.
Scott S, Clapham D, Clark A, Goodlad R and Parkey H (1993, forthcoming) *Training for Tenant Management* London: HMSO.
Scott S and Kintrea K (1992) *Tenants Rent Arrears – A Problem? Tenants Attitudes* Edinburgh: Accounts Commission.

Scottish Development Department (1977) *Scottish Housing Handbook 1: Assessing Housing Need: A Manual of Guidance* Edinburgh: HMSO.
Scottish Federation of Housing Associations and Scottish Homes (1989) *Performance Standards for Housing Associations* Edinburgh: SFHA/Scottish Homes.
Scottish Homes (1990) *Information Factsheet 4: The Scottish House Condition Survey 1991: Local Surveys* Edinburgh: Scottish Homes.
Scottish Homes (1992) *Housing Information and Advice: You Can't Ask a Leaflet Questions* Edinburgh: Scottish Homes.
Scottish Housing Advisory Committee (1972) *Planning for Housing Needs* Edinburgh: HMSO.
Scottish Office (1990) *Homelessness Code of Guidance for Local Authorities* Edinburgh: Scottish Office.
Scottish Office (1991) *ENV8/1991: Community Care in Scotland: Housing and Community Care* Edinburgh: Scottish Office.
Scottish Office Environment Department (1992) *National Planning Policy Guideline NPPG1: Land for Housing – Draft* Edinburgh: Scottish Office.
SDD (1988) *Scottish Housing Handbook: Part 2: Local House Condition Surveys: a Manual of Guidance* London: HMSO.
Secretaries of State for Health, Social Security, Wales and Scotland (1989) *Caring for People: Community Care in the Next Decade and Beyond* Cm. 849, London: HMSO.
Seebohm (Chairman) (1968) *Report of the Committee on Local Authority and Allied Personal Social Services* Cmnd 3703, London: HMSO.
SERPLAN (London and South East Regional Planning Conference) (1992) *The Provision of Affordable Housing in the South East* London: SERPLAN.
SFHA (1991) *SCORE quarterly Report: April–June 1991* No. 3.
SFHA (1992) *SCORE quarterly Report: October–December 1991* No. 5.
Smith D (1992) 'Taking the Lead' *Housing* May, 28:4, pp 9–11.
Smith M (1977) *Guide to Housing* (2nd edition) London: Housing Centre Trust.
Smith M (1989) *Guide to Housing* (3rd edition) London: Housing Centre Trust.
SOED (1992).
Stearn J (1992) 'Transferring the Homeless' *Housing* February, pp 12–16.
Stewart J (1989) 'A Future for Local Authorities as Community Government' *The Future of Local Government* J Stewart and G Stoker (eds) London: Macmillan.

Stoker G (1991) *The Politics of Local Government* (2nd edition) Basingstoke: Macmillan.
Telling A E (1990) *Planning Law and Procedure* (8th edition) London: Butterworth.
Thomas A D (1986) *Housing and Urban Renewal* London: Geo. Allen & Unwin.
Thomas A D with Hedges A (1986) *The 1985 Physical and Social Survey of Houses in Multiple Occupation in England and Wales* London: HMSO.
Warburton M (1992) 'When Competition Becomes a Lottery' *Inside Housing* 9:4, pp 8–9.
Ward C (1974) Tenants Take Over, London: Architectural Press.
Warner N (1992) 'Housing and Community Care' *Inside Housing* 9:41, p. 10.
Watson S (1988) *Accommodating Inequality: Gender and Housing* London: Allen & Unwin.
Welsh Office (1988) *Welsh House Condition Survey, 1986* Cardiff: Welsh Office.
Wertheimer A (1988) *Housing Consortia for Community Care* London: NFHA/NCVO.
Whitehead C and Kleinman M (1992) *A Review of Housing Needs Assessment* London: The Housing Corporation.
Williams G, Bell P and Russell L (1991) *Evaluating the Low Cost Rural Housing Initiative* London: HMSO.
Williams G and Bell P (1992) 'The "exceptions" initiative in rural housing – the story so far' *Town and Country Planning* Vol. 61, No. 5, pp 143–44.
Williams G, Bell P and Russell L (1991) *Evaluating the Low Cost Rural Housing Initiative* London: HMSO.
Williams N J and Twine F E (1991) *A Research Guide to the Register of Sasine and the Land Register in Scotland* Edinburgh: Scottish Homes.
Wincott P (1992) 'Cut Out the Red Tape' *Housing* 28:3, pp 10–11.
Young, Sir George (1992) 'The Big Debate' *Roof* Vol. 17, No. 2, pp 20–21.

Index

accountability, 169
affordable housing, 61, 63-9, 72-3, 76
Allen, P., 54-5
Area renewal, 42, 94
'arms length companies', 122-4
Arnold, P., 136
Ascher, K., 2
Association of District Councils, 136
Association of London Authorities, 106, 110
Association of Metropolitan Authorities, 47, 98, 116, 121
Audit Commission, 47, 49, 52-3, 55, 104, 145, 147, 154-7, 173

Baker, L., 100, 137-8
Barlow, J., 63, 72-3
Battersby, S., 94
Bedford, 161
Bell, P., 68-70
Birmingham, 13, 85, 92, 101, 120
black people, see race
Blackburn, 120
Blake, J., 47
Blakely, J., 134
Blincoe, B., 51
Bowes, A., 142
Bramley, G., 47
Brent, London Borough of, 65, 112, 141
Bright, J., 94
Brindley, T. S., 47
Bristol, 94
Brooke, R., 37-8
Brown, T., 47, 137
Bryant, C. L., 96
Bulmer, M., 131

Cairncross, L., 35, 117-8, 121, 153
Camden, London Borough of, 107, 109
cash incentive schemes, 46
Cardiff, 38, 75, 149, 157
Care and Repair, see home improvement agencies
Carter, N., 47

Centre for Housing Research (CHR), 54, 98, 109, 116, 152, 167
CHAC (Central Housing Advisory Committee), 16, 23-4
Charles, S., 5, 51
Chambers, D., 72-3
Children Act 1991, 130, 151
citizen's advice bureaux, 151-2, 154, 164
citizens, 7, 34, 146
Citizen's Charter, 34, 148
Clackmannan, 160
Clapham, D., 31-3, 35, 37-8, 117-8, 120, 121, 122, 123, 128, 132, 153
Clinton, A., 116
Cm. 214, 25
Cm. 242, 25
Cmnd. 6851, 17, 25, 45, 127
Cmnd. 6852, 17-18, 25, 45
Cmnd. 9513, 89
Colchester, 160
Commission for Racial Equality, 140, 142
community care, 37, 50, 57, 131-7, 143
community development, 121
comprehensive housing service, 16, 22-5, 166-8
Conservative government, 2, 9, 22, 36, 39, 87, 187-8, 190-3
consumers, 1, 29, 34, 50
co-operatives, see housing co-operatives
CORE (continuous recording), 107, 109, 110
corporate management, 166-9
council housing, 3, 6, 23, 25, 28, 32, 48, 98, 100, 143
Cox, A., 25
Crook, A. D. H., 96-7
cross subsidy, 61, 63-6, 76
Cullingworth, J. B., 10, 13, 14, 16, 23-4, 80, 84, 86, 88, 146

Darlington, 75
Davies, M., 167
demography, 51, 55-6

207

demolition, *see* house clearance
Department of the Environment, 24, 27-8, 29, 30, 35, 45-7, 48, 54, 55, 56, 63-5, 67, 69, 72, 75, 80-3, 90, 92, 94, 98-9, 113, 122, 135, 155-6, 175, 177, 181
Derby, 108
development control, 61-2, 64, 66
development plans, 15, 61-2, 64, 66, 68
disadvantage, 127-144
Duguid, G., 158-9
Duncan, S., 100
Dunmore, K., 60, 62, 74-5

Edinburgh, 150
enabling, 5, 6, 9, 16, 22-40, 41, 46, 50, 62-3, 75, 86, 117, 165-78, 179-93
England, 2, 5, 8, 11-12, 14, 18, 25-6, 44, 46, 55, 61, 63, 75, 82, 85, 92, 100, 113, 141
　South, 69, 72, 147
　South East, 66, 70, 83, 113, 124
　Midlands, 72, 96
　North, 83, 96, 147
Englander, D., 2
Ermisch, J., 51, 52
Estate Action, 49, 99, 116
Estate Management Boards, 99, 116, 120-2
Evans, A., 113-5
Evans, A. W., 52
Eve, G. J. R., 71-2
exceptions policy, 63, 67-70, 74, 77
Exeter, 109

Finch, H., 166-7
Forder, A., 49-50
Foote, J., 118
Forrest, R., 14, 92
Fraser, R., 60, 74, 75, 76, 100, 107, 122, 135

Garden Cities, 14
Gauldie, E., 10
gender, 137-9
General Improvement Area, 12-13, 88-9, 92-3
Generalised Needs Index (GNI), 46
gentrification, 86
Gibb, K., 46, 49
Glasgow, 38, 47, 49, 92, 98, 116, 121, 142
Gloucester, 161
Goodlad, R., 35, 117-18, 121, 153
Goss, S., 139

Greater London Council, 5
Greenwood Act, 13
Griffiths Report, 132-3
group repair, 94
Gunn, L. A., 35, 44
Gyford, J., 33-4

HAG (housing association grant), 30, 75, 106
Ham, C., 181
Hambleton, R., 45, 47, 48
Hampshire, 137
Hampton, W. A., 2, 17, 169
Hancock, K., 52
Harlow, 76
Harrison, L., 134
Hedges, A., 96-7
Henderson, J., 139-40
Henney, A., 35-6, 122
Hill, M., 181
Hillingdon, London Borough of, 157
Hodson, P., 132
Hogwood, B. W., 35, 44
Hole, W. V., 47
home improvement agencies, 161-3
homelessness, 50, 76, 106, 111, 114-5, 124, 145, 147, 155-9
Houlihan, B., 80, 93
house
　building, 1, 10, 22, 25, 28, 46
　clearance, 1, 10-11, 80, 83-4, 101
　condition, 1, 16, 42, 48, 52, 80, 100
　　surveys, 54, 80-2
　developers, 29, 46, 60, 66, 74
　fitness, 51, 55, 90
　grants, 10-13, 36, 42, 54, 90
　improvement, 1, 10, 46, 63, 80, 86, 88
　prices, 52-3
　rehabilitation, *see* improvement
　renewal, *see* improvement
　repair, 80, 82-3, 86, 89, 92, 101
housing associations, 6, 13, 22, 26, 29, 31, 38-9, 46, 48, 60-1, 65, 67, 69, 73-5, 78, 100, 105, 122, 124, 152, 172, 174
Housing Builders' Federation, 186
housing consortium, 134
Housing Services Advisory Group (HSAG), 24-5, 46, 48
housing
　allocation, 16, 28, 55, 76, 140
　co-operatives, 99, 116, 118-119, 122, 123
　demand, 41, 47, 49-50, 51-3, 55, 57-9, 64

Index 209

density, 64
information and advice, 145-64
in multiple occupation (HMOs), 14, 87-8, 94-7, 101-104
management, 23, 31, 76, 103
plans, 53
need, 16, 28-9, 31, 41, 46, 49-50, 52-3, 55, 58-9, 61, 64
standards, 41, 49, 51, 63
supply, 52, 56, 65
Housing Act 1935, 14
Housing Act 1969, 12, 88
Housing Act 1974, 12
Housing Act 1980, 89
Housing Act 1985, 95
Housing Action Area, 12, 88-9, 91, 93
Housing Action Trusts, 5, 116
housing authority
loans, 13
powers and duties, 1-2, 10-11, 13, 16, 31, 32, 95, 105
regulation, 13-16, 33, 36
resources, 1, 4-5, 41-3, 48, 143, 171, 173
strategy, 16, 31, 42-4, 48, 59
role, 16, 34, 35, 38, 51, 115, 135, 143, 146-8, 159, 181, 187-93
Housing Benefit, 28, 104
housing co-operatives, 6, 32, 34
Housing Corporation, 12, 29, 47, 61, 75, 105-6, 140, 172
Housing Finance Act 1972, 13
Housing Plan, 18, 44-5, 47, 53, 58, 133
Housing Repairs and Rents Act 1954, 11
Housing Strategy and Investment Programme (HIP), 18, 29, 44, 46-7, 53, 58, 92-3, 99-100, 133
Housing Strategy and Operational Plan, 18, 44-5, 47, 53, 58, 133
Hunter, D., 55

Inquiry into British Housing, 30-1, 33, 35-6, 39, 44, 126
Institute of Housing, 76, 126, 140, 166, 176
Islington, London Borough of, 38, 116

Jowell, J., 71

Karn, V., 139-40
Kay, A., 118
Keating, M., 47
Kellas, J. G., 2
Kemp, P., 104, 128, 132, 166

Kensington and Chelsea, 28
Keogh, G., 52
Kintrea, K., 123, 154
Kirby, K., 96, 166-7
Kirkham, A., 94
Kleinman, M., 61

Labour government 1974-79, 2, 11, 17
Lambeth, London Borough of, 141
land, 44, 52, 62, 64, 66-7, 74-5
release, 28
landlord, 11, 32, 90, 125
local authority, 22, 31
private, 10, 29
alternative, 122-124
Lansley, S., 139, 141
leasing, 112-115, 124
Leather, P., 47, 49, 88, 161-3
Leeds, 76, 108
Legg, C., 118
Leicester, 38, 76, 85, 92
Liverpool, 38, 92-3
local plans, 15, 66
local authorities, 2, 17, 35
Local Authority Housing and Racial Equality Working Party, 140-2
local government, 2-8, 34, 41, 188-193
expenditure, 2
structure, 17
Local Government Act 1988, 75
Local Government, Planning and Land Act 1980, 2
Local Government and Housing Act 1989, 9, 26, 75, 85, 89, 121, 147, 184, 186
London, 38, 63, 70, 74, 110-111, 141, 147
London Research Centre (LRC), 62-3, 67, 72, 74, 112-114, 147, 153, 159-60
Loughlin, M., 5-6, 148

McCafferty, P., 119
McCluskey, J., 142
McDonald, A., 116
Macintosh, S., 88, 161-3
Maclennan, D., 44, 47, 51, 52, 55, 56
McKay, D. H., 25
Malpass, P., 13, 26, 98
management skills, 175-7
Manchester, 113
Martin, G. J., 96
Mason, P., 122
Means, R., 134
Merrett, S., 44

Midwinter, A., 47
Morris, J., 85
Morrissey, D., 54-5
mortgage arrears, 159-161
Munro, M., 46, 49, 137
Municipal Corporations Act 1835, 2
Murie, A., 4, 13, 26, 47, 49, 98

National Federation of Housing Associations, 106-7, 134-5, 140
National Health Service and Community Care Act 1990, 130, 133
National Housing Forum, 54-5
Neighbourhood Renewal Assessment (NRA), 91
Neighbourhood Revitalisation Services, see home improvement agencies
networking, 170-5
Newcastle, 38, 92
Newham, London Borough of, 141
Niner, P., 92, 157, 167
nominations, 28, 32, 75, 104-12
Northern Consortium of Housing Authorities, 60, 74, 76, 186

Oldham, 161
'off-plan' sites, 67
owner-occupation, 25, 28, 51, 57, 61

Page, D., 136
Parker, J., 107-110
participation, 7, 68
partnership schemes, 74-7
Pateman, C., 7
performance measurement, 170, 182-7
Perry, J., 84-5, 100
Pinto, R. R., 99
planning, 28, 30, 41-2, 56, 63, 96
  planning permission, 44, 52, 62-3, 69, 71, 75
planning agreements, 63, 67, 69, 71-4, 77-8
Planning and Compensation Act 1991, 62, 70, 85
Power, A., 17, 98-9, 120
poverty, see disadvantage
Prescotte-Clarke, P., 54-5
Priority Estates Project, 98, 120
property management, 103-26
Public Assistance Board, 13
public choice, 5-6, 50
public health, 14
Public Health Act 1961, 14
Purkis, A., 132

quota policy, 65-6, 72, 74, 77

race, 139-43
Raynsford, N., MP, 123
Redcliffe-Maud Commission, 17
Registrar General, 56
renovation, see house improvement
rents, 60-1
Richardson, A., 7, 118, 173
Ridley, N., 6, 35, 39
Right to Buy, 7, 13, 26, 29, 60, 74, 85, 116
Riley, D., 119
Roberts, T., 100
Robertson, D., 91
Robson, W. A., 2
Rochdale, 85, 94
Rochester, C., 134
Rowan-Robinson, J., 71
Russell, L., 68-70

Samuel, R., 94
Satsangi, M., 120
Scotland, 2, 12, 14, 15, 18, 26, 27, 47, 55, 68, 72, 82-3, 100, 108, 131, 141, 153
Scott, S., 120, 154
Scottish Continuous Recording (SCORE), 109
Scottish Development Department (SDD), 46, 54, 55, 80-3
Scottish Homes, 82, 105-6, 147-50, 153-4
Scottish Federation of Housing Associations, 106-7, 111
Scottish Office, 56, 135, 158, 181
Scottish Register of Sasines, 53
Seebohm Report, 23-4, 131, 146
Sefton, 93
SERPLAN (London 2nd South East Regional Planning Conference), 61, 66, 70
shared ownership, 28, 61, 69, 73, 78
Sheffield, 85, 121, 161
sheltered housing, 57
Sim, D., 142
slum clearance, see house clearance
Smith, D., 137
Smith, R., 107-10
Smith, S., 128, 132, 137
Smith, M., 147, 153
social housing, 66, 72
social services, 7, 37-8, 44, 131, 134-6, 151
social work, see social services

Index

Sopp, L., 96
'special' needs, 57, 106, 130-7
Staying Put, see home improvement agencies
Stewart, J., 36, 38, 173
Stoke on Trent, 93
Stoker, G., 3-6, 35, 171, 174, 178
Strathclyde Region, 15
structure plans, 15, 66

Taylor, P., 47
Telling, A. E., 62, 71
tenancy relations officers, 96
Tenants choice, 7
tenant involvement, 31
tenant participation, 29, 115-125
tenants, 46, 61
tenants' organisations, 22, 29, 147, 152-3
Tenants Rights Etc (Scotland) Act 1980, 89
tenure, 65-6
Thomas, A. D., 9, 12, 86, 88, 91, 95, 96-7
Town and Country Planning Act 1947, 14
Town and Country Planning Act 1968, 15
Town and Country Planning Act 1990, 70
Town and Country Planning (Scotland) Act 1947, 14
Town and Country Planning (Scotland) Act 1969, 15, 70
town planning, 14, 44, 46, 60, 62, 65
trusts, see housing associations, Housing Action Trusts, village trust
Twine, F. E., 53

ultra vires, 7
Urban Development Corporation, 5
Urban Programme, 85

village trust, 67, 69
voluntary organisations, 7, 13, 29, 37, 38, 151-2
voluntary transfers, 122, 125, 148

waiting list, 54
Wales, 2, 8, 11, 14, 17, 18, 25, 27, 44, 46, 47, 55, 75, 82-3, 85, 94, 98, 105-6, 113
Wandsworth, 7, 37
Warburton, M., 47
Ward, C., 122
Warner, N., 137
Watson, S., 137-8
Webb, A., 5, 51
Welmar, C., 139
Welsh Office, 56, 82, 155, 181
Wertheimer, A., 134
Westminster, 7, 37, 157
Whitefield, L., 132
Whitehead, C., 61
Williams, G., 68-70
Williams, N. J., 53
Williams, P., 107-110, 166
Wincott, P., 109
Wood, D., 166-7
women, 137-9
Wrekin, 49, 109

Ynys Mon, 94
Young, E., 71
Young, Sir George, 60